THE RISE AND FALL OF THE
MIRACULOUS WELFARE MACHINE

The Rise and Fall of the Miraculous Welfare Machine

*Immigration and Social Democracy
in Twentieth-Century Sweden*

Carly Elizabeth Schall

ILR Press

AN IMPRINT OF
Cornell University Press
Ithaca and London

Chapter 2 is adapted from "(Social) Democracy in the Blood? Civic and Ethnic Idioms of Nation and the Consolidation of Swedish Social Democratic Power, 1928–1932," *Journal of Historical Sociology* 25, no. 3 (2012): 440–474. © 2012 Blackwell Publishing Ltd. Reprinted with the permission of Blackwell Publishing Ltd.

First published 2016 by Cornell University Press

Printed in the United States of America

Library of Congress Cataloging-in-Publication Data

Schall, Carly Elizabeth, author.
The rise and fall of the miraculous welfare machine : immigration and social democracy in twentieth-century Sweden / Carly Elizabeth Schall.
    pages cm
  Includes bibliographical references and index.
  ISBN 978-0-8014-5667-1 (cloth : alk. paper)
1. Welfare state—Sweden—History—20th century.　2. Sweden—Emigration and immigration—History—20th century.　3. Sveriges socialdemokratiska arbetareparti—History—20th century.　4. Sweden—Ethnic relations—History—20th century.　5. Nationalism—Sweden—History—20th century.　6. Sweden—Politics and government—20th century.　I. Title.
  HV338.S33 2016
  361.6'509485—dc23　　　　2015033487

Cornell University Press strives to use environmentally responsible suppliers and materials to the fullest extent possible in the publishing of its books. Such materials include vegetable-based, low-VOC inks and acid-free papers that are recycled, totally chlorine-free, or partly composed of nonwood fibers. For further information, visit our website at www.cornellpress.cornell.edu.

Cloth printing　　　　　10　9　8　7　6　5　4　3　2　1

For Rich and Roman

CONTENTS

ACKNOWLEDGMENTS

A great many intellectual debts were accumulated in the process of writing this book. I'd like to thank its many commenters, critics, and supporters, among them Mara Loveman, Mustafa Emirbayer, Ivan Ermakoff, Julie Allen, Scott Mellor, Orfeo Fioretos, Myra Marx Ferree, Pam Oliver, Rahul Mahajan, Richard Aviles, Jennifer Holland, Jason Turowetz, Jacob Habinek, and Alex Hanna. The other steady participants at the Politics, Culture and Society and Race and Ethnicity brownbags also deserve a mention. Of particular importance, too, was the research assistance of Phil Creswell. Last in this list, and certainly most important, is Chad Goldberg, whose influence can be seen on every page. In Sweden, where the data were collected and occasionally presented, I owe a debt of gratitude to Klas Åmark, Ingela Naumann, Vanessa Barker, Jens Rydgren and Elizabeth Thompson at Stockholm University, Sven Hort of Linneaus University, and the excellent archivists at the Labor Movement Archives, the Royal Library, and the National Archives in Stockholm. At Vanderbilt University, where I overhauled and rewrote the manuscript into its final book form, I'd like to thank Katherine Donato, Holly McCammon, and Dan Cornfield.

Research for this book was furthermore supported financially by the University of Wisconsin Sociology Department, a Foreign Language Area Studies Summer Fellowship, a Fulbright IIE Full Grant, Vanderbilt University, and Indiana University–Purdue University Indianapolis. Without this support, the book would not have been possible.

Finally, I would like to extend a heartfelt thanks to my family: to my parents, Nancy and Don Schall, who have always encouraged intellectual curiosity. To my brothers, Casey and Peter Schall, who are both way cooler and more creative than I can even aspire to be and, in that sense, will always be an inspiration. Finally, to my husband, Rich Holden, who has provided both intellectual and emotional support. He has always been both my harshest critic and my most enthusiastic supporter, and my work is better for that. He has also been a true partner and an amazing father—without these things, I could not have completed this book.

THE RISE AND FALL OF THE
MIRACULOUS WELFARE MACHINE

Introduction

From the end of the Second World War until the 1990s, the development of Swedish society was nothing short of a miracle. This small state on the periphery of Europe grew steadily and phenomenally. Yet, Sweden did not simply grow as all Western capitalist countries did. Equality increased along with gross domestic product. Capitalism, in the Swedish case, seemed not to be a zero-sum game where the rich grew richer and the poor grew poorer as economic development proceeded. For Swedes, the mechanism behind this view was obvious: a strong state, coordinating but not steering the economy and working to distribute its fruits. In short, Sweden's economic development has been the product of a miraculous welfare machine.

In this book I trace the cultural conditions that enabled the construction of this welfare machine and its transformation into the central feature of Swedish political and social life—the transformation of social democracy into an important part of Swedish national identity. Key to this story is the process through which the national community was constructed and reconstructed as an ethnic, class, or civic community. Indeed, if the welfare state is the outcome to be explained in these pages, then ethnicity, broadly construed, is what carries the explanatory weight. While not eschewing entirely the traditional explanations for the Swedish welfare state—chronicled in this introduction—I argue that we cannot possibly understand the Swedish "People's Home" without understanding who the people were and who they now are.

This claim is, perhaps, uncontroversial. After all, many have suggested that Sweden's ethnic homogeneity was key in its development of a universalist welfare state,[1] and many continue to argue that immigration is destroying the institutions of the generous welfare state as well as support for these institutions.[2] In fact, the incompatibility of ethnic diversity and generous, universal welfare states has become a sort of "common sense" in recent years. Yet, the way scholars and lay people alike have approached the question of ethnic homogeneity and the welfare state—both in general and in the specific case of Sweden—has been facile and unsatisfying. How, exactly, homogeneity translates into a universalist welfare state and how immigration threatens the welfare state has been, with a few notable exceptions, unexplored.[3] To explain the "how" (and along the way the "whether") of the ethnicity–welfare state nexus, I zero in on processes of national (and, therefore, welfare state) closure. The findings here indicate that there is no unidirectional march toward increased ossification of national boundaries, but rather a process that goes in fits and starts and which is subject to periodic crises of national and welfare community. The focuses of this book are these moments of crisis—and the insights that such crises provide.

The questions I address, therefore, are the following: (1) How does ethnic homogeneity matter in the development of the Swedish welfare state? (2) Does ethnic heterogeneity threaten the universalist welfare state, and, if so, in what ways? (3) What do the answers to these questions tell us about processes of national closure? These questions are addressed through an examination of the discourse around the welfare state, immigration, and national belonging during five periods of crisis in the Swedish twentieth century (1928–1932, 1945–1951, 1968–1975, 1991–1995, and 2006–2014). The key to these questions is understanding the Social Democratic Party's (Socialdemocratiska Arbetarpartiet, SAP) active and successful promotion of a cultural hegemony that makes Swedishness synonymous with social-democratic values. In the early periods, this strategy involved drawing on and policing an ethnic definition of nation, though SAP infused this definition with civic values. In the later periods, the civic aspects of this definition led SAP to pursue an expansive strategy toward immigrants, though this strategy faltered in the face of severe crisis in the 1990s and fell apart after 2006.

Nationalism, Ethnicity, Immigration, and the Welfare State

The argument many make is simple: homogeneity is good for welfare states, and heterogeneity is bad. Indeed the common sense underlying this is simple as well. People are more likely to contribute to the well-being of someone "like them" and less willing to do so for someone different. Welfare states, it is argued, rest on a basis of trust and solidarity that is supposed to be more readily found in homogeneous communities. For some scholars, this argument is nearly a self-evident truth. "There can be no doubt that migration has been little short of a disaster," writes Gary Freeman, "Immigration has tended to erode the more general normative consensus on which the welfare state was built."[4] Indeed, some research supports this view, finding that redistribution is greater in countries that are less diverse.[5] Sweden is held up on this point as a positive example: a generous welfare state forged in a context of mutual ethnicity. Even the famed Swedish economist Gunnar Myrdal thought Sweden's welfare state was only really possible in a culturally homogeneous context.[6] The classic counterexample, of course, is the United States, where divisions between white and black and between Mexican Americans and Anglo-Americans scuppered the social state from the very beginning, resulting in a patchwork and atrophied welfare state.[7]

In the exceptional case of the United States, arguments about how ethnic division threatens welfare states have been most complete, nuanced, and compelling. Quantitative studies of public opinion have consistently shown that racial division and racial prejudice have a strong negative effect on the welfare state, especially when a particular ethnic group is seen as receiving a disproportionate share of the benefits.[8] These studies are complemented by careful historical work that has documented the ways in which ethnic or racial divisions have inhibited welfare-state growth. Such explanations center on the effects of institutionalized racial barriers, divisions within labor movements, racialized labor practices and politics, or the ways in which race has affected the construction of categories of worth.[9] In the U.S. case, the effect of heterogeneity is clear: it was a barrier from the very start.

The literature on European states in this regard is less comprehensive and less conclusive. Some studies suggest that a country's welfare regime (liberal, social-democratic, or corporatist) mediates the effect of immigration on welfare-state support.[10] One possibility is that, because social-democratic welfare states do a better job of incorporating immigrants, welfare-state support in those regimes is least likely to be affected by increased immigration.[11] However, there is little evidence that universal welfare states do in fact incorporate immigrants better than residualist or corporatist regimes.[12] Others argue that immigrants place undue stress on generous social-democratic welfare states through high levels of welfare claiming, which may make these welfare states unsustainable and reduce support for these welfare systems.[13] Key to this argument is that it is not the actual high number of claims that matters, but the perception of a high number of claims and a politicization of these perceptions.[14]

On the other end of the spectrum, Markus Crepaz asserts, in his geographically wide sweeping, but temporally limited study of immigration and the welfare state, that scholars have ignored the trust-generating capacities of the welfare state.[15] Indeed, Crepaz uses Sweden as a prime case to indicate the ways in which welfare states do not just draw on solidarities, but create solidarities. At the time of Crepaz's writing, Sweden seemed to many observers to be unlikely to develop a powerful far-right xenophobic party like his other cases and to be able to maintain its welfare state intact. That Crepaz failed to foresee the cuts made by recent conservative governments in Sweden does not undermine his basic point: that welfare states may be strengthened by immigration when their social welfare apparatuses work to create trust among both the native population and the immigrant population.

Sweden is, in fact, the polar opposite of the United States both on the immigration front and on the welfare-state front. As a welfare state, Sweden is the social-democratic welfare state par excellence. It provides cradle-to-grave social services on the basis of citizenship, not need, and has high levels of decommodification, redistribution, and taxation. It is for many the go-to case of a fully realized welfare state. It was also a fairly homogeneous place when the welfare state began to take shape.[16] The opposition of these two cases would seem to provide superficial support for the linking of homogeneity to the welfare state. Yet, none of the partial explanations noted previously for European states in general provide a link between ethnic homogeneity and the welfare state tout court. Similarly, we cannot simply invert the more nuanced explanations of the stunted American welfare state to explain Sweden. If this explanation were applicable to other nations, we would expect highly homogeneous Japan also to have a universalist welfare state, which is not the case. What we can learn from these studies of the United States, however, is that to understand the relationship between ethnicity, race, and the welfare state, we have to pay attention to how ethnicity enters into labor movements and into politics at the historical moments that matter for the welfare state's development. For Sweden, this means understanding why shared ethnicity was (or was not) important at the moments of the welfare state's birth as well as how immigrants came to fit (or not) into an already-established welfare state. To obtain this understanding, it is useful to consider the factors that may mediate the relationship between homogeneity and heterogeneity and the welfare state, and in this book I look to one such crucial factor: nationalism.

From this perspective, it is not insignificant that the watchword of the Swedish welfare state is the "People's Home" (*folkhem*). Such a conception captures both a description of the welfare state and a description of the nation. Indeed, central to this organizing concept is an understanding of the nation as something like the "good home" where everyone takes care of one another and no one is left behind. The state, too, is implicated in this image as the guarantor of care. The People's Home is a familial concept—launched by Social Democratic prime minister Per Albin Hansson on the eve of SAP dominance—that captures the aspirations of the state to be inclusive of all. The initial subtext may have been one of class as much as one of ethnicity (or race), but the linking of welfare to national community is unmistakable— we have a right to welfare because we all belong to the people. Dominant modes of thinking regarding who the people are, what belonging to a people's home entails, and how the state ought to be involved have shifted over time, but the concept retains a great deal of cultural resonance to this day.

Sweden is not alone in linking its welfare state to its nation. All welfare states have necessary connections to the nation, and some argue that the welfare state is nothing less than a codification of national solidarity.[17] Andreas Wimmer notes that "the welfare state transformed the nation into a real, not just an imagined, community of solidarity, a hyper-extended family where everybody cares for everybody else."[18] The interconnectedness entailed in belonging both to the national and to the welfare states is rooted in material benefits, too. Indeed, much of the scant literature that connects the field of nations and nationalism with the field of welfare-state studies is focused on those "welfare-nationalist" or "welfare-chauvinist" movements that seek to deny the material goods of the welfare state to nonmember immigrants.[19] Yet we can conceive of the material welfare state as connected to the nation in a way that does not presume either an already-existing welfare state or a settled national community. Turning to Wimmer again, we find the argument that the development of the welfare state increases the benefits of membership in the state, which promotes national closure. Welfare-state building coincides with national closure. Decisions about where to draw the boundaries of the nation have profound effects on the welfare state not just when newcomers seek access, but from the very earliest attempts at institution building.

The nationalism I refer to in this book is not the "hot" nationalism of wars and violence. It is, instead, that of Benedict Anderson's "imagined community": the membership community bound by a "deep, horizontal comradeship" that is both sovereign and limited.[20] These limits can be drawn and policed in a number of ways. On the one hand, they can be policed directly through legislation, especially citizenship legislation, and through border control. On the other hand, membership can be policed culturally-symbolically or discursively, in terms of how people think of inclusion and exclusion in the membership community of the nation.[21] These two forms of policing may work together or separately. It is possible, in other words, to conceive of people who are formally included through citizenship or residence, but who are excluded in the ways in which people think of or talk about their nation. Although formal inclusion in citizenship and the welfare state are considered important here, it is primarily this second, discursive aspect of inclusion that is highlighted. In this book, then, I follow Michael Billig, Claire Sutherland, and Rogers Brubaker in their concern with the everyday common sense of the nation as developed through a grand discourse, or idiom of the nation.[22] Discursive or symbolic exclusion can, of course, have important consequences for material inclusion, and vice versa. I show that mismatches or potential mismatches in who is materially included and who is symbolically included may lead to corrections in one domain or the other. These corrections may have wide-ranging consequences.

Crises of Closure: A Theory of Membership under Threat

To understand how processes of inclusion and exclusion in the nation and in the welfare state are related, I draw on and develop a theory of national closure. The notion of "social closure" is Max Weber's invention, rooted in the idea that there are "open" social relations that are available to all (or most) and "closed" social relations restricted to a subset of members. This Weberian concept was meant to extend from small social groups up through societies and to function as a way of categorizing interaction.[23] Focusing on one particular aspect of social closure, for instance, we can think of citizenship as a form of social closure with formal acquisition of legal citizenship as the closure mechanism.[24] There are potentially other forms of closure focused on the same national level, and Wimmer extends Weber's concept of social closure to one of "national closure." In so doing, he connects "nation" as a membership community to the welfare state. Wimmer argues that as the collective goods of state membership (defense, security, social benefits, etc.) increase, the need to "close off" access to these goods by outsiders also increases. The nation becomes a "real community of interests," and racism and xenophobia arise out of the necessity to maintain that community of interests, which has come to be ethnically defined.[25] National closure, then, goes hand in hand with the development of the state, including the development of welfare-state institutions. We can think of closure mechanisms, as well, as either physical and legal (i.e., border control and citizenship requirements) or cultural and symbolic. Wimmer further argues that a "reorganization of the mechanisms of solidarity" that works to integrate "the labor movement into the national order of things" through the welfare state represents a key final step in the consolidation of a nation-state.[26] Wimmer writes that "the welfare state was inspired by the idea of a national community of solidarity and could not have evolved independently of the institutional framework of the nation-state."[27]

The welfare state and the nation, then, are closely connected. A welfare state cannot function unbounded. The concept of a "nation" is a device for bounding. That nations and states coincide to a great—but not perfect—extent makes the nation an ideal closure mechanism for bounding welfare states. Yet, when various shocks to the nation occur—increased immigration, demand for inclusion by previously excluded groups, loss or gain of territory—the nation ceases to be an effective closure mechanism. It either encompasses too many or two few people. It fails to match the limits of solidarity that the welfare state requires.

Therefore, I argue that the process of national closure is not unidirectional and does not end once a state has achieved closure. Rather, states face various difficulties along the way to closure, as well as disruptions to already-established national closures. These disruptions I term "crises of closure," defined as relatively short-lived, acute challenges to the agreed-upon boundaries of a membership community. Crises of closure can have a number of different causes and manifestations originating both outside and within the membership community. High levels of immigration, loss or gain of territory as a result of war, and demands for inclusion from previously excluded domestic groups may all lead to such crises. Challenges may be about "numbers"—how many members can the national community sustain?—or they may be primarily a reevaluation of what binds a membership community together. Using Wimmer, again, as our guide, who argues specifically that exclusion from territory and exclusion from access to public goods are explicitly linked, crises can be categorized into two analogous groups. Crises may be primarily about closure-as-entry and may center around policies concerning the granting of visas and work permits and the policing of borders. Crises of closure-as-entry are wholly focused on newcomers—immigrants and refugees. Crises may also, however, be primarily about closure-as-access to goods. These crises may affect immigrants, as in the many questions that arose throughout the twentieth century regarding what kind of access migrants should have to the redistributive parts of the welfare state once they are in the country. However, they may also affect all or some native-born populations, as when debates about targeted versus universalist programs arise or when the question of what goods a member has a right to in the first place become actualized. These crises are largely definitional—what does it mean to be a member of a community? Crises often arise simultaneously, but analytical separation of the two types helps us to understand better the uneven processes of closure that Wimmer's work suggests and that characterize the welfare-state history of Sweden.

Crises can also arise out of multiple kinds of causes. They may generally arise out of changing conditions within a community, be they economic, social, or political. Crises can have multiple causes and textures simultaneously: immigration or emigration may cause a nation to reevaluate what it means to be a member of the nation, while asking how much migration should be allowed. Crises may also be largely manufactured by elites, either through overstating the shocks to conditions (e.g., claiming that "hordes" of migrants are waiting to enter the country when really the numbers are quite small) or by adding salience to issues that have always been around (e.g., by heightening attention to elder poverty at a particular time despite no change in elder poverty). In that sense, crises may sometime be more like "moral panics"[28] than objective crises. The converse is that sometimes conditions that ought to provoke crisis (e.g., sharp economic downturn or massive increases in immigration) may not actually produce crisis. Both manufactured crises and noncrises appear in this book.

The goal in examining these crises is twofold. First, as Lars Trägårdh has suggested, crises make visible the often invisible assumptions that underlie national community.[29] Second, in understanding how crises of closure are resolved, we can better understand the strategies through which national communities are both changed and preserved. There are three possible strategic responses to crises of closure: (1) *restriction*, wherein access to the membership community is denied to potential newcomers; (2) *expansion*, wherein the national community accepts newcomers. Such expansion may entail either "bridging," reaching across differences to create new membership ties, or "bonding," strengthening already-existing ties between members or partial members.[30] Finally, (3) *selection* entails the development of a specific set of criteria that admits certain newcomers but denies access to others. In the end, all processes of expansion and restriction are also selective. However, a separate category of selection is useful in that it distinguishes between a strategy that only selects for those who are already members (restriction) or allows new members in with few or no conditions (expansion). As will become clear through the narrative presented in this book, the strategies actors choose to pursue may either emphasize or de-emphasize homogeneity and may define exactly what is homogeneous about a community. To a large extent, then, homogeneity and heterogeneity matter because political actors make it matter.

The strategies available to even powerful actors, are, however structured in important ways by culture. Ann Swidler's conception of culture as a "tool kit" argues that actors' possibilities for strategic action are conditioned by a set of "habits, skills and styles" that are culturally determined.[31] Culture is both a resource and a constraint. Actors participating in the public discourse are constrained in particular by the prevailing cultural idioms of the society in which they live.[32] Cultural idioms are, broadly, a form of expression and thinking that is "natural" to a group of people. Brubaker, for instance, identifies civic and ethnic "idioms of nationhood" that represent the dominant way of thinking about membership in the nation. Cultural idioms are deeply rooted in the histories, identities, and interests of society as a whole, as well as of subgroups of that society.[33] These histories, identities, and interests may be complex and even contradictory. They are always subject to interpretation, and participants in the public discourse, particularly elites, have a great degree of latitude in choosing which aspects to emphasize. Idioms, then, are fluid over time, subject to both situational and subjective forces. Both elites and competing interests have opportunities to reshape these idioms, but there are limits to this reshaping. To resonate with their audience, elites can only draw on histories that are in some meaningful sense their own.[34]

The making of public policy, too, is constrained by culture. The shared values and common assumptions that make up the common sense of public discourse serve to limit the types of public policies that policymakers perceive as effective, or even morally acceptable, and such common sense varies between societies.[35] This limiting is, in part, a function of the structure of democratic politics—voting publics will only accept change that goes so far. However, cultural constraint also operates through the construction of actors' interests. Symbolic frameworks that have developed over time and through contestation assign meanings and importance to certain goals and goods over others.[36] Policymakers may dismiss certain policy options not only because the options are unpopular but also because they may fail to see certain options.

What is remarkable about the Swedish case in this regard is SAP's historic role in forging a new cultural idiom and framework for the Swedish nation, one that privileged social-democratic values and institutions. Over the course of the twentieth century, the development and refinement of this cultural idiom not only worked to keep SAP in power but also provided SAP with mechanisms for dealing effectively with the crises of closure the nation faced. It did so because it had developed into a hegemonic way of thinking about the role of the state and the features of a "good society." SAP, in other words, became the authors of a new Gramscian hegemony. "Hegemony," in Antonio Gramsci's work, refers to the political and cultural dominance of one group over the whole of society.[37] By extension, the values, symbols, and ideology of that group also comes to be dominant, exercising control over subordinate groups through setting the limits for legitimate debate. David Laitin elaborates this aspect of hegemony, arguing that hegemony provides a "symbolic framework" within which all actors, elite or mass, must work in order to act effectively.[38] Despite this constriction of possible positions, however, hegemony is not necessarily harmful to democracy. In fact, as Dylan Riley has recently argued, by delimiting a space of competitive antagonisms where means, but not broad goals, are contested, hegemony actually lays the groundwork for the sort of compromises that are necessary to a functioning democracy.[39] The development of hegemony—be it a socialist hegemony as Gramsci predicted or a social-democratic hegemony as developed in twentieth century Sweden—allows for a relatively clear conception of the "good society," which elites can construct their positions in relation to.[40]

Gramsci further argues that while the development of hegemony is a dimension of class formation, it is not economically dependent, but rather is a function of politics and culture. In fact, that hegemony develops autonomously from economics is one of the concept's key features: groups can become "dominant," claiming to rule for a considerably broader base than simply their own narrow economic class because they express the interests of nations in ways that are not purely economic. Hegemony is also maintained autonomously from economic dominance.[41] In so doing, political or cultural hegemonies also structure context-specific concepts of "peoples" or "nations." As Rogers Smith, puts it, "Economic interests are always integral and often primary in senses of peoplehood. . . . Nonetheless, economic interests can usually be advanced through many forms of peoplehood, so that economic motives alone cannot be completely determinative of political outcomes."[42] Smith's statement highlights another key feature of the relationship between economic and cultural and political hegemony: interpretation. Economics is important, but it matters insofar as it is interpreted through cultural and political lenses. Thus, while the rise and persistence of social-democratic hegemony in Sweden was related to the economic conditions under which it developed, it was the interpretation of these conditions that allowed for the remarkable rise of social-democratic hegemony. Once this type of hegemony was established, it constrained the available interpretations of economic crisis (and gain) in a way that privileged support for social-democratic policy solutions, even for nonsocialist actors.

The process of interpretation is an elite process, carried out by specific actors in specific social roles. Gramsci ascribed, famously, to the idea that "there really do exist rulers and ruled, leaders and led."[43] Gramsci's account is primarily top-down: a small subset of elites within a class, which he calls "intellectuals," works to achieve first dominance within a class ("intraclass hegemony"), followed by cross-class (or "interclass") hegemony of the type previously discussed in this introduction. Insofar as the "nation" is made possible by an (at least symbolic) integration of multiple classes, we can think of this stage of hegemony building, when bounded by the state, as also a process of negotiating national closure.[44] It is notable that intellectuals, in Gramsci's account, are not only, or even primarily, "thinkers" or "artists," but also organizers, political leaders, and others who work toward creating and promoting the ideology of their class. Such elites may work initially in the interest of that class, but in formulating an ideology, seek to extend beyond the narrow class and make claims to be representative of the whole nation.[45] Hegemonic ideologies reach toward universality, though in practice that universality often stops at the boundaries of the nation (or the state). The idea that there is a necessary connection between interclass hegemony and national closure gives us some clues into the unique position of the Social Democratic Party, perhaps the most successful of "interclass" political parties, in the development of Swedish nationhood. I argue in this book that claims made in service of developing hegemony can, and do, come to be integral parts of national identity: indeed, in the case of Sweden, as the very thing that holds the nation together.

In sum, I propose a theoretical framework for this book that makes three broad statements:

1. National closure is subject to periods of crisis ("crises of closure"). Examining these crises gives us clues to the relationship between the national community as a membership community and as a codification of the welfare state. In the case of Sweden, understanding how the People's Home has expanded or contracted in responses to crises helps us to understand how the social-democratic welfare state par excellence was built and maintained.

2. Political elites act strategically to deal with such crises, employing strategies of restriction, expansion, or selection. Such strategic responses can coexist in a time period, and the same elites may pur-

sue multiple strategies simultaneously. In the case of Sweden, the focus ought to be placed squarely on SAP elites, given their unique dominance of the political stage for most of the twentieth century.

3. In dealing with crises of closure, elites are both constrained by culture and create new cultural constraints. In the case of Sweden, this entails the development and maintenance of social-democratic hegemony that comes to define what it is to be Swedish.

The overarching conclusion of this book's narrative is that homogeneity and heterogeneity matter for the welfare state because elites make it matter. However, elites do so within an evolving set of cultural, economic, and political contexts, even as their own actions shape and reshape these contexts.

The Case: Social Democracy and the Swedish Welfare State

Social-democratic ideology and values are key to the story told here. So, what is "social democracy," and what does such an ideology entail? At its heart, social democracy is an ideology that embeds a capitalist market economy within political institutions that are emphatically democratic.[46] With this arrangement, the productive economy in a social democracy, as in any capitalist system, relies on competition and the profit motive to create growth and encourage innovation.[47] However, that capitalist system—and the distributive and redistributive system attached to it—are subject to political control through democratic institutions. The economy is highly regulated, but not state directed. The labor market, too, is subject to regulation and support, and wages as a function of the capitalist economy are set not by employers alone, but in concert with the state and labor as an attempt to coordinate the economy across regions and industries. Redistribution decommodifies labor to increase the bargaining power of workers and to smooth the ups and downs of an essentially intact capitalism.[48] This redistribution is, like market regulation, under the control of the state and subject to democratic political influence.

Institutionally, it is important to distinguish social-democratic ideology from ideologies such as fascism, libertarianism, or communism. Unlike any of these ideologies, social democracy does not describe an ideal end state for institutions, but rather provides ideals and principles for organizing society that, theoretically if not always in practice, can be constantly adapted to new conditions.[49] Yet, where the social-democratic ideology has been most influential, a certain model has arisen and, to an extent, persisted. The social-democratic ideology underlies the so-called Nordic model, a term used to describe an economic and social system combining corporatism, a comprehensive welfare state, and an activist industrial policy, especially including active labor-market policies. Although all five Nordic countries (Iceland, Norway, Denmark, Finland, and Sweden) adhere to a certain degree to the Nordic model, Sweden is often held up as the paradigmatic example. The ideal social-democratic economy, especially before "Third Way" social democracy in the late 1980s through the 1990s, was influenced by John Maynard Keynes and focused on keeping people in employment, stimulating consumerism, and supporting those out of work.[50] Because of this Keynesian focus, the economies and political systems most directly influenced by social-democratic ideology rely heavily on continued economic growth. Much of that growth has been accomplished through an export-driven economy, relying on the international capitalist economy to support a social-democratic domestic regime—security at home with competition abroad, as Peter Katzenstein put it.[51]

That political control of the economy is, and was always meant to remain, democratic is an essential feature of the ideology. Sheri Berman's landmark work labels this essential feature the "primacy of politics."[52] Berman's term implies two concepts, equally important to understanding the argument that is to come in this book: (1) that, historically, the welfare state arose to a large extent out of party politics; that is, party political competition and consensus, as well as, crucially, the vital role of SAP, determined not just the initial shape but the course of social-democratic development in Sweden,[53] and (2) that democratic politics remained, for much of the twentieth century, determinative of economic development, and not vice versa. What Berman says of Sweden (and Germany) is also true of social democracy in general. It is not simply that the market is embedded in politics, but that politics takes precedence over markets.

Social democracy also provides a set of political values that guide policy and, in the case of Sweden, provide a sort of culture that exerts an influence over individuals, and not just policy.[54] A number of values could fall under the rubric of "social-democratic" values, but those that seem to drive political culture in particular in the Swedish case and that frame much of the content of the chapters that follow are equality, freedom of choice, and security. Timothy Alan Tilton includes a host of other values that shaped the Swedish welfare state, including solidarity, work, and efficiency alongside the three just listed. Tilton makes the case quite well that these values have concrete and specific policy outcomes (solidaristic wage policy, industrial democracy, etc.), but I argue that equality, freedom of choice, and security are more diffuse, popularly ascribed to, and resonant. They are, hence, better suited for demarcating a social-democratic cultural hegemony, which provides a cultural framework for integration in the Swedish case.

Equality, in particular, is often held to be the leading value for social democracy. Equality in social democracy encompasses both equality of opportunity and relative equality of outcomes. It figures both as a condition that enhances the experiences of individual and drives economic growth. It is a concept that has grown from being primarily about income equality and leveling between the classes to encompassing a more radical idea of both economic and social equality between different groups in society. Equality is also conceived of as, in some sense, a "prior" value for the other two.[55] Equality, security, and freedom of choice are all mutually constitutive, but a level of equality is necessary to ensure that security is truly felt and that freedom of choice entails real choice.

Security (*trygghet*) in this case is primarily economic security and refers to the sense that life is, to a certain extent, secure, predictable, and comfortable; that not only are a person's needs taken care of but that that person is not anxious about those needs. The welfare state, particularly, is the mechanism through which security is primarily achieved. Freedom of choice, the third value around which the social-democratic hegemony is built, is less apparently social-democratic than the other two. Individual liberty is, of course, essential to ideas of social democracy and provides one of the key dividing lines between social democracy and communism. Yet, it is important to distinguish the freedom of social democracy from that of classical liberalism. Liberty in the social-democratic sense is positive liberty—"freedom to"— rather than the negative liberty—"freedom from"—that characterizes classical liberalism. In that way, freedom of choice, to live one's life in the manner of one's choosing, becomes compatible with a large and powerful state.

This point brings us back to our discussion of social democracy's core tenet—that economic institutions should be firmly embedded in political institutions. A widespread understanding of the state as the primary producer of "the good life" mirrors extensive state involvement in the economic realm for individuals. This state involvement is deeply colored by values that have specific meanings, although those meanings change over time. The state—not the individual, civil society, nor any other institution—is seen as the guarantor of equality, freedom of choice, and security.[56] State intervention is seen as producing a kind of security and equality that allows individuals to live life as they choose—what Henrik Berggren and Lars Trägårdh call "statist individualism."[57]

The institutional outcome of the social-democratic ideology that promotes state intervention is the welfare state. That this book's focus is on the Swedish case specifically is no accident. Sweden is, along with being a country that moved rather spectacularly from homogeneity to heterogeneity in the twentieth century, also the paradigmatic case for studies of the welfare state. Many of the most influential explanations of welfare-state development have featured the case of Sweden at their core; for example, the "power-resources" school of explanations and the "state-centered" models of welfare-state development.[58]

The power-resources model focuses on the mobilization of working-class interests and the strength of social-democratic parties as the determining factors in the development of welfare states.[59] The basic argument is that states with strong labor movements, especially those connected with strong political parties, will have more well-developed welfare states than those without these characteristics. In overly simplified terms, labor movements and their parties function in this model as "intermediary" groups, translating the interests and demands of the working class into actual policy change—welfare-state policies such as unemployment insurance, pensions, and parental leave. Social-democratic parties are functionaries primarily for their class and only secondarily for other groups, such as the nation.

The power-resources model has been subject to reconstruction in the past few decades, however, and the impact of other class actors has been highlighted, not least in the very case the power-resources model was designed to explain. Peter Baldwin, for instance, notes that cross-class compromise, particularly between SAP and the Agrarian Party, was key in the establishing of the universalist Swedish pension system.[60] Peter Swenson, on the other hand, argues that the Swedish welfare state arose out of the balancing of capitalist and socialist interests. In his account, Sweden's powerful employer associations often had a strong positive effect on welfare-institution building, although in the United States, capitalist interests tended to work against such developments.[61] Neither downplays the importance of social-democratic actors and the labor movement more generally, however, and both emphasize the importance of political maneuvering.

Critics of the perspective, however, have pointed out that the power-resources model ignores or underestimates the role of the state. Alexander Hicks, for instance, argues that labor movements and workers' parties can successfully translate their strength into policy best when they are incorporated into centralized corporatist decision-making structures.[62] Thus, a second line of reasoning points to institutional features, particularly the level of autonomy of centralized state bureaucrats, as the key factor in the rise of the welfare state.[63] These explanations, too, seem particularly well suited to describe the Swedish case. Certainly, the corporatist pact between state, labor, and capital struck in 1938 at Saltsjöbaden set the groundwork for a social-democratic managed labor market and economy more generally. The dominance of SAP, likewise, can be attributed just as much to SAP's ability to organize the administrative apparatuses of the state as its ability to integrate labor interests with the political apparatuses of the state.[64] Indeed, studies that attempt to combine power-resources and state-centered approaches do an excellent job in elaborating the institutional and political opportunities that led to welfare-state growth, as well as identifying key actors in the story of the assembling of the Swedish welfare machine.[65]

What neither set of explanations convincingly explains, however, is why these actors became powerful enough to set the policy agenda to the extent that they have been able to do so. What I suggest is that the power-resources model succeeds in identifying the important actors (SAP, especially), but conceiving of these actors' ascendance as solely or even primarily a result of successful class mobilization ignores the crucial role that the broader national bases for SAP's ideology played in their electoral and legislative successes. Furthermore, the later power-resources theorists who concern themselves with political maneuvering of multiple parties also get part of the story right. However, once again, the puzzle of why other political actors come to wholeheartedly embrace the welfare state, not just in its particular programs (which may or may not be in their economic interests) but as a model for the good society, is left virtually untouched.

To tackle these questions, we need to understand the cultural and normative bases of the Swedish welfare state. Indeed, some attention has been paid to these factors, dating back even to Marquis Childs's famous 1936 characterization of Sweden as a "middle way" between individualism and collectivism.[66] Childs did little to explain the origin of this cultural predisposition, however. Perhaps he, like the more recent historian Lars Trägårdh, believed that the cultural support for many of the principles of the welfare state long predated the rise of social democracy and "in fact are of ancient origins and are perhaps most aptly described simply as 'Swedish.'"[67] Though Trägårdh does not see the Swedish welfare state as automatically resulting from ancient culture, he argues that many of the key goals of the welfare state are rooted in cultural characteristics with long histories (e.g., the commitment to full employment is an outgrowth of a cultural propensity to see work as an obligation; family policies arise out of a cultural statist individualism), which have been interpreted and translated by SAP, the Liberals, and the Conservatives in equal measures in response to economic conditions. Trägårdh, however, ascribes entirely too much continuity to Swedish culture, and papers over the very real conflicts in the basic worldview that existed both between and within political parties in much of the early days of the Swedish welfare state.[68] Others have made less sweeping claims about the cultural foundations of the welfare state. Such explanations have focused on Sweden's history of a free peasantry with a genuine, if limited, voice in political institutions even in preindustrial Sweden, sometimes linking this history with the particularly egalitarian version of Lutheranism predominant in Scandinavia.[69]

Of course, the arguments noted previously that link ethnic homogeneity to the universal Swedish welfare state are also cultural arguments. For instance, Offe's assertion that a "sameness" underlies the Swedish welfare state by reducing the occurrence of conflicts and making consensus easier, is an argument about Swedish culture primarily.[70] Likewise, arguments that point to the overlap of the concepts of "state," "society," and "people" in the Swedish language and culture as contributing to, perhaps even constitutive of, the high level of trust in the state also provides a cultural link between ethnic homogeneity and the welfare state.[71] Most of the explanations have some truth to them. Yet all of these explanations, both those that focus on ethnicity and those that focus on other factors, assume a preexisting and relatively stable culture that is somehow transmuted into a generous welfare state. In this book I attempt to modify these explanations by focusing on the role of SAP, not just in drawing on culture, but in creating culture, something that is vital to understanding the remarkable success of the social-democratic welfare state in Sweden.

Focusing on the dynamic nature of culture and the role of elites in creating culture, the explanation set forth in this work leaves room for understanding how cultural change may threaten the welfare state. In fact, much of the literature on welfare states in the last decade has been focused on explanations for potential or actual welfare-state retrenchment. Paul Pierson famously dubbed the modern era one of a "new politics of the welfare state" operating under conditions of "permanent austerity."[72] Although Pierson initially found little evidence of wholesale reversals of welfare-state institutions, he has since found that smaller cuts and modifications have worked to ensure that social protections are slowly eroding. Recent swings toward austerity in many European countries have perhaps proved him correct. Pierson contends that the power-resources theory of welfare state development tells us very little about welfare-state retrenchment: the sources of retrenchment are more precisely found in the transition to a postindustrial economy. Yet, he and others find that very little actual retrenchment has occurred, though economic liberalization certainly has.[73] Until very recently, this lack of welfare-state retrenchment has been the case in Sweden, too. The last period of center-right governance has begun to change this, as Sweden has been knocked off its "top spot" in terms of replacement rates for certain social insurances. Whether this program of austerity is connected to, as Pierson would argue, a shift toward a postindustrial economy, increased immigration, or another factor is, as of yet, hard to tell. The main action of this book, however, sets the stage for this decline, and perhaps by the end, the mechanisms may become clearer.

Part of the explanation might be found in changes in the 1990s that scholars of retrenchment have largely ignored. Walter Korpi challenges the notion that retrenchment had not, by 2003, occurred, arguing that scholars of retrenchment have been working with an incomplete picture of welfare-state institutions. In particular, he argues that the abandonment of the goal of full employment by Western European states, including Sweden, represents a fundamental challenge to welfare states.[74] Whether this significant retrenchment is a result of traditional left-right politics is a matter of intense debate, however. Some insist that the power-resources model continues to hold in the face of retrenchment,[75] whereas others see very little effect of partisan politics.[76] Others argue that bureaucrats have much more latitude to make cuts and will do so in response to a complex set of interests. Anders Lindbom, for instance, finds that, in the case of Sweden, bureaucrats have been much more instrumental in cutting social expenditures than any political party.[77] Korpi and Joakim Palme, however, argue that in the case of Sweden, partisan politics continued to matter in retrenchment, especially in the abandonment of full employment. However, it is not true that nonsocialists cut and socialists preserve social rights. Rather, left and right parties are engaged in a "reworking of the European postwar social contract" that may have radically different distributive consequences than that which they came to earlier in the twentieth century.[78] The notion of a radical overhaul seems to hold some weight in the case of Sweden, where the social-democratic hegemony that characterized much of the twentieth century seems to have finally loosened and found a viable challenger in the shape of the current center-right parties.

Of course, there are those who place the blame for retrenchment squarely on the shoulders of increased diversity. These critics are not limited to welfare chauvinist populist politicians, although they certainly argue this way as well. Klaus Offe, for instance, attributes retrenchment—or in any case lack of welfare-state expansion—to a "destruction of collectivities" that attacks the solidaristic "sameness" that forms the foundation of support for the welfare state. He states that "even in the rather exceptional case of Sweden, new divisions, antisolidaristic strategies, symptoms of lack of trust in the welfare state's administration and particularistic tendencies . . . put into question major achievements of public policy."[79] Critics point to a number of dimensions of diversity that may be bad for the welfare state, but the majority focus on ethnic diversity and especially immigration.

Likewise, the shape of the state also affects integration. "Welfare regime," for instance, may have an effect on both integration policies and integration outcomes. Stephen Castles and Mark Miller, for instance, find that social-democratic regimes are most likely to pursue "interventionist" integration strategies. In other words, social-democratic states are more likely to have an integration strategy that involves active attempts to bring immigrants into economic and cultural institutions rather than simply letting them "sink or swim" in a free-market system. This combination of social democracy and active integration is a "hallmark of the Scandinavian approach."[80] Some have suggested that, because both involve high levels of state intervention and have aspects of a social-engineering ethos, commitment to a universalist welfare state requires that immigrants be drawn into the system.[81] As the final chapters of this book will show, this strategy has both strengths and weaknesses for the immigrants themselves and for the society.[82]

What is lacking from most immigration studies and what I seek to remedy here is a picture of the relationship between immigration and the welfare state in the long run. Most studies focus on either the present or a single historical time period, or, alternatively, rather narrowly on discrimination and racism alone. What is sought in this work is inflection points between social policy discourses and immigration discourses. Ultimately, connecting the processes of social closure that immigration and integration policies entail and the national closure processes that welfare states require will help in understanding how the relationship between homogeneity, heterogeneity, and the welfare state has developed over time, building a more precise explanation of their effect on one another.

Data and Methods

Research Design and Case Selection

The work described here is a single-case study, but with a series of internal comparisons across time periods. Although case studies have been criticized for, among other things, lacking generalizable results and being "pure description," they also have a number of advantages. First, case studies, precisely because they are focused on a single case, can provide a level of details that is difficult or impossible for other methods to provide. As Anthony Orum, Joe Feagin, and Gideon Sjoberg put it, a case study "provides information from a number of sources and over a period of time, thus permitting a more holistic study of complex social networks and complexes of social action and social meanings."[83] Further, because of this close engagement with a number of sources, the case study is well suited to provide explanations and understandings that are meaningful within the context of the case. Second, case studies are particularly amenable to the use of narrative, both as a style of presentation and as an analytical tool (i.e., to provide explanations of events or phenomena). As such, case studies have a relatively straightforward mechanism for bringing time into the analysis—a distinct advantage for a study like the one proposed that ranges over a long historical time period.

In addition to the use of narrative to bring time in, the use of internal comparisons across five time periods highlights the effect of time on the objects of study. Using internal comparisons somewhat limits the number of variables to be controlled for, helping to isolate the effects of the variables of interest (level of immigration, idiom[s] of nation). At the same time, I do not assume here that each of these time periods is independent, recognizing that what happens in each of the earlier time periods affects the later ones.

The use of a single-case study does not, furthermore, imply a lack of transferability to other cases. Case studies are often meant to illuminate parallel cases, or at least aspects of parallel cases. Although it is likely there is no case that is similar enough to the Swedish case that one could lift the arguments wholesale and apply them to another, the experience of Sweden may indeed suggest solutions to the problems of diversifying welfare states elsewhere. Indeed, the final chapter, where Sweden is becoming less and less exceptional both in terms of immigration and in terms of welfare-state politics, may prove of particular value for understanding other cases. This case study, therefore, not only has value in itself but provides an excellent launching point for comparative work.

Sweden has specifically been chosen for this case study both because of its status as the social-democratic welfare state par excellence and because of its late experience with immigration. Sweden's welfare-state pedigree has been previously described and does not need to be repeated in this section. Chronologically, however, we can generally trace a broad narrative of the welfare state's origins: SAP abandoned orthodox socialism in the 1910s and formed its first government in 1920. By 1932, SAP had become Sweden's biggest party, ushering in an era of SAP rule that was unbroken until 1976 and dominant until the 1990s.[84] SAP managed to achieve many of its early reforms through coalition building, especially the 1933 Red-Green alliance that arose out of the "cow trade" with the Agrarian Party.[85] The historic Saltsjöbaden compromise between Landsorganisation (LO) and the Swedish Employers Association also laid the ground for the high-level collective-bargaining agreements that became a central tenet of the Swedish welfare model. SAP used its position of strength before and during World War II (when they led a Grand Coalition government) to essentially dictate the building of social policy in the postwar period; it put into effect both flat-rate universal programs such as child allowances and a basic pension, as well as income-related programs such as unemployment and sickness insurance that, given SAP's commitment to full employment, had the character of universal programs. By the mid-1950s, the ground was laid for the universalist social-democratic welfare state.

In terms of immigration, large-scale immigration from outside the Nordic area has occurred in Sweden largely after the institution of the Swedish welfare state. The number of foreign-born residents has increased steadily from about 4 percent in 1960 to about 14 percent in 2008. Furthermore, the number of foreign-born residents from the Nordic countries has decreased significantly, from about 58 percent in 1960 to less than 25 percent in 2004. In contrast, the number of foreign-born from refugee-sending countries has increased from about 20 percent in 1960 to about 53 percent in 2004.[86] More specific numbers on immigration can be found in their respective places in the chapters that follow. Thus, Sweden represents a case wherein relative homogeneity characterized the time period in which the welfare state first grew up, but where immigration, and therefore heterogeneity, increased rapidly once that welfare state was firmly entrenched.

Time periods in this work have been chosen because they frame moments where national closure is threatened or unstable, or, in the case of time period 3, where objective conditions seemed likely to produce a crisis. Although ongoing and normal processes of closure are, of course, important to national identity, crisis makes closure mechanisms and strategies more visible and hence more suitable for a work of this type. The time periods selected are as follows:

Time period 1, 1928–1932: Starting with Per Albin Hansson's famous *folkhemstal* ("People's Home Speech") in parliament in 1928, and ending with the first SAP victory in a long string of virtually uninterrupted victories in 1932, this time period is a period of SAP power consolidation. In the process, the SAP works to construct a national closure that is favorable to its electoral position.

Time period 2, 1945–1950: Following World War II, Sweden accepts a large number of war refugees, who present a challenge to Sweden's national closure-as-entry. At the same time, SAP is pushing for a universalist welfare state, building many of the institutions that are a realization of P. A. Hansson's People's Home ideal (a crisis of closure-as-access to goods).

Time period 3, 1968–1975: Increased labor migration pushes immigration and integration into the public debate (a crisis of closure-as-entry).

Furthermore, the oil crises of the 1970s prompt an economic debate that poses a potential challenge for the welfare state, although SAP hegemony largely averts that challenge (a potential, but not realized crisis of closure-as-access to goods).

Time period 4, 1991–1995: Economic crisis, coupled with high unemployment and ideological incoherence within SAP leads to the first major challenge to its dominance since the 1940s, a crisis of closure-as-access to goods. Furthermore, a refugee crisis (closure-as-entry) occasioned a wide-ranging debate on migration, multiculturalism, and Swedishness.

Time period 5, 2006–2014: The final time period represents the rise of the center-right as a truly counterhegemonic, internally consistent force in Swedish politics. This change provokes crises of closure (both of entry and of access to goods) as the welfare state is scaled back and as the debate on immigration shifts drastically, most obviously seen in the success of the far-right xenophobic Sweden Democrats.

The choice to examine such a broad swath of time has necessitated some sacrifice of detail. Entire books could be written on each of these time periods (indeed, there have been). However, the comparisons of periods during which Sweden had a homogenous population to periods when the population was heterogenous and of building to maintaining to challenging the welfare state are intended to provide answers to the bigger questions about closure over time. In this book I do not follow one particular set of social policies through history, but rather I consider the welfare state holistically and conceptually. Although I reference certain policies throughout, these references should not be considered either a history of or an explanation for any one specific social policy.[87]

Data and Analysis

The main data source for the first four time periods consist of newspaper data from three major newspapers: *Arbetet* (*ARB*), a Malmö newspaper affiliated with SAP; *Dagens Nyheter* (*DN*), a Stockholm newspaper affiliated with the Liberals; and *Svenska Dagbladet* (*SvD*), a Stockholm newspaper affiliated with the Conservatives. For the fifth time period, *Arbetet*, which went bankrupt in 2000, is replaced with *Norrländska Social-Demokraten* (*NSD*), the largest surviving nontabloid SAP paper. All of these papers are chosen for their large readership, as well as their status as relatively mainstream papers for their particular political slant. There were multiple newspapers associated with each of the three orientations, some of which were more radical than the three chosen.[88] The choice to consult mainstream-oriented papers allows me to use these papers largely as a proxy for party speech in the first three time periods when these papers are directly connected to political parties. For these three periods, the papers have organizational links to the parties through funding as well as through personnel. The editors of all three papers were drawn from party members, many of whom had sat in parliament at one time or another. Newspapers are relied on more heavily than other sources because hegemony cannot be reduced merely to political culture as practiced in the halls of governance. Newspapers are uniquely suited to evaluating the operation of cultural and political hegemony in that they act as speech that links between the public and the political. Swedish newspapers, because they are so closely tied to political parties, do this linking job particularly well.

Using parliamentary debates as a check on these papers reveals that party speech in parliament and in the papers is nearly identical in the first two periods. In the third, there are increasing differences, with more independent voices coming through despite the continuing organizational links between the parties and the papers. This variety is particularly true of *DN*. I have noted within the main text when writers are not affiliated with the Liberals in *DN* or the Conservatives in *SvD*, or when the position taken in the paper is substantially different from those taken by the party within parliament.

In the last two time periods (1991–1995 and 2006–2014), both *DN* and *SvD* are "independent" although they retain their political leanings, becoming "independent-liberal" and "independent-conservative," respectively. I have attempted in the final time period to note the political positioning of the writers whenever possible, especially when these have differed from the overall orientation of the papers. *ARB* remains a steadfastly mainstream SAP paper until its demise, and *Norrländska Social-Demokraten* is also closely associated with SAP.

For the first three time periods, a manual examination of every eighth issue of each newspaper was carried out. In addition, issues on dates of particular

Table 1. Search terms for time periods 4 (1991–1995)
and 5 (2006–2014)

Swedish	English
MIGRATION:	
flykting*	refugee
invandr*	immigrant/immigration
asyl*	asylum(seeker)
rasis*	racist/racism
minoritet*	minority
utlänn*	foreigner
främlingsfientlig*	xenophobia/c
SOCIAL POLICY:	
välfärd*	welfare
socialpolitik	social policy/politics
pension	pension
daghem	day care
föräldra*	parental (leave, insurance)
bidrag*	benefit
arbetslöshet	unemployment
NATION:	
folkhem	people's home
nation*	nation(-al/-alism/-ality)
fosterl*	homeland/patriotism/ic
IDEALS:	
jämlikhet/jämställdhet	equality
valfrihet	freedom of choice
trygghet	security
solidar*	solidarity

* Search was performed with a truncation at this spot.

interest (May 1, the weeks leading up to elections, etc.) were also searched.
Article indices are available for time periods two and three for the papers in
question. However, these indices are not exhaustive and particularly exclude
most unsigned opinion pieces, which formed a large part of my data. I did,
however, use the indices to cross-check my hand examination, in order to
ensure that I did not miss any major pieces of relevance. For the period 1991–
1995 and 2006–2014, I used the database ArtikelSök to search for relevant
articles. See table 1 for a list of search terms. Articles and editorials were

Table 2. Article totals by paper/year

Time Period	Arbetet	Dagens Nyheter	Svenska Dagbladet	Total
1928–1932	213	110	76	399
1945–1950	168	215	97	480
1968–1975	222	234	121	577
1991–1995	103	159	138	400
TOTAL	706	718	432	1,856

selected using theory-driven purposive sampling, that is, articles and editorials were selected for their relevance to the research question.[89] Although editorials and other opinion pieces are often left out of newspaper content analyses, I have chosen to leave them in. The reason for this inclusion is that the reason-giving speech that is most relevant to the project is most likely to be found in opinion pieces. This process resulted in a database of 2,321 articles. See table 2 for the number of articles by newspaper and by time period.

In addition to the newspaper data, relevant parliamentary debates on social policy initiatives and immigration or integration initiatives were analyzed. This analysis functioned as a check on the use of the popular press as a proxy for party speech as well as an additional source of data. In the first three periods, the debate in parliament was substantially similar to that in the popular press. For the fourth time period, some important differences are noted in that chapter. I furthermore consulted a number of documents from the Labor Movement Archives, and National Archives, including personal correspondences, internal party meeting minutes, and documents from relevant committees.

I performed a qualitative analysis on all documents. The initial coding was carried out according to a framework developed from the theoretical literature. Over the course of analysis, the coding structure was adjusted and refined throughout the coding process. Main themes coded for include nation (nation-as-people; nation-as-class; nation-as-state), inclusion-exclusion, (immigrants as members, Swedes as members), welfare (support for/opposition to reforms, morality of welfare state/particular programs, economic efficiency of welfare state/programs), portrayals of SAP (as class party, national party, as idealistic, as self-interested), portrayals of nonsocialist parties (as class parties, national parties, as idealistic, as self-interested), promotion of values (equality, freedom of choice, security, democracy) and attitudes toward immigrants (immigrants as welfare abusers, immigrants as good citizens, immigrants as in need of charity). Articles were also coded by source, both by author (where possible) and by stated political orientation, which as previously noted nearly always aligned with the source newspaper for the first three periods, but not for the last.

In addition to primary sources, a wide range of secondary sources were consulted in order to understand the broader context for the processes examined in this work, as well as to help build a narrative of welfare state and national development. Secondary sources included work from several disciplines (history, sociology, and political science, chiefly) by both Swedish and other scholars. Narrative, that is, the retelling of complex events set in their sequential ordering is considered vital. Each of the individual empirical chapters attempts to tell the story of that time period, while building an overarching narrative for all four time periods. Thus I take seriously William Sewell's statement that "giving a causal account of something . . . means telling a story of how it came to be."[90]

The Structure of the Book

This book is organized chronologically, starting in 1928 and ending in 2014. Each chapter is organized according to the logic of that particular time period. This book can furthermore be divided into two main parts: the first two empirical chapters fitting loosely under the title of "Homogeneity in the People's Home" and the third, fourth, and fifth chapters under "Heterogeneity in the People's Home." Each of these two parts is followed by an interlude. The focus of the interludes is primarily on conclusions about the specific case, rather than the theoretical implications of these findings, the latter of which can be found in the final conclusions.

A Note on Terminology

Within this book, I have tried not to conflate the Social Democratic Party and the set of values and policies that make up "social democracy" as an ideology. To indicate when I am talking about the former, I use the abbreviation "SAP" or the capitalized phrase "Social Democrats" when appropriate. When discussing the latter, I use the uncapitalized phrases "social democracy" or "social-democratic." All other parties are referred to by their standard international names. As noted within the chapters that follow, each of the four main parties (excluding SAP) changes names over the course of the time periods considered in this book. I use the following terminology to describe the parties, following international convention:

SAP or Social Democrats: Socialdemokratiska Arbetarpartiet (the Social-Democratic Worker's Party).

Liberals: Frisinnade Folkpartiet Liberalerna (Freethinking People's Party Liberals) changed to Folkpartiet Liberalerna (People's Party Liberals) in 1934. "Liberals" is used for both variations of the party name.

Agrarian Party/Center Party: Bondeförbundet (Agrarian Party) changed to *Centerpartiet* (Center Party) in 1957.

Communist/Left Party: Sveriges Kommunistpartiet (Swedish Communist Party) became Vänsterpartiet Kommunisterna (Left Party Communists) in 1967 and finally simply Vänsterpartiet (Left Party) in 1990.

Conservatives: Högerpartiet (Right Party) became Moderata Samlingspartiet (the Moderate Coalition Party, or simply "Moderates") in 1969.

Greens: Miljöpartiet de Gröna (Environmental Party the Greens), founded in 1981 and active in parliamentary politics starting in 1988.

Christian Democrats: Kristdemokraterna, founded in 1964 and active in parliamentary politics starting in 1985.

New Democracy: Ny Demokrati, founded in 1991 and in parliament from 1991 to 1994.

Sweden Democrats: Sverigedemokraterna, founded in 1988 and in parliament since 2010.

Alliansen: Alliansen för Sverige (the Alliance for Sweden), a partnership between the Conservatives, the Liberals, the Center Party and the Christian Democrats, active since 2004.

Given the way in which Swedish politics has largely (though not entirely) functioned through the opposition of two blocks, usually referred to in

Swedish as a socialist block (SAP and the Communists/Left Party) and a *borgerlig*, or bourgeois block (Conservatives, Liberals, and Agrarians/Center, later joined by the Christian Democrats). The latter term has generally had a much broader meaning in Swedish that roughly equates to "non-Socialist," and many scholars adopt this term even in English. However, given that it is misleading as a category of analysis (an agrarian party does not have its class bases in the bourgeoisie, for instance), I have chosen to avoid this label except in direct quotations. It is replaced with a disaggregation of specific parties where possible, and the broader term "nonsocialist" where it is necessary to speak of the three parties together. In the final chapter, this block is referred to as either "center-right," following international reporting norms, or by its proper name (Alliansen).

PART I

Homogeneity in the People's Home

Chapter 1

1928–1932: Ethnic Nation and Social Democratic Consolidation

Sweden's Social Democratic Party (Socialdemokratiska Arbetarpartiet, or SAP), was founded in 1889, growing out of and primarily backed by the trade union movement.[1] The early party had a particularly close, formal association with the blue-collar trade union federation, the Landsorganisation (LO). In its early days, SAP was dedicated first and foremost to revolutionary class struggle. The party initially modeled itself after the German Social Democrats, whose manifesto provided not just the inspiration, but the actual text for SAP's own first party program. Though some within the party—notably, Hjalmar Branting, SAP's first elected representative—supported social reform, most were in favor of revolution. Even the supporters of a more moderate program of reform did not dismiss the usefulness of force as a way of bringing about the revolution.

The focus remained primarily on militant class struggle into the early 1920s, but alternate views, more optimistic about the possibility of reforms as an end in themselves, began to surface in the mid-1910s. In 1917, differences of opinion on these two perspectives on reformism led to a split in the party, with the Social Democratic Youth Organization leaving for a new, left-wing socialist party with ties to Russian communism. The loss of the more radical element of the party left room for collaboration with other parties. SAP formed a close cooperation with Liberals in the campaign for universal suffrage and, later, the eight-hour workday. By the time universal male suffrage was achieved in 1918 (1921 for women), a commitment to work within a democratic system had replaced revolution at the heart of SAP's program.[2] As Herbert Tingsten put it, "With each year the party's perspective shifted a little until . . . the word 'democracy' was accorded the sacred position once reserved for 'socialism.'"[3]

The cooperation between Liberals and SAP was never entirely smooth. SAP's desire to retain the classical Marxist view of class struggle, furthermore, prevented the party from supporting many of the Liberals' preferred reforms. Yet, the coalition remained strong so long as democratic, and not social, reform remained the focus of Swedish politics.[4] Cooperation between the Liberals and SAP broke down following the success of the suffrage campaign in 1918, and SAP formed their first government alone in 1920. The reason for the official break in 1920 was, nominally, a dispute over municipal taxes. However, SAP's desire to pursue the idea of socialization weighed heavily in the decision to break up the coalition. Following this disintegration, the Liberals quickly became the main object for Social Democratic opposition as the Liberals realigned themselves with the Conservatives.

By 1932, SAP had become Sweden's biggest party, ushering in an era of Social Democratic rule that was unbroken until 1976, and a dominance that continued into the 1990s (for a timeline of Swedish governments, see table 3). Some have credited a shift to "moderate reformism" as the reasoning behind SAP's breakthrough,[5] and others a change in SAP's concept of democracy.[6] Both of these changes probably were important, as were SAP's attempts to build cross-class alliances with the rural proletariat and smallholders.[7] It is also true, however, that SAP's rhetoric shifted in this time, and the party no longer profiled itself solely as a "working-class party." Rather, SAP began to claim that it was a party of the whole nation—a *folkparti*.[8]

This chapter focuses on the process by which SAP became a national party, and how it began to position itself as the architect of the welfare state. I focus on SAP as a party, rather than welfare-state development, which makes sense given the role that party politics played in creating the Swedish economy and considering that most of the foundations for the welfare state

Table 3. Swedish governments

Year	Prime Minister	Party
October 10, 1928–June 7, 1930	Arvid Lindman	Conservatives
June 7, 1930–August 6, 1932	Carl Gustaf Ekman	Liberals
August 6, 1932– September 24, 1932	Felix Hamrin	Liberals
September 24, 1932–June 19, 1936	Per Albin Hansson	SAP
June 19, 1936–September 28, 1936	Axel Pehrsson	Agrarian Party
September 28, 1936–December 13, 1939	Per Albin Hansson	Coalition: SAP, Agrarian Party
December 13, 1939–July 31, 1945	Per Albin Hansson	Coalition: SAP, Agrarian Party, Liberals, and Conservatives
July 31, 1945–October 6, 1946	Per Albin Hansson	SAP
October 11, 1946–October 1, 1951	Tage Erlander	SAP
October 1, 1951–October 31, 1957	Tage Erlander	Coalition: SAP, Agrarian Party
October 31, 1957–October 14, 1969	Tage Erlander	SAP
October 14, 1969—October 8, 1976.	Olof Palme	SAP
October 8, 1976–October 18, 1978.	Thorbjörn Fälldin	Coalition: Center, Conservatives, and Liberals
October 18, 1978–October 12, 1979	Ola Ullsten	Liberals
October 12, 1979–May 19, 1981	Thorbjörn Fälldin	Coalition: Center, Conservatives, and Liberals
May 19, 1981–October 8, 1982	Thorbjörn Fälldin	Coalition: Center, Liberals
October 8, 1982–February 28, 1986.	Olof Palme	SAP
March 1, 1986–October 4, 1991	Ingvar Carlsson	SAP
October 4, 1991–October 7, 1994	Carl Bildt	Coalition: Conservatives, Center, Liberals, and Christian Democrats
October 7, 1994–March 22, 1996	Ingvar Carlsson	SAP
March 22, 1996–October 6, 2006	Göran Persson	SAP
October 6, 2006–October 3, 2014	Fredrik Reinfeldt	Alliansen (Conservatives, Center, Liberals, and Christian Democrats)
October 3, 2014–present	Stefan Löfven	SAP, Greens

were put into place after 1932.[9] It is also worth noting that Gramsci considered the intellectuals' transition from claiming to speak for a class to claiming to speak for a nation to be a key step in the building of a new hegemony.[10] To achieve this transition, SAP drew on ethnic, civic, and mixed ethnic-civic definitions of the Swedish nation. This use of multiple and mixed idioms represents a strategy to solve a potential crisis for the Social Democrats in a context where they are balancing national and class interests. SAP is responding, essentially, to the demand for the working class to be integrated into the national whole, and it achieves this integration through controlling the definition of the nation. SAP's definitional efforts, were, thus, an expansive response to a crisis of closure-as-access to goods, although one with certain restrictions at the margins. SAP aimed to establish the Swedishness of the nation on partially ethnic grounds, but this strategy turned out to be expansive as a context where ethnicity is more—not less—inclusive than class categories. The party achieved success by providing a set of highly resonant conceptions of the nation, but these were conceptions that privileged SAP and their ideas about the social system.

The Swedish *Folkhem*

In 1928, SAP's party chairman, Per Albin Hansson, gave a speech that called on Swedes to treat Sweden as a good home and the Swedish nation as a single family. The *folkhemstal* was a speech that marked SAP's separation from revolutionary class struggle, signaling the party's aspirations to become a national party. In presenting such a cohesive, resonant vision for Sweden's future, the speech set the tone for SAP's (and Sweden's) politics for most of the rest of the twentieth century. Though Hansson did not coin the term "People's Home," his use of the term made SAP and *folkhemspolitik* (people's home politics) synonymous. But, what, exactly did the concept mean?

The term "People's Home" historically had a wide variety of meanings. When *folkhem* was first used is unknown, but the term came into wide usage in connection with a Liberal campaign to extend access to newspapers in the 1890s. The term *folkhem* as referring to the Swedish nation was of a later mint. Rudolf Kjellén, a political scientist and Conservative politician, is credited for first using the term as such. Kjellén did not give the term a very precise meaning, however, using it generally to represent a strong, traditional national community.[11] The Liberals, as well, laid some claim to the term and continued to use it to refer to Sweden throughout the 1920s. For the Liberals, the "People's Home" was an expression of their specifically *democratic* conception of the Swedish nation and state. The party tended to use *folkstat* (people's state) interchangeably with *folkhem*, indicating that perhaps the social aspect of the concept was less well-developed among Liberals. The equation of the *folkhem* with the more complex set of obligations and expectations required in a social state was a wholly Social Democratic innovation. And it was highly successful. As SAP ascended to their place of dominance, the People's Home idea became entirely bound up with social democracy (and with Hansson personally), eclipsing all previous uses of the term. When Hansson launched *folkhem* as the organizing principle of a new national Swedish social democracy, he offered some insight into who ought to be a part of the Swedish nation.

The primary image in the speech was one of "the good home," an image of familial harmony and solidarity. It is that sentiment that underlies the most famous passage of the speech:

> The foundation of the home is fellowship and feelings of togetherness. The good home doesn't admit privilege or backwardness—neither favorites nor stepchildren. There one doesn't look down on the other. There, one doesn't seek advantage to another's cost. The strong do not oppress or pillage the weak. In the good home there is equality, compassion, cooperation, helpfulness. Adapted to the great *people's* and *citizens'* home this would mean the breaking down of all the social and economic barriers that now divide citizens into the privileged and the backwards, the ruling and the dependent, the looters and the looted.[12]

Because Swedes were all members of the great Swedish family, Hansson argued, they ought to take care of each other. The People's Home was rooted in *equality, compassion,* and *cooperation.* The familial imagery calls to mind a rhetoric of blood ties that necessitates mutual obligation. Though civic nationalisms sometimes use a language of family—brotherhood, especially— the holistic notion of nation-as-family sounds more like a language of ethnicity than of citizenship. There is more than just a touch of paternalism in the family metaphor, too. In Hansson's *folkhem*, the state is a kind of guarantor of happy (and equal) family relations.

But the *folk* (people or nation) were also, notably, citizens. The state may have been the fatherly guarantor of equality, but citizens were also bound up in a network of mutual obligations and rights. Crucially, the realization of the *folkhem* was both enabled by, and supportive of, democracy. Hansson reportedly agonized over terminology, unsure of whether "People's Home" or "Citizen's Home" (*medborgarhem*) should be used. Indeed, the speech retained the title "People's Home—Citizen's Home" despite his choice of the former.[13] The idea of the people as democratic citizens pervaded the speech. Hansson highlighted the requirement that democracy be built on a foundation of actual (not just formal) equality, conditioned on positive liberty, a key social-democratic value: "If Swedish society is to become a good citizens' home, class differences must be removed, social care developed, an economic leveling occur, working people be given their share in economic administration, democracy implemented and adapted even socially and economically." Democracy was likewise necessary to ensure equality: "It [was] the major task of a true democratic politics to turn society into the good citizen's home." The *folk* was formulated as a body of citizens, made equal because of their connection to a protective state. Attaining equality, and making the nation into a "good family" was possible, according to Hansson, only with the guidance of SAP as the party of true democracy and the ultimate guarantor of equality. In launching this new politics, what was conspicuously scarce (though not absent) in this speech were references to SAP's traditional base: the working class.

SAP, from Class to Folk Party

Writing on the anniversary of the founding of a southern branch of SAP in 1931, one Social Democrat celebrated the increasing unity and universality of the party as such:

> Like birds, who one by one took off in a storm, they flew against the wind, eventually gathering together in a great flock. That the light fell differently on each of them doesn't mean that they didn't take off with the same colors on their wings. *They have all borne the colors of social demo-*

cratic ideals and have had the welfare of the whole nation as their goal (emphasis mine).[14]

Class-struggle politics, Hansson had realized, would only take SAP so far. To stand on their own, separate from the Liberals, SAP needed to appeal to a broader base. That SAP would reach out to a broader base is not surprising. As mass democratic participation increases, as occurred with the granting of universal suffrage from 1918 to 1921, the need for parties to appeal to the greatest possible number of voters increases. Parties seek to minimize calls to action that would divide the electorate, including calls to class struggle,[15] and many "workers' parties" are actually organized along "peoplehood" lines.[16] What is interesting in the case of SAP is, on the one hand, their remarkable success, and, on the other, how they achieved it. That SAP, in Sweden where working-class interests are thought to have been best promoted, was actually working outside the class-struggle frame, is significant.

In general, SAP's language of class struggle declined, and appeals to the whole nation increased between 1928 and 1932. The language of class never fully disappeared, but the contexts in which it was used became more restricted. In the 1928 parliamentary election campaign, SAP mixed class politics with appeals to the broader *folk*. Consequently, Social Democrat Gustav Möller declared at the 1928 May Day demonstrations in Stockholm that "the workers stood under the command of a foreign class" and that SAP's responsibility was first to the working class,[17] while in Malmö, Zeth Höglund argued that SAP did not represent solely the working class, but rather "aimed, on the whole, for society's best."[18] Similarly, the 1928 program not only spoke of an obligation for workers specifically to mobilize and to "battle the true terror" of a nonsocialist regime but also reached out to those who "desire a politics in the spirit and meaning of true *societal* solidarity."[19]

SAP's claims to be a national party intensified in the 1930 elections. It claimed it was the only party that would, in its "political action, strive for what will benefit and promote the entire nation's and people's interests."[20] SAP was still clearly a party in transition, though. The party continued to project itself as "the political expression of the property-less classes who lack the means of production."[21] This language was meant to include the rural proletariat and smallholders in addition to industrial workers. Yet, it was different from the strain of discourse which appealed to voters with a rhetoric focused on "peoplehood." The party leadership, too, recognized that the transition would take time and work:

> [SAP] should seek to establish our party on an even wider base, to make it into the great national party, which with support of a majority of the nation can realize the dream of the good *folkhem*. The expectations of such a union is a politics which meets the needs of different groups and without prejudice attempts to satisfy the legitimate demands, from which these needs are expressed. We don't need to go searching for that type of politics. We have enough guidance in our own experience, and truth be told, it is not really a question of anything other than a realization of our current politics with adaptations to the social and economic development of society.[22]

Ultimately, "SAP [wanted] to show that it [was] responsible to society" and "all Swedish citizens,"[23] but was loathe to give up the language that had changed "a spiritually sleeping, politically disenfranchised, socially enslaved and economically hamstrung mass into a spiritually and culturally awakened, politically enfranchised, conscious class, aware of its own human worth."[24]

This mixed discourse left the party open to attack from nonsocialist parties, especially SAP's former allies, the Liberals. Along with the Conservatives, they engaged in a campaign that sought to discredit SAP by highlighting the more radical syndicalist and communist elements within the socialist block. They accused SAP of "[marching] out to the battlefields, side by side with men from Moscow."[25] These attacks were relatively tame in 1928, but reached fever pitch in the 1930 elections as SAP's attempts to rebrand themselves as a national party intensified. The Liberals depicted SAP as an "out and out class party,"[26] covertly steered by "Bolsheviks" lurking within their ranks. They argued that SAP's new politics was a dangerous dividing force in Swedish politics. An editorial from *DN* expressed fear that the breakdown of the Liberal-SAP cooperation was a sign of an "unraveling of democracy":

> The bourgeois parties' collaboration on the one side and the socialist-communist coalition on the other easily leads one to believe the nation is divided into two nations, which exist to battle each other and between which no common ground exists. It's likely, then, that class differences will sharpen through such alliance politics. If this is the only lasting result of this alliance-

making, it would be sad. Among those, who hold a political world-view in which class struggle has become near enough a metaphysical necessity, this division must be greeted with relief as if something which is destined to be now is. But among those, who see the unraveling of modern democracy in this feeling of class enmity, this battle-readiness cannot be greeted with any enthusiasm at all.[27]

The nonsocialist parties' discrediting campaign seemed to work. SAP lost ground in the 1928 election, and although they recovered somewhat in 1930, they fell far short of being able to build even a minority government. The Social Democratic press attributed this loss largely to the use of scare tactics both about the composition of the party and what they would do in government. As an example of this type of tactic, the nonsocialist parties encouraged the rumor that SAP wanted to collectivize agriculture.[28] In fact, SAP had no intentions of doing so. SAP's response to these losses was, on the one hand, resigned, because "if one is a democrat, then one must accept all of democracy's consequences."[29] Yet on the other hand, there was a sense that the democratic will of the people had been perverted.[30] According to party leadership, SAP was the only party that had the interests of the whole nation at heart, and properly informed voters would have unquestionably backed SAP.

By the 1932 election, language appealing to "the general good," "societal interest," "all of the Swedish people," and "the whole nation" had become the dominant discourse from SAP. The preelection party congress "called for a rallying around a politics which, without regard for group or class interests, desires in all areas to assert and develop democracy as a tool for the general good . . . a call which will bring victory in all of Sweden's communities."[31] This choice of language represented a conscious avoidance of the narrow language of class politics. The strategy appears to have worked for SAP; the year 1932 marked a major victory for the party. Although it did not attain a majority, it did form a solid minority government—a favorable position from which to make allies in parliament and enter into a long, stable period of governance.

One should not take this interpretation too far, however. SAP was not a completely new party. Appeals to socialism were still made. The framing of socialism was different, though. SAP claimed to promote socialism not because it benefited the working classes specifically, but because "socialist

solutions" were the only solutions that served the "general interest." Furthermore, the new SAP government was "not going to, for the sake of
appearances, pursue politics of a radically socialist shade" but rather
would "decide their course of action dependent on what is for the good of
the country and the people." That this course of action "by itself will give a
more or less socialist tone to their politics" was merely a consequence of the
current economic crisis.[32] Yet the party was different in demonstrable ways.
It emphasized democracy and SAP as the party of "true" democracy more
forcefully than ever. This position meant, too, that attacks on the nonsocialist parties focused on these parties as antidemocratic "class dictators." It
is also true that SAP's newfound national focus encouraged its members to
speak not just to an abstract democratic nation, but to a particularly *Swedish* nation.

As Tingsten points out, SAP's view of democracy evolved in the early
twentieth century from viewing democracy as the preferred tactic for bringing about socialism to a value in and of itself.[33] Thus, SAP attempted to
rebrand itself, not just as a national party, but more specifically as the party
of true democracy. For SAP, "democracy's goals shone like a beacon and
urged people to fight for freedom, against oppression."[34] SAP also set itself
against the disingenuous democracy of the non-socialist parties. Thus, the
1928 parliamentary elections were framed as "a choice between genuine
democracy, represented by the social democratic party, and some formal,
'apparent' democracy, represented by the other |parties|."[35] Socialist victory
was presented as a sign of "democratic maturity"—a sign that the Swedish
people were ready for democracy, unlike other nations whose people
"wandered around, driven by vague emotional impulses."[36] SAP was a true
"democratic people's movement" (*demokratisk folkrörelse*), whose members
were stewards of a great project of democratization inherited from a now-
defunct left consensus.[37] Although a "party of democracy" could potentially be a more traditional, class-struggle-focused socialist party, such was
not the image SAP sought to project. Democracy was a replacement for
endless class struggle: "The revolution |could| not be a goal in a society
where democracy reigns."[38]

The nonsocialist parties, of course, challenged SAP's claim to "true" democracy, countering that SAP's attempts to portray themselves as the party
of national democracy were simply disingenuous *valfiskeri*—fishing for
votes. SAP itself, their adversaries noted, was made up of "shortsighted vote-

counters."[39] Although the party's rhetoric was "worthy and impressive," it was "paired with a content which is all smoke and mirrors and nothing—except, of course, politics."[40] Further, "a social democratic government would," in fact, lead to a "situation where democratization's progress would be distorted and obstructed."[41] SAP "stands in the way of a just society," and it was the "good Swedish citizen's . . . enemy."[42]

An opposite depiction of the nonsocialist parties as enemies of democracy occurred in the Social Democratic press, as well. One editorial stated that nowhere in the nonsocialist parties' election "pamphlets does one find signs of a general interest; the societal viewpoint, solidarity are missing."[43] The Conservatives, in particular were singled out as "class dictators" and "emperors in miniature."[44] ARB argued that the Conservatives' "warning regarding class politics [fell] back on the ones doing the warning themselves, when the newly called parliament shows the strongest evidence of class politics from the Conservatives themselves."[45] For the nonsocialist parties, it was argued, "citizenship rights come from money."[46]

SAP recognized that the nonsocialist parties, too, had aspirations to represent the nation. SAP argued that their opponents' nationalism was a false *punschpatriotism* (punch patriotism), reflected only in a festive glass raised to the nation among the upper classes. It was bourgeois *fosterländskhet*[47] rather than true, popular *folklighet*, although not for lack of trying: "Against the bourgeois programs one cannot direct the criticism that they don't make the effort to *appear folklig*, but evidence of *folklig* reforms are missing entirely."[48] Inherent in this bourgeois nationalism was a romanticization of the upper classes, for instance, within historical writings that glorified the deeds of kings and the aristocracy while minimizing the contributions of the "people."[49] Thus, in SAP's construction, their own *folklighet* was based on a unifying principle—that social democracy was beneficial for the nation as a whole. The nonsocialist parties' *fosterländskhet*, in this interpretation, was an essentially upper-class phenomenon dependent on ignoring certain (industrial) classes and romanticizing others (e.g., farmers).

The democracy to which SAP appealed, furthermore, was a particularly Swedish democracy, built on a uniquely Swedish nation. That SAP could and would work within the bounds of the nation was acknowledged by the opposing parties, as for instance in this statement in an unsigned *DN* editorial in early 1928: "The expectations for mutual or, more precisely said, general fair play is a social democracy on Swedish and democratic grounds, a Social Democracy which isn't supported by, or makes secret deals with democracy's foes or obvious enemies of Swedish habits and Swedish traditions. The Social Democrats know this."[50] Beyond the need to avoid "enemies of . . . Swedish traditions" (Russian communists especially), SAP presented themselves as, in fact, more in harmony with Swedishness than other parties. "As a Swede, one wishes for the country's improvement, growth and expansion of the general well-being. . . . *As a social democrat, one wishes everything that a Swede wishes for.*"[51] Here the wishes of the Swedish people were equated with the wishes of the party. To be a social democrat, the party argued, was to be Swedish. The achievements of SAP were painted as achievements of and for the Swedish people. To make this a credible position, however, SAP needed to clarify who, exactly, were the "Swedish people" in the "People's Home."

Who Are the Folk *in Hansson's* Folkhem?

It was not always clear how SAP in this early period imagined the nation to which it was appealing. SAP's idea of the proper size and shape of the national closure that would restrict access to the new societal goods it was intent on producing was up in the air. An egalitarian sense of state-based citizenship is one candidate. This sense is often thought to underlie the modern sense of Swedish citizenship, and some have traced it back to the late nineteenth and early twentieth centuries.[52] However, the popularity of and state funding for an extensive program of race biology and a sometimes-related eugenic program also point toward a more ethnic conception of belonging in the *folkhem*. A third, mixed civic-ethnic conception, too, was present and actively used by SAP for political gains. This third conception was an image of the Swede as ethnically predisposed to democracy—the idea of Swedes as a people with "democracy in the blood."

From the early twentieth century, Sweden's national self-concept was based, at least in part, on egalitarianism. Attempts at nation building aimed in this period to include previously excluded parts of the population, especially the working class, in a democratically defined nation. The universal suffrage campaigns of SAP and the Liberals, in that they sought to extend citizenship rights to the working class, should be understood as a manifestation of this form of nation building.[53] Social Democrat Arthur Engberg, furthermore, contrasted SAP's freedom-enhancing nationalism with that of the nonsocialist parties:

> The nation as an expression of freedom's ideal, the nation as a tool for humanity's striving after a higher culture, a cooperative order, in which individual nations participate as members in international unity, the nation as a duty, a goal for the fight for justice as a collaborator in a true people's association—for such an idea is their blue-yellow hurrah-patriotism wildly foreign.[54]

Thus, Engberg saw the nation as progressive and liberating. Notably, too, the nation was an "association"—a voluntaristic, not organic body. The ties that bound the nation were shared ideals, not shared ethnicity. Engberg's formulation is an almost textbook description of the civic nation.[55] It is also worth repeating that Hansson's own *folkhemstal* pointed toward citizenship as a basis for membership. Part of SAP's own conception of the People's Home was that it was state mediated. People were members, at least in part, by virtue of their relationship with the state.

Yet, purely civic depictions of the nation were relatively rare in this period. Romantic notions of Herderian "folk souls"[56] that had only vague and fuzzy affinities with geographic boundaries and political identity still lingered in the national consciousness, and SAP could not ignore this notion. In fact, Sweden's sense of nation was particularly influenced by the notion of a unique "folk soul" in this period. Sweden had only within a few decades shed themselves of the last vestiges of empire, and the need to prove that Swedes were their own people with their own unique and positive qualities still drove some of the national reimagining found in this period. Thus, alongside the civic definition of nation existed an ethnic, even racial, definition, materialized in a popular, state-supported race biology program, coupled with a SAP-driven eugenics initiative. Sweden's relative homogeneity, a product of its peripheral geography and low levels of immigration, made common ethnicity relatively easy to call upon. The coincidence of territorial and ethnic closure, furthermore, hid the apparent inconsistency between the two. Yet, the ethnic community was not as neatly bounded as it might first seem. Some boundary work was still necessary.

Perhaps the most important boundary-making institution in this sense was the State Race Biological Institute, the first race biological institution to be fully state funded. The institute was founded in 1921 with broad support from across the political spectrum, although Member of Parliament Arthur Engberg, notably the same civic-minded SAP member quoted previously, was the most vocal. Engberg clearly linked racial homogeneity to positive outcomes, writing, for instance, that "the fact that our population is a highly homogeneous and uncontaminated race constitutes a value that is hard to overestimate."[57] The aims of the institute Engberg so vociferously supported were, in addition to scientific exploration, expressly stated as "race preservation," referring to the preservation of the quality of the Swedish racial stock.[58] Allan Vougt, SAP member of parliament and chief editor of *Arbetet*, justified the continued existence of the institute and its importance to SAP's program in a 1925 pamphlet entitled "Race Biology and Socialism," in which he states that "race hygiene doesn't have a goal of setting the races against each other, only to safeguard what is the best within each of them and to hinder the occurrence of dangerous combinations."[59] Herman Lundborg, a supporter of so-called mainline eugenics—the position that states that certain races held inherent worth and ought to be kept pure—was appointed as the first director of the Institute.

The institute's first and most important publication, a massive anthropometric study entitled *The Racial Characters of the Swedish Nation*, was published in 1926. The major task of this volume was to define the racial makeup of the inhabitants of the Swedish state. Lundborg and his coauthors sought to demonstrate that Sweden was, racially, the *most* Nordic of the Nordic states. Sweden was, according to the report, the original homeland of the Nordic race and had remained the most racially "pure" throughout its history.[60] The other racial groups found most commonly in Sweden, according to Lundborg, was the "East Baltic" race and the "Lappic" race. The latter referred to the Sami—the indigenous people of northern Scandinavia, who were confined, both in actuality and in the report, to a specific region and to a few socially marginal occupations. The former was described as a "Slavic" race, native to both Finland and Russia rather than to Sweden. Though Lundborg and his colleagues admitted that the Swedish nation was "racially mixed," both at the level of individuals and at the level of society, it is clear that they looked on the Nordic race as the "true" Swedes. Only the Nordic race is referred to as "our ancestors" in the volume.

Notably, Finns constituted one of few significant minorities in Sweden, and the position of Finnish speakers in northern Sweden, in particular, was an area of contention. Furthermore, the attempt to distance the Nordic race from a mostly Slavic race was significant. Swedish socialists often saw Russians as a backward people, and their brand of socialism as rash and "immature."[61] From nonsocialist corners, there was fear of creeping Russian influence, sometimes expressed through accusations of Russian blood infiltrating the Social Democratic ranks.[62] Thus the "scientific" standard for distinguishing Nordic from East Baltic/Slavic laid out in massive anthropometric tables and photographic plates in *Racial Characters* can be seen as one manifestation of a more generalized Russian fear, as well as an attempt to manage the presence of the Finnish and Sami minorities within the (Nordic) Swedish nation.

The book was well received at home and abroad and, when republished in a streamlined Swedish translation, sold well to the general public. There were some detractors, however. For instance, one reviewer questioned the nationalism in the book, not because it was wrong per se, but because nationalism had no place in a scientific publication.[63] The perceived overrepresentation of Sami was also criticized, indicating perhaps a belief that they ought not be considered a significant part of the national community.[64] The existence of a Nordic race, and the necessity of a race biological program with "race-hygienic" aims, however, was not questioned by either the social-democratic press or by the bourgeois press. The only major objection the social-democratic press seemed to raise was regarding the appropriateness of the photographic plates in the book—particularly the inclusion of famous Swedes among the other subjects.[65]

That the work of the institute had prescriptive and not just descriptive aspirations was intended to be clear. The race biological program of the institute carried with it a concern with "race hygiene." *Racial Characters* did not make any explicit recommendations, but assessing the "quality" of the Swedish race was one of its stated goals. It is no coincidence that the first calls for a legally codified program of sterilization occurred in the same year as the institute's founding. Such a law did not pass until 1934, but the discourse producing it was clearly active during the years under study. The 1934 Law on Sterilization allowed for the sterilization of women who were thought to be a threat to the quality of the Swedish "stock." Though in the text of the law, sterilization was only to be carried out on a voluntary basis, sterilization was often made a condition for release from mental health or correctional institutions (including schools for the "feebleminded").[66] Sterilization for racial reasons was not specifically indicated, although being a member of the racialized group called the *Tattare* was often a strike against a woman in her case. The *Tattare*, notably, were a social group who were believed by most at the time to have Romani blood, but who probably were simply social outsiders.[67] Instead, the "quality" of the race was often linked to some vague measure of the "productivity" of the population, and the women targeted were often mentally ill or poor.[68]

Indeed, class featured into decisions on racial classifications perhaps more than the Social Democrats who promoted the institute would have liked. *Racial Characters* portrayed the upper classes as fitting a distinctly more "Nordic" profile—taller, with a higher incidence of blue eyes. Lundborg argued explicitly that class position was an effect of racial differences: "Decided systematic differences exist between the different occupational groups and different social strata. . . . There is no occasion to doubt, however, that these differences . . . depend to a major extent on different racial compositions in the respective populations."[69] Further evidence of the racialization of class differences can be found in the "ethnographic plates" included in *Racial Characters*. Lundborg included several photographs of the major racial types—Nordic, East Baltic, Lappic (Sami), and various individuals identified as "mixed race." Among the Nordic race, one finds primarily professionals, military officers, and aristocrats. The East Baltic and mixed-race plates, by contrast, depict almost entirely farmers, laborers, and squatters. The Lappic plates depict nomads and farmers. Interesting, as well, are several plates depicting people in "national" or regional traditional dress—all of the Nordic race. Similar to language claiming the Nordic race as "our ancestors," the photographic plates clearly depict the Nordic race as the true Swedish nation. The conflation of race and class can be seen as an attempt to draw racial boundaries excluding the working classes and some agricultural workers from full membership in the nation.

SAP, of course, was attempting to integrate the working class into a national whole. The party had little interest in a racialized concept of nation that rested on class difference. Some of the criticism of the photographic plates noted earlier, perhaps, can be seen as a protest against this concept. Nonetheless, many within SAP expressed support for the race biological project, and continued to support sterilization laws well into the second half of the twentieth century, although sterilization became increasingly less racialized following World War II.[70] Social Democratic support for race biology may be rooted in the *potential* for racial discourse to be more inclusive than class discourse in Sweden, so long as that discourse focused on national homogeneity vis-à-vis other states (i.e., the focus on Sweden as the "most Nordic" of Nordic states). Excluded groups could be constructed as peripheral or marginal. The Sami, for instance, were geographically isolated in the North and thus almost entirely ignored as potential polity members. Other populations targeted for sterilization, like the *Tattare*, were small and socially peripheral, and thus easily excluded. Finnish speakers in the North, meanwhile, were objects for active "Swedification" and therefore inclusion in the national community. As such, the racial definition of the Swedish nation included, in practice, most Swedes in the early twentieth century. The use of a racial definition of the Swedish nation could, paradoxically perhaps, be considered an expansive strategy. In fact, there is strong reason to believe that racial definitions were used in just that way.

Evidence for this expansive strategy can be found in the third way that SAP talked about their nation. Beyond simply ethnic and civic definitions of *folk* was a blended civic-ethnic definition rooted in the idea of Swedes as a people with "democracy in the blood"; that is, the idea that Swedes were naturally, ethnically, hereditarily predisposed to be democratic citizens. In other words, Swedes were ethnically civic. This construction relied on a romanticization of Sweden's "free" peasants. The Swedish peasants, because they were included early in quasi-representative bodies, were bearers of democracy. The peasants, at the same time, were the most *folklig* of the Swedish *folk*. They were depicted as the purest representatives of the Swedish ethnicity and as the root of true Swedishness.[71] It followed, then, that Swedes were ethnically predisposed to be freedom- and equality-loving citizens of a democratic state. Democracy, in this view, was not something that flowed institutionally from the early foundation of representative bodies, but was a trait genetically passed down from democratically inclined "free peasant" ancestors.

Even Herman Lundborg, the quintessential racialist, read democracy far back in history—"From the very beginning to the present time [Sweden] has been . . . a constitutional kingdom, not an absolute monarchy"[72]—linking this narrative to Swedish national character. Lundborg expressed a sentiment rooted in the historiography popular at the time, especially in the work of historian and poet Erik Gustav Geijer. Geijer's *Svenska folkets historia* (A History of the Swedish People, 1832) was exceedingly popular, and his narrative was found in textbooks across the country. Geijer propagated the image of the free peasant as the chief stock of the Swedish people. These peasants were fiercely independent and deeply committed to democracy. Geijer's account is rooted to an extent in fact. Peasants were included as one of the four estates in the Swedish diet, a precursor to the modern parliament, since the fifteenth century, and they enjoyed considerably more power than in most other states. Romantic-era historians, however, took this participation as evidence that democracy was a feature of the Swedish national character—the heart of the Swedish *folksjäl* (national soul), and that peasants were actually bearers of enlightenment.[73]

Lundborg, too, connected peasants to the Nordic race. He does both in the text and through the extensive use of children in national or regional dress, in idyllic peasant settings in the photo plates. These plates depict *only* the Nordic race. Of course, "farmers" were depicted in the East Baltic and Lappic plates, but these were labeled differently from the "peasants" and were neither dressed in national dress nor placed in the idyll of the Swedish countryside. Thus, although these non-Nordic farmers may have shared a profession with the idealized Nordic peasants, they were held as distinct from them. Note, too, that although the use of "famous" Swedes in the plates was objected to by the press, the use of national "peasant" dress was not.

SAP's calls for a democratic reform campaign called on this national Romantic image of the "freedom-loving, individualistic, and principled peasant."[74] SAP encouraged a view of the peasant village as "the cradle of democracy," wherein the Swedish character took on its progressive shade.[75] In 1929, for instance, in an unsigned *ARB* editorial celebrating SAP's role in Sweden's progress toward democracy, the author writes that "when trouble is brewing in the depths of the nation, the national soul may follow different impulses. Already in the middle of the 18th century broke forth a striving for freedom which, comparatively early, fulfilled this role."[76] Similarly, *Arbetet*'s editor Vougt wrote in 1931 that although other nations may fall to fascists, such a development was impossible in Sweden. Vougt argued that those who attempted to bring fascism to Sweden called themselves the "Swedish-est of the Swedes," but that the Swedish national character, being deeply committed to democracy, "lacks completely the psychological prerequisites for such movements."[77] Being a good democratic citizen was clearly linked to national character. This link by itself does not necessarily demonstrate a connection between democracy and *ethnicity*. However, seen juxtaposed against the idea of the democratic will of eighteenth-century peasants, and the simultaneous construction of the peasants as the "purest" members of the Nordic race, we begin to see evidence of overlap. Race, or at least ethnicity, and civic democratic values become conflated in such overlaps.

The *folkhemstal* itself could also be seen as an attempt to promote a particular national heritage rooted in both familial blood ties and in shared democratic values. The use of a family of "people" and a community of "citizens" side by side is telling. Racial and civic discourses could even be seen as mutually reinforcing. Ethnic heritage can only be associated with democracy and equality on a national scale when that ethnic heritage can be plausibly extended to the whole nation. It was useful for SAP to be able to tap into a racial discourse that emphasized Sweden's homogeneity and effectively incorporated some groups into the *ethnos* (e.g., Finnish speakers), while pushing peripheral groups (socially isolated *Tattare*, marked for sterilization, and geographically isolated Sami, ignored except as an anthropological curiosity) outside the boundaries of the nation. Thus, SAP was able to convince the electorate that they were a *folkparti* through claiming the mantle of democracy, because the Swedish nation could be defined narrowly as ethnic, but simultaneously inclusively, in terms of shared democratic principles.

Questionable Swedes: Finnish-Swedes, Swedish-Finns, and Gammalby Swedes

We can partially test these conceptions of nation by comparing cases where inhabitants (or potential inhabitants) were questionably Swedish. It should be noted that, because migration to Sweden was rare, there are few cases where new groups attempted to claim Swedishness in this period. Yet, three cases illustrate very well the ethnic and mixed civic-ethnic conceptions of nationhood that underlay SAP's ways of talking about the nation: Finnish-speaking Swedes (Sverigefinnar), Swedish-speaking Finns (Finlandssvenskar) and the Gammalby Swedes.

The last case provides the clearest illustration of the ethnic conception of nation. The Gammalby Swedes were a small community of Swedish speakers descended from a group of settlers who had migrated to Ukraine from Swedish Estonia in the late eighteenth century. The community held on to their language and traditions long into the twentieth century. In 1929, a group of about nine hundred settlers sought to relocate to Sweden. Some settled in Sweden permanently, others moved to Canada, and still others returned to what was by then the Soviet Union. To illustrate both the extent to which an ethnic definition of national membership was at work in early twentieth-century Sweden and what benefits accrued to those who belonged and were denied to those who did not, it is fruitful to compare the reception of these Gammalby Swedes to that of another migrant group in the early twentieth century—the Galicians. The Galicians entered Sweden in the first decades of the twentieth century, imported as labor for an already tight agricultural market. Although the number of migrants was not overwhelming (about one thousand at its height),[78] the response was very hostile, and the migrants were seen, particularly, as a hindrance to the claiming of rights for the working class. *Karlstads-Tidningen*, a Liberal paper, declared that "it is treason to bring in foreigners to take bread out of the mouth of our country's own children, just because they demand citizenship rights."[79] The Social Democratic press, too, condemned the Conservatives' support of this migration as a betrayal of the Swedish nation.[80]

The Gammalby Swedes, by contrast, were welcomed, at least initially, with open arms when they "returned" from Ukraine in 1929. The Gammalby Swedes entered Sweden under even worse economic conditions than the Galicians. However, they were given assistance in entering a tight agricultural market. Keeping in mind that the Swedish economy was in severe crisis, the efforts made to incorporate this population and the positive press they received from diverse political directions were remarkable. The Gammalby Swedes' return to Sweden was heralded as an opening "of the warm embrace of Mother Sweden, which invited in the windswept Swedish folk tribe (*folkstammen*)."[81] When it became clear that the Gammalby Swedes would not be able to adapt to the conditions of their erstwhile fatherland and that they would either move on (mostly to Canada) or return to Ukraine, both *Arbetet* and *Dagens Nyheter* saw the loss of what was portrayed as an integral part the Swedish people as a "tragedy."[82] In *Arbetet*, this sadness over the loss of this part of the Swedish nation became an indictment of the reigning capitalist mode of production.[83]

Although the two cases are not perfectly comparable, the difference in treatment of the two populations, both emigrating from Eastern Europe and attempting to enter at a time of economic difficulty, is striking. The Galicians—ethnic others—were seen as a distinct threat to the progress of workers' rights. In the case of the Gammalby Swedes, in contrast, socialism was posited as a means to maintain the integrity of the Swedish nation, ethnically defined. In other words, even in the words of those most pushing for an egalitarian society, membership in the ethnic nation was required for the affordance of rights that would have been accorded under more civic bases of membership.

Another comparison can illustrate, however, that ethnicity alone could not explain the terms of "membership" in the Swedish nation: a comparison between Finnish-speaking Swedes and Swedish-speaking Finns. Ethnic nations tend to pursue exclusion of ethnic others at home and inclusion of co-ethnics abroad. Civic nations, on the other hand, tend to grant national membership by virtue of residence in the territory and to pursue assimilatory policies toward ethnic others at home.[84] Regarding these two "Finnish" populations, however, there is evidence of a policy of protectiveness toward Swedish speakers abroad, coupled with an assimilative policy toward Finnish speakers at home.

Most of both Swedish speakers in Finland and Finnish speakers in Sweden at this time were long-standing national minorities. Most Swedish speakers in Finland had been there since the 1500s, and the Finnish speakers, concentrated largely in northern Sweden near the Finnish border, often in areas that were primarily Finnish speaking, were likely the original inhabitants of the area. Despite long periods of residence for both populations, there continued to be conflicts with the dominant populations. These conflicts provoked different reactions on the part of the Swedish press and politicians.

Both *DN* and *ARB* devoted serious attention to the Swedish-Finnish language conflicts in Finland during the period under study. One conflict, for instance, centered around the right of Swedish-speaking students at a Finnish university to be represented as their own group in student associations and to use Swedish in the classroom. In these cases, Swedish newspapers universally took a protective stance toward Swedish-speakers abroad, insisting that Swedish speakers be allowed to maintain their language. Finnish speakers' attempts to limit the use of Swedish or to demand the use of Finnish were dismissed as "marked by spitefulness" and "naive nationalism."[85]

By contrast, the Finnish-speaking population in Sweden were largely expected to "Swedify"——to learn Swedish and fully integrate into Swedish society, although demands for Finns to give up their own language were rare. This integration was accomplished mostly through Swedish-only schools and workplaces, even in "pure Finnish" areas.[86] This assimilatory pressure occurred despite protests from abroad similar to the ones launched by Swedish newspapers. The implication was that Finnish speakers in Sweden were in fact Swedish, whereas Swedish-speakers in Finland were part of the Swedish nation. Thus the Swedish nation seems to act in one case like an ethnic nation by being open to and protective of (perceived) co-ethnics abroad, but in the reverse case to act like a civic nation by pursuing assimilative policies toward ethnic others at home.

Conclusions: Inclusion or Exclusion and Early Social Democracy

The concept of the nation, thus, is decidedly mixed during the late 1920s and early 1930s. Despite the interesting cases of ethnic others noted previously, there was no real crisis of closure-as-entry given that there was very little migration into Sweden at the time. Closure as access-to-goods, however, was acutely important for SAP who was attempting to position itself as the architect of the welfare state. SAP had a pressing interest in lifting the working class into the status of members of the nation, thereby reconfiguring Swedish national closure. For this, bourgeois notions of upper-class patriotism were insufficient. Although the nonsocialist parties, too, sought to represent the nation, the bourgeois nation subordinated the working class, pushing it discursively out of the nation rather than seeking its integration.[87] A racial or ethnic definition of nation, thus, was more integrative and inclusive than class-based definitions, especially in the largely homogeneous Swedish context. However, the ethnic definition of nation that SAP reached for could not only be the scientific race biology discourse, whose strictly racialized class distinctions excluded SAP's primary base. Definitions writing off the working class as racially inferior hardly fit the inclusive sense of nation SAP strove for. SAP's desire to be the party of democracy and to build the "great People's Home," on the contrary, was enabled by a definition of people linking the inclusiveness of an ethnic nation with the state-guaranteed egalitarianism of a civic nation, which proved to be an excellent fit with the party's needs. This mixed discourse allowed SAP to include the working class, racially, as Swedes, and thereby claim for them the mantle of "citizen," fully included in the democratic polity. It also pointed to some of the ways in which SAP could transform this conception of nationhood into an ideology supporting the welfare state.

It is difficult in this early period to connect national idioms closely with welfare-state development. Yet, it is possible to identify some of the seeds of a universal welfare-state culture. In this period, SAP sets the scene, so to speak, putting down a foundation for the social-democratic hegemony that comes later. Most simply, the ability of SAP to gain and to hold power using this rhetoric put them in a position to push welfare legislation. Furthermore, the way in which the Social Democrats appropriated and shaped the *folk* concept not only gave SAP a strong anchor in the Swedish political system but also affected the organization of Swedish society.[88] The general principle of universalism, one that was to be refined in the later periods, fit substantially with the nationalizing approach taken by SAP during in the 1930s. More specific links between the use of idioms of nation and the welfare state may also be traced, however. For one thing, the presence of a race-hygiene program with "productiveness" as a goal has affinities with the welfare-capitalist system, which later developed. Furthermore, the requirements of Finns to "Swedify" in northern Sweden in order to gain access to services indicates that the boundaries of the budding welfare state also were drawn, at least in part, with the boundaries of the nation as SAP understood them. Most importantly, though, the conception of the nation that SAP called on in this early period was uniquely compatible with the welfare-state idea they continued to push in the years to follow.

Others have highlighted the potential connections between the Swedish sterilization program and the welfare-capitalist system of governance pushed by SAP.[89] Efficient production was a key part of the Swedish welfare model, and the sterilization program, aimed primarily at "unproductive" members of society, could be seen as a part of this model. The same impulse of rationalization and state control or planning evident in the welfare state also underlay the sterilization program. Much more generally, the birth of the program in a time when "mainline eugenics" and "race hygiene" were strong currents of thought both within and outside government points to a probable racial component to the "rationalization" impulse of sterilization. The connections here are tenuous, but they suggest at least a conceptual harmony between the race-hygienic goals of the sterilization program and the broad outlines of the "rational," technocratic social system that SAP wanted to create.

Furthermore, it is also true that one can trace the beginnings of a closing-off of the welfare state to those who do not belong in the requirement that Finnish speakers, even in wholly Finnish-speaking areas, speak Swedish in order to gain access to public education—according to T. H. Marshall, the first step toward social rights.[90] Despite the legal status of Finnish-speaking Swedes as citizens, their inclusion in state-provided services was contingent on them *becoming* Swedish, at the very least in a linguistic sense. Where the boundaries of the nation were drawn—how and under what conditions ethnically "Finnish" citizens were included—was an important question for how the goods of the state were to be distributed. This problem, a true and classic crisis of closure, becomes clearer—indeed magnified—as refugee migration comes in the postwar period.

For the most obvious connection between national closure and the welfare state in this early period, one need only look as far as Per Albin Hansson's *folkhemstal*. In addition to the promotion of particular boundaries of national inclusion, the *folkhemstal* also presented a vision of a universalist welfare state. The "great family" Hansson wished Sweden to become was not simply a vision of the nation but also a statement about how that family should act. The "good home" is one wherein members *take care* of each other. Hansson then goes on to clearly state that it is the responsibility of the state to ensure that this happens. "It is decisive, too," he says, "for the large masses of our people who have dreamt of the creation of [social and] political democracy, that the state powers should seriously take up the task of halting oppression and insecurity."

Following Hansson's speech, the idea of the *folkhem* became the main organizing cultural principle of the Swedish welfare state and was on its way to becoming the cornerstone of a wide-reaching social-democratic hegemony. This idea of the welfare state as an integrative People's Home closely approximates Marshall's classic conception of the welfare state as the nation given concrete form.[91] That is, the horizontal bonds of membership crucial to national identity were in the ideal social-democratic *folkhem*, made up of a feeling of inclusion in a system of social caring between members that is mediated through the state.[92] Hansson's speech, then, attempted to convince the Swedish people that Swedes indeed were a people who had as a national characteristic this propensity toward state-mediated caring—and that the boundaries of the nation drawn by SAP and others, based on the civic and ethnic traditions outlined earlier in this chapter, are also the extent of this network of care.

This process of convincing, however, continued for several decades. The next chapter devotes itself partially to that process, which can be thought of as the development of the cultural hegemony of social democracy. SAP's expansive strategy, designed to solve their issue of closure-as-access to goods and to draw the working class into a cohesive national "whole" based not only in both ethnicity and democracy, laid the groundwork for this process. SAP, as a truly "national" party with a particular claim to "Swedishness," was positioned to make social-democratic values synonymous with the character of the Swedish nation, something which they pursued actively following World War II.

Chapter 2

1945–1950: Making the "People's Home"

On October 6, 1946, Per Albin Hansson died unexpectedly while riding a streetcar in Stockholm. Between SAP's first major victory in 1932 and his death, Hansson had become a sort of *landsfader* (father of the nation), and SAP the clear leaders in Swedish politics. The quality of SAP's leadership was a key feature in SAP's ascent, but it was also the party's ability to make coalitions, especially the famous so-called cow trade agreement made between SAP and the Agrarian Party in 1933 that propelled them to the top.[1] This agreement allowed SAP to put into practice much of their crisis package for dealing with unemployment and positioned SAP to oversee economic recovery in second half of the 1930s. Similarly, the labor movement, closely connected with SAP, had reached a compromise with employers in 1938 in the historic Saltsjöbaden agreement that allowed for high-level collective bargaining and generally organized the labor market in a way that was favorable to SAP's programs for employment and social insurance.[2] This success set the stage for World War II's SAP-led Grand Coalition that included all Swedish parties except the Communists. Hansson remained throughout the war as prime minister, and SAP maintained and increased its popularity during these years. Some even suggested that the consensus-oriented Grand Coalition government with SAP at the lead should continue to rule after the war ended.[3]

By the time of his death in 1946, Hansson had become synonymous with SAP and the People's Home ideology. After his death, the party could not simply claim the legacy of the great statesman, but had to work to reclaim the *folkhem* ideology for the party and to turn it into an ideology of a people. For instance, this necessity is evidenced in the way that *Dagens Nyheter* mourns the loss of Per Albin's holistic perspective on Swedish society. In so doing, they connect Hansson personally to a patriotism and broadmindedness that, they argued, did not inhere in either SAP or social-democratic ideology in general. For example, one *DN* editorial proclaims that the *folkhem* was P. A. Hansson's "personal magic" (*personlig förtrollande*), and any attempt to lay claim to it by SAP now was simply empty "politics."[4]

The choice of who was to replace Hansson was colored by the popularity and charisma of the previous leader, and there was no obvious choice. In the end, Tage Erlander, a young and relatively untested former minister of education, was chosen over the older and more experienced social minister Gustav Möller. This choice was not without controversy. Erlander, despite his later image as a pragmatist, had at the time of his selection a reputation that placed him to the left of Hansson and Möller, and many doubted his ability to hold the party together through the loss of leadership.[5] Erlander's initial task, then, was on the one hand to keep the party itself unified and on the other to reassert SAP's claim, established in the 1930s, to be a party of the whole nation.

What was not challenged at this juncture was the moral correctness of the concept of Sweden as a People's Home. The idea that Sweden was to be a good home with cooperation (and the state) as its foundation had become fairly uncontroversial by the end of the Second World War. How that was to be achieved and who was to be allowed to truly be (or become) a member of the "family" that the People's Home concept entailed was, however, up for serious debate, given the reorganization of society that the end of World War II occasioned.

Postwar reorganization threw the Swedish "People's Home," with SAP as creator and helmsman, into crisis. More accurately, two coinciding crises, one of closure-as-entry and one of closure-as-access to goods, appeared at the end of the war. The first involves the management of refugee migration. The end of the war brought a large number of refugees, both Nordic and non-Nordic, to Swedish shores. The second crisis to be understood arises as part of SAP's efforts to reclaim and to retain its title of "national party" and to use that position to begin to build a social-democratic welfare state. This struggle was framed by postwar fears of unemployment and by the need to capitalize on wartime unity to build a strong sense of solidaristic "people-hood." SAP (and some other actors) used all three strategies—restriction, selection and expansion—available to them to resolve these crises. More specifically, during the period 1945–1950, there continues to be an ethni-cized notion of nation, but one that is considerably less explicit than that of the previous time period. The dividing lines between "member" and "non-member" shift to include Nordic refugees (and labor migrants), but not Baltic or southern European ones. Concurrently, SAP works more directly to make social democracy and social-democratic values into a Swedish national characteristic, with considerable success. Restated, SAP strengthens the cross-class social-democratic hegemony it began to build in the earlier period and moves to translate this cultural hegemony into actual structural change, building a better pension system and an expanded cash child benefit. We see, as well, how the other Swedish parties, especially the Liberals, begin to adopt this hegemonic way of thinking about the role of the state, coming into line with SAP's way of thinking.

The "Threat" of Migration

The final years of WWII brought an unprecedented flow of refugees into Sweden. Previously, Sweden had maintained a highly restrictive immigra-tion policy, wholly retaining the right to grant or to refuse refugee status. No person had a "right to asylum" under Swedish law. The officials in the Foreigner's Bureau (Utlänningsbyrå), furthermore, had a large degree of dis-cretion, making decisions on an individual, case-by-case basis. Labor-market protectionism played a large role in the design of this policy.[6] Toward the middle of the 1930s, the Swedish state began to consider granting asylum on a group-by-group basis. The issue was made salient by the increasing per-secution of Jews in Germany, and the resultant increase in the number of Jewish refugees seeking to enter Sweden. Most argued that defining these asylum seekers en masse as "political refugees" deserving of asylum was a bad idea—not just because it would lead to unacceptable numbers of (Jewish) refugees, but also because it would adversely affect Sweden's relationship with Germany, an important trading partner.[7] High degrees of discretion meant that individual prejudices—anti-Semitism in particular—were allowed to creep into the process of deciding who was to be granted the protection of the Swedish state.[8] At the same time, Sweden began to carefully track the small number of refugees who were in the country and to restrict their movement. Refugees were also required by law to note if they were Jewish when seeking asylum starting in 1938. Sweden's compliance with certain of the 1932 Nuremberg laws—for instance, the prohibition of marriage between Jews and non-Jewish Germans—is also worth noting. In fact, in some ways, the mid to late 1930s were more restrictive vis-à-vis refugees, especially Jewish refugees, than previously.

The major turning point came in 1942, when Nazi Germany deported eight hundred Norwegian Jews to Auschwitz-Birkenau. Sweden did nothing to prevent the deportation and made no proactive moves to save Norwegian Jews in the immediate aftermath. Despite this lack of action, close to a thousand Norwegian Jews fled to Sweden on their own and were allowed to stay. Sweden's inability to do more to help Norwegian Jews in 1942 was likely a major factor in the decision to actively rescue the Danish Jews, who came in numbers topping seven thousand—nearly all of the Jews living in Denmark at the time.[9] Coupled with daring rescue missions by Raoul Wallenberg and the rescue of thousands of Finnish children during the so-called Winter War, the tide seemed to be turning in favor of refugee acceptance. This turning point included a generous refugee policy in general, at least temporarily, and a massive increase in the number of foreigners in Sweden. Figure 1 gives an overview of the number of migrants coming to Sweden during the period under study. The majority of these were Nordic migrants. In all, a little over fifty thousand Nordic refugees (Norwegians, Danes, and Finns) were in Sweden by 1946. In addition, about eighty-three thousand Finns, including forty-five thousand unaccompanied children, were evacuated to Sweden at the end of the war, though many of these stayed only for short periods. The other major group of immigrants were refugees from the Baltic countries (Lithuania, Latvia, and Estonia), whose numbers reached as high as approximately thirty thousand, including six thousand so-called Estonian Swedes—ethnically

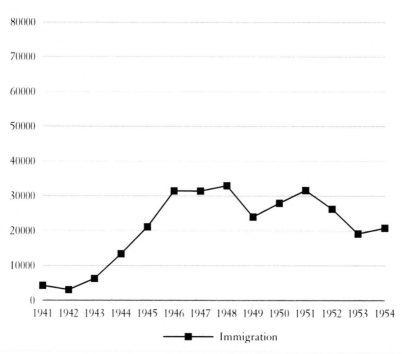

Figure 1. Immigration to Sweden, 1941–1954. Source: Statistiska Centralbyrån.

Swedish Estonians. There were also smaller numbers of other Europeans, totaling a bit over ten thousand.[10]

The increased number of migrants can be understood, on the one hand, as a relatively straightforward consequence of the material conditions prevailing at the end of the war. Sweden remained a safe and economically stable state while much of Europe still faced the horrors of active war and its aftermath. On the other hand, the increase in migration was also a result of changing attitudes and policies toward refugees. A highly restrictive refugee policy was replaced temporarily with one that was considerably more inclusive; at the same time, widespread xenophobia and anti-Semitism began to be replaced by increasingly inclusive attitudes,[11] as they were in a number of other European countries that found themselves in similar positions vis-à-vis refugees, notably Britain and Switzerland.[12] Explanations for these switches tend to revolve around reactions to the horrors of Nazism and around the exigencies of World War II. In the case of Sweden specifically, the occupation of Denmark and Norway may have provided the impetus to become more accepting of refugees, Nordic and non-Nordic alike.[13] Marcus Byström suggests a similar, but slightly more refined thesis in arguing that it was the increased presence of Nordics as refugees that led to greater inclusion in both policy and attitude for all refugees. He astutely points out, however, that an ethnic hierarchy that placed Nordic refugees above other refugees was retained.[14]

Even after the refugee crisis subsided and Sweden reverted to a more restrictive policy toward these refugees (although one within the purview of the 1951 Geneva Convention), migrants continued to come in fairly large numbers into the 1950s, drawn by labor shortages that accompanied the growth of the Swedish economy. The majority of these continued to be Nordic, primarily Finns, who faced few barriers to migration or work in Sweden. Organized imports of Hungarian, Austrian, and Italian workers began in 1946. The total yearly migration in the period between 1946 and 1950, which was mostly labor migration, was fairly stable, remaining just above or below thirty thousand migrants per year.[15]

Despite the phenomenal changes in migration and attitudes toward migration, the discussion of migrants tended to take the form of separate discussions of individual migrant groups. Thus it is difficult to speak of a unified "refugee" or "migrant discourse" during this period. It is possible, however, to develop descriptions of a separate "Nordic refugee discourse" and "Baltic refugee discourse," and then to compare these. Doing so illuminates the ways in which the character of the Swedish nation shaped policy decisions as well as how the nation was reshaped by the challenge that migration presented.

Swedish Self-Image

Although Swedes admitted their mistakes, particularly regarding the maintenance of restrictive policies against Jews at the beginning of the war, overall they built up a self-image for themselves as a leading refugee-accepting state. Their role in what was deemed a daring rescue mission in Denmark and elsewhere in Europe was lauded continually in the Swedish press as active and generous. This sentiment was echoed in the international arena, not least of all in the nascent United Nations.[16] At times, Sweden went so far as to claim for itself a tradition as a "right to asylum country" (asylrättsland),[17] an interpretation of Sweden's past migration policies that is, at best, overgenerous given their restrictive prewar policies, but one which served Sweden's emerging national image well. Swedes reported pride in their country's willingness to help. *Arbetet* points out the consensus around welcoming refugees:

> Every responsible party in our country is firmly resolved that—as also the Swedish people in general have understood the refugee question—we show these refugees who have been forced to make demands on our hospitality a real sanctuary within our borders, safe from their persecutors in the Gestapo or other pursuing groups.[18]

A related embarrassment and anger were expressed whenever improprieties regarding the treatment of refugees surfaced, as well. In particular, outrage appeared over the so-called Paulson affair. Robert Paulson, a civil servant within the Immigration Commission, acting through the Swedish consul in Germany, John Lönnegren, had given sensitive information about refugees to the Gestapo, resulting in many of these refugees being turned over to German authorities.[19] The reaction to these revelations were unqualified condemnation. *ARB*, for instance, declares that "the press corps is unanimous in its condemnation of the unqualified treachery that the main actors in this horrific affair are guilty of. How the feeling among many of the refugees in our country must be is not hard to guess."[20] Similarly, a *DN* editorial called Paulson's actions (the link with Lönnegren was not yet known) "inexplicable" and a threat to "trust for authorities" in these matters,[21] and *Svenska Dagbladet*'s coverage of the event is similar. Frequently, the press mentions how this scandal worsened Sweden's image in the international arena.[22]

At the same time, as the war reached its close, revelations of the horrors of the concentration camps were filtering through the press. Nazism's gruesome results radically called into question the legitimacy of the racially and religiously exclusive language that had flourished in the interwar period. Humanitarian language emphasizing the obligations Sweden had to oppressed and persecuted people based on their common humanity became dominant at the end of the war. A *DN* opinion piece, for instance, about the so-called intellectual refugees who proved more difficult to place in work called for "help for people who are, after all, fellow human beings."[23] In the social-democratic *ARB*, similarly, one reads that "we ought to show refugees the greatest hospitality and humanity possible, as well as a real sanctuary within our borders."[24]

This switch to humanitarianism is particularly evident in the thorough-going repudiation of anti-Semitism found throughout all three papers studied in this work, a complete reversal from the pervasive, if somewhat subdued, discourse of anti-Semitism that dominated the prewar and early war years.[25] The Liberal *DN*, in particular, devoted considerable space to condemnations of anti-Semitism, which it denounced as an "illness," "primitive," and a "horror."[26] This rejection of anti-Semitism was replaced with a pride in having "treated the Jewish refugees *as people*."[27] For instance, the Swedish authorities' willingness to adapt refugee camps to the religious needs of a group of Orthodox Jewish refugees is justified through appealing to the "basic human right to freely practice one's religion."[28] The discourse here is one of humanitarianism and universal human rights above all. Indeed, much of the criticism that surfaced regarding the restrictive migration policy pursued in the early years focused on the inhumanity of restrictions on Jewish migration, in particular.

Refugees: Nordic and Otherwise

Although there was a general switch to humanitarian language that accompanied shifts toward more open migration policy, not all refugees were treated the same. Differences existed both in concrete policy aimed at them and in the language used by press and politicians alike to describe them. Put simply, the obligation to help Nordic refugees (again, those from Denmark, Norway and Finland) was insisted on with greater force and more conviction than other groups.[29] Migration and migrant laws reflected these "greater obligations" to the Nordic people, transforming the symbolic boundary formed by the embracing language into a social boundary by allowing Nordic refugees access to opportunities denied non-Nordic refugees.[30] The most obvious manifestation of this preference is the Nordic refugees reduced time to citizenship. Nordic citizens were required to wait five years before gaining citizenship in Sweden, whereas other refugees were required to wait ten years.[31] Similarly, Danish and Norwegian refugees, though not Finnish, were routinely granted so-called general work permits which allowed them to legally seek work in any field in any part of Sweden, a freedom not granted to any of the non-Nordic refugees. Laws such as this militate against the explanation for differential treatment that focuses on the perception that Nordic refugees were more likely to return home within a few years. It is true that a large number of them did, indeed, move back to their country of origin—a consequence of their geographic proximity and their home-lands' good prospects for economic recovery. However, the easy path to citizenship and work demonstrates a willingness to accept Nordic migrants as permanent members, even if that invitation to permanent membership was infrequently taken up.

It is a key point that Nordic citizens were not to be helped simply because they were "fellow humans" as the more general discussion of refugees insisted, but because they were members of "brother peoples" (*bröderfolk*; occasionally "sister peoples," *systerfolk*, as well).[32] Humanitarian language certainly was deployed in service of Nordic help, but alongside it was a discourse drawing on the ethnically tinged language of common family, or the closely related language of common culture. An unsigned editorial in *DN*, for instance, argues that there is a "special understanding" between the Nordic peoples, rooted in "cultural affinities" that entails an "urgency to help one another."[33] Per Albin Hansson expressed this concept of brotherhood clearly in a parliamentary debate regarding help to Nordic neighbors:

> We have fulfilled what we consider natural obligations, and we have done so with a warm heart and desire to assist. We were able to do so because we managed to stay out of the war. The warm appreciation of our neighbors has delighted us as an expression of confidence and brotherhood.[34]

Rather than performing "exceptional rescue actions" as the Red Cross's humanitarian actions were sometimes framed, Hansson claims that taking in Nordic refugees was a "natural obligation" and an expression of "brotherhood."

What potentially complicates this picture of ethnic or cultural brotherhood as a basis for greater obligations is that many of the refugees from Norway and Denmark were Jews. Marcus Byström argues, on this point, that Nordic Jews were, at best, "half siblings."[35] In the ethnic hierarchy, they figured in a position somewhat above Balts, Eastern Europeans, and Germans, but below ethnically Nordic refugees. This ranking is reflected in, for example, the ways in which the Swedish Red Cross made decisions about whom to rescue from concentration camps: ethnically Nordic prisoners first, Nordic Jews second, and others afterward (a hierarchy that, notably, flagrantly violated the Red Cross's mission of help to all regardless of nationality).[36] The status of Nordic Jews as "brothers" or merely as "fellow humans" was indeterminate. At various points these refugees' "Nordic" or "Jewish" aspects were emphasized depending on the context in which their migration was discussed. Most *general* discussions of Nordic refugees, however, did not distinguish between ethnically Nordic and ethnically Jewish refugees; the title of "Nordic brothers" seemed to include even these "half siblings" for all intents and purposes most of the time. This inclusiveness did not always hold true when *specific* rescue actions were reported on. For instance, Byström correctly points out that when the Jewishness of the refugees is made salient, often in discussion of specific refugee groups, there is a distancing, including a tendency to revert back to the language of human rights rather than of fraternity.[37]

The saliency of the Nordic/non-Nordic divide, however, acquires new dimensions viewed from the vantage point of those refugees from entirely outside the Nordic area. The majority of these refugees were from the nearby Baltic countries (Lithuania, Latvia, and Estonia), all of whose fragile interwar independences had been shattered by German occupation, and which were beginning, by the end of the war, to come under Soviet influence. Baltic refugees were accepted in Sweden in large numbers toward the end of the war. On the one hand, these refugees received work permits and access to employment services, as well as assistance such as cash grants and housing assistance (through both the government and through nongovernment aid societies). Thus acceptance and subsequent good treatment of Baltic refugees was one side of Sweden's self-image as "good humanitarians" at the end of the war. On the other hand, waits for citizenship were longer and initially work permits were considerably more restricted for Balts than for Nordics—with the exception of a group of ethnically Swedish Estonians—though these restrictions began to loosen up as Sweden faced postwar labor shortages. Long residence requirements for Baltic citizens who wished to marry Swedish citizens also existed (seven years, until 1947 when this term was reduced to two years), requirements that did not exist for Nordic migrants.

Quite apart from the policies that made it more difficult for Baltic refugees to become permanent members was the difference in attitudes toward

Baltic refugees, both from the general public who were less willing to make sacrifices to support Baltic refugees and from officials who subjected Baltic refugees to greater scrutiny and suspicion regarding their political loyalties. All three newspapers suggested, for instance, that Baltic refugees ought to (indeed, were expected to) return home voluntarily once the war ended, even if that meant returning home to Soviet occupation.[38] Furthermore, concerns about the use of public buildings for refugee housing and public funds for support of refugees, specifically in reference to Baltic refugees, were raised.[39] Similar concerns were not raised for Nordic refugees.

Extending these observations to the more explicitly political field of discourse, we see distinct suspicion from those in power. These suspicions, along with geopolitical concerns, culminated in the deportation of 146 Baltic refugees back to their home countries—countries which had in the meantime come under Soviet occupation. The deportation had come in response to pressure from the Soviet Union, who claimed that large numbers of the refugees were German sympathizers or even war criminals. Although there were, indeed, some German sympathizers (and possibly war criminals) among the refugees, the Soviet Union's claims were greatly exaggerated and failed to take into account that many of those who fought in the German army were coerced into doing so.[40] The Swedish government, however, gave into the demands of the Soviet Union, although not without some resistance; the number of deportees was considerably lower than the Soviet Union had demanded. The Swedish government cited the desire to maintain reasonably good relations with the Soviet Union, a key part of Sweden's program of neutrality in defense of the deportation.[41] At the same time, many in the Swedish parliament expressed genuine suspicion of Baltic refugees as a group.[42]

Yet, such geopolitical caution and generalized suspicion did not extend to Nordic refugees, even under roughly similar circumstances. Although Finland did not come under Soviet rule, for instance, the Finnish loss in the Finnish-Soviet "Continuation War" resulted in Soviet claims to parts of Finland's Eastern Karelian province, as well as a precarious independence for the Finnish state that entailed continued Finnish deference to the Soviet Union on a number of points.[43] Yet Sweden granted asylum to refugees from Karelia (including even Russian citizens), actions which may have provoked Soviet displeasure. Deporting these refugees was considered "unthinkable" given the Swedish "obligation to the Finnish people."[44] In this instance, commitment to Sweden's Nordic brothers—even the more culturally and ethnically distant Finns—trumped other geopolitical concerns.[45]

There were also Nazi sympathizers among the refugees from Denmark and especially from Norway. Their presence did not escape the attention of either lawmakers or the press. However, the generalized suspicion that characterized the debate on Baltic refugees did not extend to Nordic refugees. In the case of Norwegians, rather, care was to be taken to discover individual "quislings" (e.g., traitors such as Nazi collaborator Vidkun Quisling) in order to deal with them appropriately, most often through deportation. An unsigned editorial in *ARB*, for instance, presents the following argument:

> In other words, one ought not to forget completely that, at least among the most recent refugees from the west, there is an out-and-out quisling-element, which we all agree ought to be held in quarantine if a deportation cannot be effected. Quite aside from this, however, it must be said that it is better if such actions take place under strict regulation of law, and with the greatest care for the refugees' rights.[46]

Suspicion against quislings was weighed against individual rights for Nordic migrants, and Nazi sympathizers were simply "bad apples" in a good bunch. This view led to a mass deportation of Baltic refugees but not Norwegian refugees.

Despite generalized suspicion and probably very real geopolitical pressure regarding the deportation of Balts, however, the decision to comply with the Soviet Union's demands was controversial. The press as a whole expressed outrage at the deportation of Balts, primarily because they were being deported to the Soviet Union where they were likely to face persecution. These objections were framed, once again, in humanitarian language. Baltic refugees were, after all, human beings with human rights, and geopolitical concerns ought not, members of the press argued, to take precedence over those human rights.[47] A few years later, a *DN* editorial labeled the deportations "from a moral perspective, the worst thing that the current government has done."[48]

Reactions to the deportations reflect the often contradictory responses to refugees overall: a desire to prevent or lessen human suffering, yet wariness and suspicion over the "otherness" of some migrants. This contradiction is also evident in the way in which Sweden's more open attitude and policies toward refugees proved temporary—when the war subsided, so too did Sweden's "generous and active" refugee policy to a large extent.[49] During World War II, Sweden was prepared to accept non-Nordic refugees within their borders as people in need of protection, but not prepared to accept them as full members. This attitude carried over even as the refugee crisis subsided and labor migration increased. Indeed, the same split between Nordic and non-Nordic migrants, potential and actual, is observed during this period.

Labor Migrants: Nordic and Otherwise

As the war ended and conditions improved all over western Europe, the flow of refugees to Sweden slowed to a crawl. As before the war, smaller groups of refugees made their way toward Sweden, but these were handled on a case-by-case basis and under the strict guidelines of the Geneva Convention. Sweden's economy improved, too, with the end of the war. Despite widespread fears that the end of the war would bring mass unemployment, just as the end of World War I had, Sweden instead found itself with labor shortages in a number of key industries. As a response, industry leaders and some politicians began calling for the import of labor from outside of Sweden. Labor imports from a number of countries were suggested, though most frequently from Denmark, Norway, Finland, and southern Europe (especially Italy).

Workers from Denmark or Norway, and to a lesser extent from Finland, were often singled out as acceptable imports into the Swedish labor market. Measures designed to create an open labor market between Norway, Denmark, and Sweden are the clearest example of this preference, but the prospect of the direct import of Nordic workers, mostly from Denmark, was viewed favorably by nearly all commentators. That Denmark had its own labor shortages and was therefore in no position to send workers was noted with regret, but calls for Danish workers continued regardless of the prospects for success.[50] Again the language of cultural similarity was marshaled in defense of either a relatively or a completely open labor market. An editorial in social-democratic *ARB*, for instance, noted that an import of workers from Denmark, "whose people, temperament, and language are close to ours would be desirable."[51] Liberal *DN* similarly contained approval of an import of Nordic doctors, who "from a general cultural standpoint would be desirable."[52] An open Nordic labor market was even seen as a foundation for social welfare because "our goals are the same: social security, economic justice and equal opportunity in cultural respects."[53] Indeed, some even suggested making social insurances portable across borders in the Nordic region.[54]

Despite this emphasis on brotherhood, the view of the Nordic neighbors was not always so inclusive, especially as the acute refugee crisis reached its end. Finns in northern Sweden, for instance, continued to be the object of suspicion in this period, often because of the high number of communists among them and, therefore, their supposed ties to Soviet Russia.[55] Likewise, elite enthusiasm for Nordic migrants was not always backed up by popular enthusiasm. A Gallup Poll in 1946, for instance, showed that only 22 percent of Swedes were "unconditionally" in favor of a completely open labor market, though an additional 21 percent supported it with some reservations regarding the availability of work.[56]

The rosiness of the reception for Nordic labor migrants becomes crystal clear when we examine the response to plans to import workers from elsewhere. The response to the idea of bringing in workers from southern Europe was almost entirely negative. This type of labor import was labeled a "drastic measure" or a "last resort."[57] Objections were largely couched in cultural, not economic terms. Although Nordic workers came from a people whose "customs and language were near to ours," Italians had a "lifestyle and mentality |that was| completely different from ours."[58] Furthermore, it was argued that southern European workers were likely to act as a wage depressant because they were unlikely to have the same "cultural expectations for standards of living."[59] In other words, even what is normally an economic argument drew on the idea that southern Europeans were too different *culturally* to integrate into Swedish working life. In *DN*, one finds concern perhaps once the labor market cools down, problems will arise between Swedish and foreign workers. It would be worthwhile, the writer argued, to be "cautious in approving residence permits, with the idea that the number of foreigners in the Swedish labor market now is quite large, and that serious clashes may occur if work becomes scarcer in an economic downturn."[60] Notably, this concern was also expressed by the LO, indicating some consensus across ideological boundaries.

Occasionally, it was suggested that the government should invest money in programs which made it possible for more women to get into work, including flexible working hours or help in completing domestic duties and caring for children, rather than importing foreign laborers.[61] The costs associated with such programs would likely be considerably higher than the costs of importing temporary workers. This proposal indicated a strong preference for further integrating Swedish workers through social reforms, rather than bringing in potentially cheaper "outsiders." This preference was perhaps indicative of the historical moment the social state found itself in as much as it was an outgrowth of continued hostility toward ethnic others. In some ways, the solution to the crisis of closure-as-entry that the threat of migration represented was heightened by the coinciding crisis of closure-as-access to goods that the movement toward a social-democratic welfare state presented.

Building Solidarity for a Social-Democratic Welfare State

While Sweden wrestled with the question of who would be allowed to become a member of the Swedish nation, the question of what, precisely, that membership meant was also becoming acute. Fear that the end of World War II would result in high levels of unemployment enabled SAP to capitalize on a potential crisis of closure-as-access to goods and to build the Swedish welfare state. SAP emphasized the potential crash to make urgent their program of social rights. In particular, Swedish lawmakers began to push for (and achieve) sweeping social reforms that could only function with the support of most of the Swedish population. These reforms included large-scale expansions to the universal national pension (*folkpension*, or "people's pension") approved in 1946 to come into effect in 1948, as well as a cash-grant child allowance (*barnbidrag*) that came into effect the same year. At the same time, active labor-market policies and the general level of state regulation of the economy increased during this period. These reforms required solidarity that went beyond the intraclass solidarity that characterized relations among workers and within a social-democratic movement. These reforms, the institutional basis of the social-democratic welfare state, required truly national solidarity.

This section considers the nature of this solidarity, asking especially who is included in the imagined community invoked in the justifications of reforms. The imagined community was a distinctly Swedish national community, although this Swedishness is rarely explicitly invoked. This section begins with a comparison of refugee and social reform discourses that highlights how the target for the latter was understood. Following this comparison is a discussion of how the process of consensus building for social reforms attempted to make social-democratic values into national values, thereby constituting the Swedish nation as a social-democratic nation. Social democracy as an ideology was, in the immediate postwar period, becoming hegemonic, with even liberal and conservative parts of Swedish political society acquiescing to certain aspects of that hegemony.

Solidarity for Swedes, Humanitarianism for Others

The key difference between the way support for refugees was justified and the way that the new social reforms were justified was that the former was seen as a form of charity and the latter an expression of solidarity. This distinction is not a benign one. Emile Durkheim wrote of "charity" that charity and justice "derive from ideas and sentiments that have nothing in common."[62] Yet Durkheim also believed that "social solidarity" could be the basis of justice, even of redistributive justice.[63] Underlying this distinction is the notion that aid motivated by charity is unlikely to either bond or to bridge a community the way that support motivated by solidarity, based in a notion of common fate or shared risk, has the potential to do. It is precisely for this reason that the labor movement, including SAP, opposed both "charity," named as such, and "means-testing" as a solution for poverty.

In contrast, the task of building support for social-democratic reforms was carried out by lawmakers and the press by invoking concepts of solidarity and community. Phrases such as "national cooperation" (*nationell samverkan*), "security for all" (*trygghet åt alla*), and "justice for the whole society" (*rättvisa för hela samhället*) recur in discussions about both the need to pass reforms at all and the shape those reforms ought to take. Means-testing for child allowances, for instance, was rejected because it would create divisions and thus "ruin the foundations of solidarity on which our national cooperation is built."[64] A national pension, on the other hand, was seen as a path to equality and as necessary in order to "make secure our entire people,"[65] while a *DN* editorial asserts its support for the pension because it will "promote cross-generational solidarity."[66] Erlander, meanwhile argued that active labor-market policies, too, were seen as promoting "general security" alongside the individual benefits to work. Erlander, for instance, in his May 1, 1950, speech argued for state intervention in labor markets, saying that "full employment is the foundation of society, the home and the individual's well being."[67] This solidarity language is neither interesting nor unexpected taken by itself, though perhaps the fact that this language was common even from the nonsocialist parties is. Yet, set side by side with the language used to justify some very similar programs for refugees, the language becomes striking.

"Humanitarianism" characterized the language used to justify programs of aid for refugees, particularly aid to non-Nordic refugees. This concept provided little to no room for the kind of expansive strategy of bonding that the new social reforms aimed at Swedes entailed. Refugees deserved "help" (not "support") because they were needy human beings, not because they were part of the national whole. For instance, even programs to get refugees into jobs were labeled "humanitarian programs."[68] unlike the very similar active labor-market policies aimed at Swedes or the common Nordic labor market, which were about solidarity. "Hospitality," "humanity," and "sanctuary" (as noted previously) rather than "solidarity," "cooperation," or "security" provide the justification for what gets framed, essentially, as "charity" for refugees.

Social policy reforms in Sweden could have been justified with a language of "help" for targeted groups such as the unemployed, the elderly, or families with children. The choice of solidarity language for national members and of humanitarian language for refugee "others" is significant. The language of solidarity draws people together in a common community, whereas the language of help holds the helped at a distance from the helpers. In the case of a strategy aiming at universality, like that which underlay the Social Democrats' drive for social welfare policy, the language of help means being kept outside the community of full (national) membership. Just as the poor could not become full members so long as they relied on charity, refugees could not become members so long as they relied on help. In this way, symbolic distance between members and nonmembers is maintained, despite the similarities between the two sets of policies.

This distinction between the support coming from the new social programs and charity was one that was not lost on the Social Democrats or

Liberals of the time. A writer in *DN*, for instance, argues that "support for new mothers must have the character of a right, not charity."[69] An editorial in *ARB* points out that even the nonsocialist parties recognize that "the right of the elderly to respectable support without relying on poor relief is an obvious and inalienable right in a democratic society."[70] Nor was it lost on the refugees who were made objects for help at the time. Refugee Rickard Schwartz wrote, in a 1948 letter to the Workers' Movement's Refugee Aid (Arbetarrörelsens flyktingshjälp), that being on poor relief made it all too easy for the Swedish press to degrade refugees and the authorities to deport them. Schwartz further writes that "poor relief is given out to all poor people, to the asocial, to the criminals, to the drunks and strikebreakers, etc. so that they won't go hungry and lead a life that is dangerous for the state and human togetherness." His argument tapped into a belief that poor relief was reserved for the less savory elements of Swedish society. Schwartz suggested, instead, that the organization should aim to get refugees into work and along the path to citizenship, so they could take part in the more "honorable" (*hederliga*) forms of social support, such as the national pension.[71]

The direct connection between migrants and the new social reforms that Schwartz makes is rarely made by either the press or politicians. The discussions of principles of universalism and basic security (*grundtrygghet*) would seem to be a natural place to discuss whether, or to what extent, to accept more potential beneficiaries into such a generous system, either by including noncitizen residents or allowing migration. It is true that the text of, for instance, both the national pension and child-allowance laws specified that these were benefits for citizens (noncitizens could receive poor relief, as noted earlier, and refugees received some aid in searching for work from the government).[72] Those migrants who could become citizens then (recalling the differential ability for migrants to become citizens) were, of course, eligible for benefits. The press, however, rarely used the word "citizen" to describe the recipient of pensions or child allowances. Instead, headlines proclaimed "pensions for every *Swede*."[73] This formulation emphasizes ethnicity over other forms of membership. Although some have argued that the concept of "citizenship" as separate from resident or other terms of belonging was underdeveloped at the time in Sweden,[74] the slippage between the language of the law, which read "citizen" and the press which read "Swede," is significant.

Making Sweden a Social-Democratic Nation

Solidarity language, of course, had existed in earlier periods, as well, and had been a mainstay of social-democratic and socialist rhetoric since the beginning. The postwar period differed from the prewar period, however, in its more conscious and vigorous linking of social reforms to Swedish national identity. Elites not only called on already preexisting notions of Swedishness but also actively used their position of power to reshape Swedishness. It was primarily SAP that had such aspirations, though the Liberals helped in the mission as well. One part of this effort was to build consensus for both reforms themselves and the ideals that lay behind them. *ARB*, for instance, contained this statement in connection with the ongoing debates over the new national pension:

> During the 1930s, we followed a line that became generally accepted. Our Social Democratic reform politics, for which the Liberals now want to claim credit, became common property.[75]

The Social Democratic reform line became "generally accepted" and "common property." In fact, SAP's liberal opposition saw value in attempting to link themselves with that line. Bertil Ohlin, a professor of economics and leader of the Liberal party, engaged in a letter-writing campaign to several daily newspapers, both Social Democratic and otherwise, trying to convince the paper's editorial staff to consider the role that the Liberals had played, first, in bringing about the national pension and, later, in working to increase the child allowance. Ohlin saw his party as, at the very least, co-architects of these seminal social reforms.[76] This campaign was largely unsuccessful. Ohlin's party was consistently represented in the press, even of his own political persuasion, as a supporter more than an originator in social reforms, perhaps because this image fit reality better.[77]

Assertions of consensus regarding social reforms, however, recurred frequently in both the social-democratic and liberal press, particularly as regards the national pension and child allowances, although SAP themselves are quick to point out that it was they who not only built the pro-

grams but also built the consensus behind them.[78] Tage Erlander, for instance, proclaimed that SAP had "led the nation to consensus about full
employment and social policies, and surely they would do the same with
tax policy."[79]

In regards to ideals, an *ARB* editor wrote that SAP had achieved in
great measure consensus behind "support for democracy, both political
and economic, and a more fair distribution of wealth."[80] Although *DN* at
the same time contained warnings of the danger of promoting blind compliance in response to some of SAP's more aggressive consensus seeking,
the Liberal party espoused many of the same principles, even if their chosen methods often differed.[81] One editorial, for instance, reads that SAP's
supporters wanted "an active reform program which increases quality of
life in society, gives security in work and life, effective protection against
sickness and unemployment, increased welfare and a comfortable old age.
But this program is also the Liberals'."[82] The Liberals also joined SAP in the
general call for "economic democracy," although preferred methods differed.
Economic democracy was framed as supporting both equality and freedom
of choice.

SAP was not, however, the only generator of policy. Indeed, social
reforms were proposed by other parties (the Liberals especially) that were
framed around some of the same values—equality and security especially—
that SAP claimed as "Social Democratic." The Liberals, for instance,
framed tax relief as a social reform that was part of the move toward a
welfare state,[83] and which better fulfilled the aim of redistribution and even
leveling (*utjämning*) that SAP pushed for:

> Our tax reform is also a reform for redistribution, but one which puts more
> power in the hands of individuals, and less in the hands of a potentially abu-
> sive state.[84]

That SAP was against this tax reduction is unremarkable in the face of their
drive to increase the state resources directed toward social programs. It is also
clear that a traditional negative liberty (freedom from an "abusive state") is
at work here. However, the Liberals' use of an equality or redistributive
rationale as well is remarkable. The Liberals framed this shift toward redistributive frames as part of a narrative of the Liberal party that shows

increasing consensus around "social sympathy" in the last half century that manifests itself in legislation:

> When 40 years ago, a proposition regarding the 8-hour workday was put forth in the Swedish parliament, it was received with scorn and sarcasm, but now social legislation of incomparably more radical and interventionist nature has become a self-evident good to everyone.[85]

In fact, the Liberal paper *DN* expressed the opinion that "expansion of state power has been valuable both from the perspective of justice and of social security" and that such an expansion had increased freedom for most individuals, but the paper also warns that it is a "difficult balancing act" given the individual's right to autonomy.[86] This statement was significant coming from a party whose ideological roots lay in individual freedom and autonomy. Even the Conservatives, who provided the strongest resistance to reforms, was part of the consensus behind the largest of them:

> There is no question of worsening national pensions, stopping child allowances or dismantling any other of the welfare state's reforms which were put into place under general agreement.[87]

Even Conservative leader Fritiof Domö agreed that, in general, the state was the proper provider for the securing of "a citizen's right to help and protection on the occasion of old age, sickness, injury, disability and unemployment," and, indeed, that the state's responsibility in such matters was one of "Swedish society's foundational principles."[88] In other words, SAP pushed successfully for consensus on questions of the big social reforms of the late 1940s (despite disputes within the party as to the details of these reforms), as well as for the principles of security and state responsibility, and the major parties to a large extent positioned themselves within that consensus, even those parties who had initially been opposed.

Even more telling, however, were the ways in which social democracy—both as a movement and as an ideal—became connected to the nation. The imagery of Sweden as the good people's home is picked up from the prewar period. In particular, SAP saw itself in its reform work as "carrying bricks to the building of the people's home" (*att bära sten till folkhemsbyggandet*) in regard to both pension reform[89] and child allowances.[90] SAP also wanted "to build a social democracy on Swedish grounds, one that has equality as its goal."[91] Social minister Gustav Möller, for his part, called Sweden "social-Sweden" in contrast to the "poverty-Sweden" that existed before SAP took control:

> We [SAP] have through decisions in last year and this year's parliamentary sessions taken care to lay the foundations for a society that evolved from poverty-Sweden to social-Sweden.[92]

Occasionally, this claiming to be the national party spilled over into calling the opposition *onationell* (unnational) when they failed to support SAP's line, but SAP largely positioned itself as the leader of a unified Swedish nation, papering over oppositional forces.[93]

DN, too, linked SAP to the nation, for instance, in likening the possibility of a crisis in the Social Democratic Party to a "national breakdown."[94] It is notable that danger in this "national breakdown" that would result from a crisis in SAP would be increased class antagonisms, a fear that recurs throughout the period under study.[95] A writer in *DN* notes as well that SAP's brand of socialism is no longer socialism, but rather has become an expression of "all that is proper, appropriate or possible. The word can hardly defined other than by pointing to the reforms pushed through by SAP or with their cooperation, or simply even the direction that society itself seems to be following," a clear equation of SAP's policies with "society" as a whole, although the writer intends the piece to be a criticism of SAP's continued use of the label "socialist" for themselves.[96]

At the same time, social policies are touted as a source of pride and, indeed, as something unique about the Swedish nation. Many during this period began to call Sweden a "model society" (*mönstersamhälle*) because of its advanced social policy[97] and, indeed, a "model for Europe."[98] In fact, even in tourism materials that sought to draw people to Sweden, descriptions of social policy advances, especially the pension program, were given equal place with descriptions of the beautiful Swedish landscape and Swedes' freedom-loving patriotism.[99] Thus, one begins to see a linking of social policy with something integral to the Swedish nation, alongside older forms of national identity, such as love of nature and democratic tendencies.

The close association of social policy with national identity seemed to be linked to Social Democratic electoral dominance and, indeed, their successful setting of the political agenda. The consensus building that proved useful in passing legislation also acted as a way to define the nation, to, in their phrase, "build the People's Home." SAP attempted, in other words, with much success, not just to turn Sweden into a welfare state, but to make the welfare state into something especially Swedish.

Conclusions: Two Crises of Closure

To return to the central theme of this book, then, we have to ask ourselves the question: What effect did the crises of migration—a crisis of closure-as-entry and the crisis of closure-as-access to goods that the of postwar economic reorganization occasioned—have on the size and shape of the nation? One part of the answer, perhaps, is that external boundaries erected against ethnic others remained fairly solid, even as refugees were permitted to enter Sweden at record numbers. Where the line between ethnic groups was drawn, however, shifted. Nordic migrants were considered "brothers" who—while not perhaps automatically—became members when they migrated to Sweden, but were offered paths to membership. Baltic (and later southern European) migrants, however, were at best invited to reside in the country temporarily, but largely as objects for "othering" charity. Baltic and southern European immigrants were viewed with generalized suspicion in a way that Nordic migrants were not.

Another part of the answer was that SAP continued the drive to become internally inclusive that had characterized the immediate prewar period. Now that the working class was relatively well integrated into the political sphere and SAP was able to parlay its intraclass hegemony into a broader ideology under which they could claim with some credibility to be a national party, SAP focused on giving institutional shape to its cultural framing of Sweden as a People's Home. The move toward nationally solidaristic policy gave the national community SAP was trying both to build and to draw on a particularly social-democratic character.

Thus, the political actors involved, especially those of SAP, used all three strategies for dealing with the crises of closure that this period entailed. The first was a selective strategy: the use of specific criteria to allow or to disallow membership in the community. In this case, this strategy manifested itself as the sorting of refugees into potential members, who came from Nordic countries, and nonmembers, who did not. The second was a restrictive strategy, one that closed off access to outsiders. In this case, this strategy entailed the maintenance of symbolic distance between members and nonmembers through the justification of programs to aid refugees as "charity" and those to aid Swedes as "solidarity."

Finally, an expansive strategy was used to deal with the specter of postwar reorganization and the potential for economic crisis. In this strategy, SAP sought a basis for Swedish identity in universalism. It should be noted that this "crisis" of closure-as-access to goods, driven by postwar fears of unemployment and lack of direction, was one that was largely manufactured by SAP in support of the kinds of policies they wished to build. This strategy involved a process of bonding (as distinct from expansive strategies that bridge) that sought extend equal rights to greater portions of the population, thus making them into "fuller" members of Swedish society. SAP sought to make support for social policies into a national characteristic, defined welfare as Swedish, and Sweden as a welfare state.

A Swedish Welfare State, a Welfare State for Swedes

The miraculous welfare machine was well on its way to being built by 1950. To extend the metaphor a bit, in the first time period, SAP acquired the contract to build the machine. They convinced the Swedish people that their broad vision for the future was a vision worth pursuing and that they were the right party for the job. In the 1945–1950 period, SAP, with some collaboration, began to draw up the blueprints and to construct components for the miraculous machine. In both time periods, homogeneity was a crucial ingredient in getting the machine built and up and running. In the 1928–1932 period, this effort entailed an explicit ethnicization of the envisioned welfare state. An ethnically civic idea of the nation resting on racial homogeneity was valued. This value was called on in support of a vision of Sweden as "the good home" that would later come to underlie the Swedish welfare state. In the later period, with the horrors of Nazism looming in the background, this explicit ethnicization gave way to a more subtle sorting of ethnic groups into "members" deserving of solidarity and "others" only worthy of charity. This sorting process worked to keep the welfare state "Swedish" (or Nordic, at least).

The driving impetus behind the Swedification of the welfare state (and, eventually, the welfare "state-ification" of Swedishness) can be found in the strategic choices of SAP. Homogeneity mattered, in other words, because SAP made homogeneity a part of their political strategy as a response to the crises, both material and manufactured. Though Social Democrats were certainly not the only ones to do so, they did so more successfully than any other group of political actors. In the first time period, Per Albin Hansson and other Social Democrats chose to use a racialized discourse in order to move SAP from a class to a national party. It is important to remember that this option was *more* inclusive than alternative (class-based) choices and thus was in many ways a democratic and civic way of defining the nation. Of course, that it could be so was dependent on Sweden having something approximating an ethnically homogeneous population. Sweden was perhaps as close as anywhere to this ideal, but even on this point, some adjustment was necessary. Those ethnic minorities that did exist within Sweden at the time needed to be actively marginalized, and both Social Democratic and other actors did so. Thus, SAP pursued a strategy that was mostly inclusive (in that it integrated class groups), but exclusive at the margins (pushing Finns, Sami, and Tattare outside the community of members).

In the second time period, SAP was focused on maintaining its popularity after the Second World War and building consensus behind a universalist welfare state. This consensus building, which was conscious on the part of SAP, entailed both deciding who the Swedish welfare state was for and convincing the populace that the welfare state was something valuable. The former was especially crucial given the particular exigencies of the postwar climate and the increasing value of the goods the Swedish state had to offer.[1] SAP sought to sharpen both the ethnic and the civic aspects of membership in the Swedish nation. Indeed, given the events detailed in chapter 3, this sharpening of the civic aspects of membership is especially crucial.

SAP, as the intellectuals working as functionaries for their class, were engaged during these two time periods in the building of a new cultural hegemony. In the first time period, the party reformulated their class politics into a national politics, a process that Gramsci notes is essential to the development of interclass hegemony—the second step in the building of new cultural hegemonies.[2] In the second time period, the party was invested in giving specific form and content to that hegemony. They worked to establish not only the values that would come to underlie social-democratic hegemony (equality, solidarity, cooperation, especially) but also the means by which such values would be realized. Namely, SAP was creating (or laying the groundwork for creating) the early institutions of the welfare state. This process relied heavily on homogeneity, although a homogeneity that was in large part constructed by SAP themselves. In fact, the bases of homogeneity differed in the first period and the second. In the first, it was a narrowly defined racial definition of Swedishness as distinct from other Nordic countries. In the second, the Nordic migrants were constructed as brothers whose membership was almost taken for granted. The latter construction was useful in a situation where Sweden was in need of labor and was concerned for its international image as being on the right side of World War II (despite the country's neutrality and some questionable wartime activity).

Social-democratic actors, essentially, developed into a dominant party through the use of a distinctly Swedish idiom and then used their position of political dominance to create a hegemonic set of social-democratic values. SAP pursued choices that emphasized the Swedish or Nordic bases of solidarity and worked toward a value consensus that effectively worked to disallow not only differences of opinion but also ethnic differences. By 1950, in other words, the welfare state was both a Swedish welfare state (i.e., a unique national trait) as well as a welfare state for Swedes. The degree to which this idea became rooted will become evident in the analysis of the 1968–1975 period, where there were basically no meaningful departures from social-democratic orthodoxy from any political parties.

From this position the increased importation of labor from outside the Nordic countries that accompanied the subsequent economic booms would come to present a challenge to the Swedish welfare state. How would a welfare state, forged on the basis of ethnicity and, indeed, increasingly bound up with the very definition of that ethnicity, respond to increased heterogeneity?

PART II

Heterogeneity in the People's Home

Chapter 3

1968–1975: Security, Equality, and Choice

Expanding the People's Home

Judging strictly by objective conditions, the next major crisis of closure should have come sometime in the early 1970s. Any number of precipitating events could have triggered such a crisis. Despite a spectacular victory in the 1968 election, SAP's dominance appeared to be slipping, as the nonsocialist parties enjoyed a string of good electoral results. Tage Erlander, who had been prime minister uninterrupted for twenty-three years, finally retired in 1969. The worldwide oil shocks of the early 1970s caused an economic crisis of considerable depth. Immigration numbers were up, and immigration debate more public and more fraught than ever. Yet, it does not appear that these political shifts, economic crises, or increased attention to immigration actually caused much of a crisis of closure. Certainly, each of these events was significant and notions of belonging had to be renegotiated to a certain extent. In contrast to previous (and subsequent) periods, however, these seemed to be matters of adjustments rather than wholesale reorganizations. This chapter, then, is as much about the "dog that didn't bark" as the dog that did. Why did these changes not provoke a crisis of closure-as-access, but only a minor crisis of closure-as-entry?

A large part of the answer can be found in the groundwork laid in the postwar era. By the late 1960s, social-democratic hegemony was firmly in place. Consensus around an expansive, wide-reaching welfare state was well established. Perhaps more crucially, consensus had been reached around a set of social-democratic values that supported an unprecedented role for the state in securing the welfare of the Swedish people. It was universally accepted that Sweden was a welfare state and that this state was, generally, a good thing, even by the Conservative party at the rightmost edge of Swedish politics.[1] This consensus was perhaps attributable to the institutional framework of the welfare state, much of which was already in place, and the right's accommodation of a new policy status quo. The welfare machine was already up and running; it was not necessarily a good strategy to seek to dismantle something that seemed to be working. It is also undoubtedly a result, at least in part, of SAP's long tenure. The party had remained in government continuously since the end of World War II and, therefore, had set the political and cultural agenda for a very long time.

For nearly all of that period, Tage Erlander was prime minster. Though a surprise at the time of his choosing and not always popular with the nonsocialist parties, Erlander himself was firmly committed to consensus building. He was also detail oriented and pragmatic—qualities that served to make compromise and accommodation easier for the nonsocialist parties to swallow, even in the face of ideological differences.[2] Per Albin Hansson, with his fortuitous appropriation of the *folkhem* idea had, perhaps, been the ideological architect of universalism, but Erlander oversaw its practical realization and all of the conflicts, great and small, that had entailed. Toward the very end of his tenure, as Olaf Ruin points out, a sort of romanticism and mythology about Sweden's "longest Prime Minister" (both in height and length of tenure) had grown up around Erlander, and much of the rancor of his tenure was forgotten. Erlander had, instead, been transformed into the same kind of *landsfadder* that Hansson had been before him.[3] Even the bourgeois press ran flattering and kind profiles about him when he finally retired.

Erlander handpicked Olof Palme, his former secretary, as his successor.[4] Palme was popular within the party and his selection as Prime Minister was expected by all. He shared much of Erlander's thinking on domestic issues, but was far more ideologically oriented and outward looking than Erlander had been. He also inherited a party that was much less secure in its political position than it had been. Although the 1968 election had been a spectacular success, it had come as something of a surprise after recent losses. In the 1973 elections, changes to the electoral system that had been put into place two years prior,[5] along with the onset of an oil-shock induced recession, resulted in the socialist block splitting the seats in the newly established unicameral legislature exactly 175 to 175 with the nonsocialist block right. That SAP was able to form a government was down to prior claim, essentially. Because SAP already held power, the opposition would have had to pass a motion of no confidence to get rid of them, which required a full majority. When consensus could not be reached, the parliament drew lots to solve the impasse, though every effort was made to compromise rather than resort to this measure.

Yet the political vulnerability SAP experienced did not really indicate deep division between the two blocks on issues of domestic economic and social policy. Palme and the party's commitment to the *folkhem* and to its underlying idea of solidarity and universality were widely shared. As he did just before the 1973 election, Palme argued that *folkhem* was alive and well: "The idea that has been foundational for the workings of democracy in our country is solidarity. People feel a common responsibility for each other."[6] Palme's contention that the conservative parties were asking the Swedish people to "give up" these "fundamental ideas that they have held fast to for decades," however, could not really be sustained.[7] To most politicians at the time, "solidarity" and "common responsibility" were cornerstones of their understandings of Swedish society. Other values, some of social-democratic providence, some of other origins, came to be seen as defining characteristics of the national community. This chapter looks closely at three key values that underlay both the Swedish welfare state and Swedish society: equality (*jämlikhet*), security (*trygghet*) and freedom of choice (*valfrihet*). All three values had driven reform in earlier periods, but they took on an explicitness and clarity that was new during this period. By this time, these three values were widespread, but also open to interpretation. These interpretations had an effect on how the national community—how solidarity—was to be defined.

A Secure, Equal, and Free Welfare State

*Security (*Trygghet*)*

The welfare's state's core policies—such as the national pension, unemployment insurance, sickness insurance, and child allowances, among others—were designed first and foremost to create *trygghet* (security).[8]

> When the Swedish people go to the voting booth, there's no real question of a fateful choice. The results may lead to a change in government, but they won't lead to a change in "security" policies in Swedish society. The three opposition parties have collaborated on these policies, and stand behind them today just as SAP does. On the other hand, new men who aren't complacent with their own performance can contribute to a more efficient economic plan that would benefit the whole country and increase employment and resources.[9]

By the mid-1960s, *trygghet*, as a goal for social policy was not only accepted but taken to heart across the political spectrum. Self-satisfied, SAP officials occasionally noted that the other parties had come around to their way of thinking. Gunnar Sträng, for instance, remarked that the Liberals had come to value many of the same things as SAP, writing that "something has happened within the Liberal party, SAP's arch-enemy for many years. There is a new generation, more responsive to those values that social democracy entails" and that chief among these values is that "security is a good for all members of society."[10] Even the Conservatives, who differed sharply when it came to policies (discussed later in this chapter), agreed that "security" was a value, although they argued that material security should be combined with a conservative "moral security" as well.[11] Johannes Antonsson of the Center Party, too, claimed that they were "the party of genuine security" (*den äkta trygghetsparti*).[12] What *trygghet* entailed, beyond a minimum acceptable living standard, however, was disputed. Even more disputed was how, exactly, security could be achieved.

Take, for example, the evenly matched 1973 parliamentary elections. Four of the five major parties featured "security" as a main theme of their electoral campaigns. SAP's posters exhorted the electorate to not "Vote

Away Security!" (*Rösta inte bort tryggheten!*). Conservatives at the other end of the political spectrum warned against the "New Insecurity" (*den nya otryggheten*). The Center Party, meanwhile, argued that economic decentralization—the party's preferred unemployment cure—was the sure path to security. Liberals, finally, promoted "security for society, and security for the individual."[13] An unsigned editorial in *Dagens Nyheter* summed the consensus up nicely in writing that "everyone agrees that we should pursue social reforms" with security in mind and that "all parties are working within the same general welfare ideology."[14]

This consensus behind "security" as a concept or value was reflected in consensus regarding many of the policies that sat at the heart of the Swedish welfare state. These security policies can generally be divided into three categories: social insurances (i.e., pensions, unemployment insurance, health insurance), family polices (i.e., child allowances, parental insurance and leave), and full-employment policies (active labor-market policies such as relocation and training services, as well as macroeconomic stimulus policies). High levels of consensus regarding social insurances and some family policies (especially child allowances) were well established by the mid-1960s.[15] Much of the nonsocialist parties' election rhetoric in both 1970 and 1973 centered on their assurances that they would not undo any of the reforms that Social Democratic governments had put into place. Center Party leader Thorbjörn Fälldin, for instance, said that it was "obvious that Center would be a driving force in social security and equality politics."[16] The Liberal party, as a matter of fact, even engaged in a heated exchange through editorials and print advertisements with SAP over which party had actually put in place the basic pensions, which escalated following the release of former Liberal Party leader Bertil Ohlin's autobiography, in which he personally took credit for the reform. The truth of the matter actually lay somewhere in between the two parties' positions. The program was a SAP reform from the beginning, but it was the Liberals who gave the pensions their final institutional form. In any case, the reform was most accurately a result of cooperation between the two parties.

In fact, the Liberals and the Center Party, who were often collectively referred to as the "middle" parties, critiqued SAP's social reforms as not going far enough. The Liberals were in favor of outright increases to both basic pensions and child allowances and, by 1975, extending parental insurances to both parents. When child allowances actually were increased in 1973, the

Liberals clearly took credit for the shift. An unsigned editorial in *DN* crowed that "Palme's adjustment to *our* position is worth noting."[17] The Liberals were not the only ones pushing for expansions, either. The Center Party argued for indexing pensions to inflation and for making unemployment insurance more generous and universal. Center Party member Karin Söder linked this directly to *trygghet*: "Security policy must of course even include those who don't have a job."[18] It had become necessary, in other words, by this time period, to appear "reform friendly" (*reformvänliga*), a term that meant, universally, willing to create new social programs or to extend the existing ones.

Only the Conservatives and Communists diverged somewhat from the "reform friendliness" that characterized the debate on social policy in the late 1960s and early 1970s. The Conservatives did not dispute that successive SAP governments had improved the material well-being of Swedish citizens. However, they argued that a "new insecurity" (*den nya otryggheten*) had taken the place of old material insecurities. A moral insecurity had arisen from the rapid erosion of traditional mores and values and resulted in crime, violence, and hopelessness. Social democracy and the fast pace of reform in Swedish society were, according to Conservatives, directly to blame. "The new insecurity," party leader Gustav Bohman argued, "exists in the midst of welfare. The winds and storms of change have blown too hard. And sometimes in the wrong direction. Too many have been ripped up at their roots. Their norms and values have broken down. And now they stand uprooted and homeless in the midst of material well-being."[19] Even the Conservative party, however, was careful to point out that social reforms had done much that was positive in Swedish society. Indeed, even its members acknowledge the positive changes that SAP had effected. Rather than denounce social democracy as entirely bankrupt, Bohman talked about SAP as "building up of a sense of community that we can be proud of" but which had certain "cracks."[20]

The Communists, meanwhile, staked out a position to the left of SAP, though they, too, had disavowed revolutionary socialism. Yet the idea that reformism, according to the Communists, only unnaturally prolonged the life of the capitalist system continued to receive some lip service from the party. SAP, in its turn, and Finance Minister Gunnar Sträng, in particular, accused the party and its members of "living in a fantasy world" and more or less ignored their arguments on this subject.[21] SAP was able to do this comfortably because the Communists nearly always voted with SAP on social reforms despite their rhetorical disavowal of reformism. Indeed, the party even suggested their own decidedly nonrevolutionary reforms from time to time, including, for instance, a reduction on sales tax on food. In other words, the Communists were considerably more "reform friendly" than their rhetoric let on. The "Communist" moniker that party members still held onto, though they had become by now the "Left Party Communists," was becoming increasingly anachronistic.

Public opinion did not, it should be noted, entirely track political consensus. On the one hand, opinions on a generous family policy were broadly favorable across the political spectrum. On the other hand, support for "social reforms" more generally was considerably more split. Among voters for the Communists and SAP, support for social reforms remained consistently high throughout the period, particularly if this support is couched as not wanting to reduce transfer payments. Among voters for the nonsocialist parties, however, most believed social reforms had "gone too far," though many fewer were interested in cutting back on what had already been achieved.[22]

Thus some points of difference between SAP and the other parties should be highlighted; the level of consensus between the nonsocialist parties—even the middle parties—and SAP on policy goals should not be exaggerated. Tax relief, especially aimed at "correcting" high marginal tax rates on middle-income families, for instance, was a nonsocialist cause that was not shared by SAP. Liberals couched this occasionally as giving individuals greater control over their incomes—a classic liberal position. More often, however, tax reforms were presented with the same language of security that characterized defenses of pensions and other social insurances. Liberals contended that high marginal taxes were "a threat to the security of the middle class, especially families with children."[23] Indeed, the threat to security from taxes was not just a threat to particular families, but to society as a whole: "There are serious risks" to high taxation that inheres in the breakdown of a strong "tax morality" that upholds the "security of the welfare state." Indeed, "tax-discontent can be a fertile ground for those who wish to harm our societal community."[24]

Employment policy provided even more room for dissension, even as security in some form was the goal of all the parties. On broad objectives, the parties were more or less agreed. The goal of full employment was universally accepted, and no one advocated a high level of structural unemployment, nor that women, the elderly, or the handicapped should be dissuaded from seeking work. Employment fit comfortably under the rubric of "security" for all parties because work was considered the first and most essential path to security. Despite this agreement on a very general level, however, there was sharp disagreement over which policies would best lead to and sustain full employment. In the low-unemployment years between 1968 and mid-1971, the arguments centered on job security measures (*anställningstrygghet*). SAP, along with the LO, pushed for policies that gave workers greater job security. Liberals, especially, however, worried that enforced job security would decrease the flexibility of Swedish labor markets. Lack of flexibility, they noted, hampered the entrance of youth and underrepresented groups onto the labor market.[25] SAP, on the other hand, argued that job security was a key issue in job satisfaction, and that the problem of flexibility was overstated in an economy with full employment.[26]

The discourse shifted away from job security, however, when economic recession hit in the middle of 1971. Unemployment rose quickly and remained high (by Swedish standards) until the second half of 1973. At this point, how to reduce unemployment became the most important issue. This was a problem both of macro-level economic development aimed at the labor market and of micro-level traditional "security" measures aimed at workers. On this issue, the parties differed sharply in both their diagnoses of the causes of the problem and their proposed solutions. The nonsocialist parties argued that SAP had mismanaged the economy during the recession years, delaying recovery and ensuring that the new unemployment would become permanent. Their solutions, then, lay in economic stimulus to businesses. The Center Party, in particular, made "decentralization" the focus of their political project and argued that the solution to unemployment lay in stimulating regional economies as a response to unequal unemployment between counties.

Although SAP did not deny that the recession had an effect on employment, the party argued that it had weathered that period of reduced economic activity better than most European countries. In fact, Social Democrats pointed out, overall levels of employment were higher in 1973 than they had ever been.[27] High unemployment numbers simply indicated that more people were seeking to enter the labor market—in particular, people such as women and disabled people who had traditionally not participated in the open labor market. SAP's preferred solutions, then, were to step up the "traditional" active labor-market policies (relocation assistance, retraining, sheltered work, etc.) and to focus those policies specifically on new populations of workers. SAP was essentially defending what had become a key part of the Swedish model—direct state involvement in the labor market.

Direct involvement in the labor market was widely supported in certain areas. Perhaps surprisingly, all parties except the Conservatives were in favor of using public-sector growth as a way of combating unemployment, although with some disagreements over how much growth and how fast. The argument, essentially, was that public-sector employment would increase security both through reducing unemployment (direct job creation) and through providing more efficient and better management of state services and goods. As a liberal commentator noted in *DN*: "Differences exist, of course, but all parties assent to a large public sector and the power that this gives a central government."[28] For a party with its roots in classical liberalism (if a particularly socially conscious liberalism), this kind of statement is particularly telling. SAP itself understood this adjustment as a natural consequence of this line of economic thought seeming to function fairly well. A report about the low-income problem put it this way:

> Contentment with increased material welfare and the major social reforms lead to a widespread contentment with that state's efforts. People see the economy as an alliance between the private and public sectors, meaning that the public sector could come to the rescue to remedy problems such as unemployment, sickness and old age.[29]

During the economic crisis, SAP mostly continued to follow its traditional active labor-market policy line. The gains that the nonsocialist parties made in the 1973 elections, however, encouraged SAP to engage in economic stimulus of the kind preferred by the nonsocialist parties. This stimulus was, of course, justified primarily with the statement that the economy had to be productive in order to support the welfare state. This view was something that all parties, now firmly welfare statist, were in essential agreement with. The concessions made to the nonsocialist style of economic governance, in other words, presented no real challenge to the Swedish model or the values underlying it. Whether as a result of the ramping up of active labor-market provisions, economic stimulus, or improvement in the global economic situation, unemployment fell precipitously starting in the second half of 1973.

It did not begin to rise again until the 1980s. The central place of work as a guarantor of *trygghet* (and the state as a guarantor of work) was reaffirmed alongside the continued commitment to security outside of work.

Equality (Jämlikhet)

Security was a value that approached universality. All parties understood and used the term in a roughly similar sense, and it was a central, integral piece of each party's political program. In contrast, the value of equality came to be especially closely associated with SAP, an association that was strengthened as Olof Palme took over from Tage Erlander as party leader, and the party adjusted its goals and profile. This is not to say, of course, that equality was unimportant to the Communists or the nonsocialist parties. On the contrary, equality enjoyed a great deal of passive support from all of the parties. It was SAP, however, that most clearly articulated the concept. The party also devoted more concerted attention to the practical steps necessary to realize equality—both equality of opportunity (*jämställdhet*) and equality of outcomes (*jämlikhet*).

Considered from some angles, this initiative to bring about equality was a natural progression. Many in SAP considered much of the work on security to be accomplished. A basic standard of living had been reached. The next step was to ensure that all were sharing in this security equally. Equality in this sense had always been a goal of the Swedish welfare state, at least as far back as Hansson's *folkhem* speech in 1928. This equality was a product of social policies that aimed at poverty reduction and at increasing the general material well-being of the Swedish population at large. Essentially, it was a secondary goal of *trygghet* policies. However, by the late 1960s, "equality" had taken on a very broad meaning, referring to a whole host of things: income equality, but also power equality, equality before the law, equality in education, gender equality, and others. Drawing on this broader meaning, SAP sought to use equality as a total organizing frame through which social democracy could be refined and reconceptualized. Although the idea of equality as the special province of social democracy was long established within the party, SAP saw their use of equality as a master frame as something new. Olof Palme, then not yet prime minister, described the shift toward a new concept of equality:

> We have for many years discussed the question [of universal versus targeted
> solutions], but finally now reasoning around this issue has loosened up,
> thanks to new demands and new concepts. No party has ever tried to ana-
> lyze society from the perspective of equality.[30]

This new emphasis resulted in a pair of reports on equality jointly authored by an LO-SAP committee, the Committee on Equality, led by Alva
Myrdal. "Equality: The First Report from SAP-LO's Working Group for
Equality Issues" came out in 1969, shortly before SAP's party congress,
the first with Olof Palme as prime minister. A second, shorter report came
out in 1972 ("Equality—Everyone's Participation in Working Life and
Politics") and was authored by much the same committee. Equality
dominated both SAP's internal machinations and its external in Palme's
first few years. The 1970 parliamentary election focused on this message,
though in the midst of the recession, equality was trumped by security-
focused campaigning in 1973.

Crucial to this new perspective was the idea that equality was not only a
sign of progress, but an *engine* for progress in and of itself. SAP contrasted
their concept of development with center and right concepts of development
rooted in "development optimism" (*utvecklingsoptimism*). Within the nonsocialist worldview, they argued, technological development and market dynamics would lead to economic growth and therefore a higher standard of
living. The security policies that the nonsocialist parties stood behind acted
as correctives and safety nets for an imperfect market. Some degree of
redistribution was, perhaps, necessary, but such policies were generally not
believed to be conducive to economic growth. The nonsocialist parties were
not unconcerned with equality altogether. The Liberals, for instance, framed
their programs for tax relief as an "equality reform," arguing against SAP's
contention that tax relief would exacerbate inequality. The Liberals coun-
tered that the reform would make markets more efficient, which in turn
would lead to greater equality.[31] Equality, in this argument, was an outcome
of sound economic policy, not a prerequisite for it. SAP, on the contrary, saw
the arrows of causality running in a different direction. Active promotion of
equality, many within the party argued, would stimulate economic growth.[32]
This contrast between free-market mechanisms and active government
mechanisms for creating economic growth is, of course, nothing new. However, the strong statement that the very creation of equality in and of itself

would increase efficiency in the economy and therefore lead to growth was new. SAP's ultimate goal was to "combine rapid economic development with full employment, security for the individual and a more just distribution of incomes and wealth," a distribution that was fundamental to "building a strong society."[33]

In other words, equality, always a part of SAP's program, shifted into the party's very center, both as a value and as a policy goal. Poverty reduction and prevention certainly remained a goal, but party leaders emphasized that "the demand for leveling (*utjämning*) concerns everyone" not just the poorest in society.[34] Policies that simply aimed to improve the situation for the worst off, in other words, were not truly in line with society-wide equality. Palme, in particular, argued for the adoption of a sort of "societal" concept of equality for two reasons: (1) most voters would not "identify" with a program that is targeted at the bottom 5–10 percent, but more importantly, (2) it was a poor economic tactic.[35] Tage Erlander, drawing on his years of experience in the day-to-day activities of building the welfare state, added to this the requirement of a strong state to guarantee equality.[36]

Although equality was a goal in and of itself, SAP also saw the new direction as a way to extend and maintain solidarity. This concept, indeed, is one of the key reasons that Palme, Erlander, and Myrdal gave for not thinking of equality as simply bringing up the bottom 10 percent, but as a sort of "total" equality—because solidarity must be not only something that exists within classes but also between classes. This view of equality was not a new idea, as the SAP leadership recognized.

> We would be wrong to say that we're coming out with something altogether new. This solidarity [between classes] is something that has always existed, but we perhaps have a special reason to emphasize it now when certain groups lag behind in society. I don't think we should depict this as a new situation, but rather as an expression for the situation that the party has always stood behind and will always stand behind so long as we make solidarity demands.[37]

As previous chapters have demonstrated, SAP rhetoric had been steadily aimed at a nationwide solidarity since the late 1920s. The universalism that characterized the postwar welfare-state building was the institutional manifestation of this drive. Yet, it is significant that this commitment is repeated in the context of the refocusing of social democracy toward equality. Rather than emphasizing sameness across classes in service of solidarity building, as was the focus of this type of rhetoric in previous eras, the emphasis within the new "equality" frame was on *bridging differences*. Solidarity, in other words, was to be extended not just to those who were similar but specifically and purposefully to those who were different.

"Difference," as understood by SAP and the Committee on Equality, took a number of different forms. At first, perhaps as a result of the composition of the Committee on Equality, solidarity between women and men was the main focus. Rhetorically at least, women had always been key to social-democratic solidarity and had made significant inroads into political power within the party. Yet, in terms of a number of concrete measurements of inclusion, the Swedish welfare state had failed them. Astrid Bergegren, a SAP member of parliament since 1957 and a member of the Committee on Equality, for instance, took umbrage with the oft-repeated statement that Sweden had "full employment." She asked, "Should we really talk about 'full employment' when we have large numbers of women who can't find work?"[38] The case was similar for some other areas of difference, notably disabled versus able-bodied and rural versus urban Swedes, where the rhetorical commitment to maintaining solidarity through equality was somewhat established, even if policy had lagged behind. Both the 1969 and 1972 equality reports took pains to point out the disconnect between rhetoric and reality in these areas. Prescribing policy for fixing these discrepancies was a major part of these documents. In these areas, there was little need to adjust overarching values; rather, the view of who was to be equal merely needed to expand. Put differently, perhaps SAP merely needed to adjust its focus in order to see the edges of the community more clearly. Yet the prescription to promote group rights (and attendant expectations) rather than to provide "general solutions" was a fairly new way of thinking about things.[39] Indeed, it is perhaps paradoxical that just as the "totalizing" frame of equality was used to speak against solutions targeted at the bottom 10 percent class-wise, the targeting of groups defined in other ways (by gender, ability, or geography) was beginning to gain some traction.

Also new in SAP's refocusing efforts was an increased concern with solidarity across national borders. Of course, international solidarity, as applied to the global proletariat, had been a feature of social-democratic rhetoric from early days.[40] The application of the master frame of equality, however, meant that the international solidarity SAP aimed for was not necessarily about the global proletariat. SAP's emphasis was on creating equality between developed (i.e., Sweden) and developing countries, rather than on uniting the Swedish working class with other working classes. Reflecting SAP's new ideas and commitments, the main motivation for international aid was stated as "solidarity with developing countries"[41] or "the third world."[42] Aid that was humanitarian in nature was specifically to be avoided whenever possible. As Myrdal put it, "If one just followed the principle that one helps only the poorest lands, then our aid would likely become ineffective, humanitarian aid. Which, naturally, is desirable in some cases, but it can hardly be called 'equality.' "[43] Instead, SAP sought to give aid primarily to those countries that worked for both economic growth and a more even distribution of societal goods. The role of the SAP was, in fact, to be didactic: they would both model and teach developing lands how to work toward equality and—perhaps more importantly—to *value* equality.[44]

Such a didactic role was given to the program for equality domestically as well. Palme argued that it was "ideas that we must teach the population, and our own. This is more important than any concrete propositions we've discussed."[45] The stated goal was to teach Swedes to value equality and, specifically, to value the kind of equality embraced in the Social Democratic Party programs—the totalizing, inclusive sort of equality that sought to bridge divides. This effort was part of the much longer drive to create consensus around social-democratic values. Like the reworking of "equality" itself, the meaning of "consensus" itself had come to have new nuances. Previous consensus-building rhetoric was aimed at defining Swedishness as social democratic and, in the process, drawing on ready conceptions of the nation. As is obvious by the widespread agreement on "security," much of this project had already been completed. The new task, then, was to build consensus across new populations. This new consensus building used a resonant value to extend the boundaries of the community—to bridge, not simply to bind.

Freedom of Choice (Valfrihet)

A third value came to define the Swedish welfare state during the 1960s and 1970s. *Valfrihet*, or "freedom of choice," as applied to the welfare state, was not of Social Democratic provenance, nor was its embrace as unproblematically widespread as either *trygghet* or *jämlikhet*. At times, despite the fundamentality of positive liberty to social-democratic ideology, "freedom of choice" was even set up as oppositional to equality. As such, SAP's attitude toward the concept (and the term) was often skeptical. The idea of "freedom of choice" in the context of the welfare state in the 1960s was much more closely associated with the nonsocialist parties than with the socialist ones, who often saw freedom of choice as a value that tended to benefit the rich and powerful. SAP, of course, was not against freedom of choice in principle. For instance, in SAP's 1969 report on equality, "freedom of choice" was mentioned as a subsidiary principle of equality—as something that would eventually be possible under conditions of true equality.[46] SAP's ambivalence, as well as that of other bureaucratic forces, pushed for the standardization of services and benefits as a way of ensuring equality, a strategy not really consistent with the promotion of choice.[47] Alva Myrdal's attempt, in 1968, to come up with a list of those "fundamental sectors which must be organized collectively *without freedom of choice*"[48] is perhaps indicative of such skepticism. Myrdal's argument was that a certain fundamental set of services and expectations could not be fulfilled without a lack of choice. Myrdal's proposed list (which remained incomplete) was not a short one. It was not so surprising, for instance, that she considered primary education as not subject to free choice, but her placing of policies such as obligatory sterilization somewhere "on the border" is. She concludes the internal memo containing this list by stating that "freedom of choice is not a useful motto" in the drive for equality.[49]

The nonsocialist parties argued, meanwhile, that freedom of choice was emphatically *not* secondary to equality, but rather equally important within the welfare state. For the Conservatives, in particular, freedom of choice was often aimed at families, not at individuals per se. For example, the party argued for devolving choices about how to use parental leave benefits down to families, rather than mandating that some portion be used by either parent. While supporting the seemingly progressive goal of offering parental leave to fathers, the Conservatives were actually seeking to place power into the hands of the family rather than the state. Such an understanding of freedom of choice which allowed the "family" as a unit to make decisions could actually promote the continuation of a patriarchal family structure.[50] SAP, indeed, was worried that the exercise of freedom of choice in the way the Conservatives envisioned it would have this (and other) illiberal consequences.[51]

For the Liberals, however, freedom of choice was rooted in an ideological commitment to *individual* freedom, and, therefore was less clearly linked to illiberal outcomes. This conception is clear, for instance, in their support for individual taxation over family taxation (the Conservative position), where they pointed to freedom of choice. Liberal Cecilia Nettelbrandt, in a 1969 report on family taxation, put it in this way:

> I would like a formulation of the tax system that is so neutral as to make *freedom of choice* possible without favoring domestic work or wage work, nor different marital statuses. This means a principled formulation of individual taxation.[52]

Liberals linked individual taxation to women's choice especially, including the choice to seek work outside the home and the choice to marry or to remain single. The contrast between Liberals' and Conservatives' conceptions of freedom of choice for families is striking.

The Liberals saw freedom of choice as essentially compatible with equality. In fact, they saw freedom of choice as *necessary* to equality. To take one example, the Liberals supported a flexible retirement age by gesturing to both individual freedom of choice and to equality. An unsigned *DN* editorial decried the standardization of retirement ages, arguing that "individuals should be free to choose when to end their working life, within certain guidelines, because people are the own best judges of their interests."[53] Just a few days later, the same policy was linked to equality: "The flexible retirement age is basically an equality reform. Under such a system, those who have done hard physical labor and those who have not can retire with basically the same quality of life."[54]

The nonsocialist parties' focus on *valfrihet* had some traction, and SAP was beginning to adapt itself somewhat cautiously to this line of thinking. SAP, for instance, which had long been in favor of individual taxation, adopted to a certain extent the Liberals' freedom-of-choice-focused justification, alongside their equality-focused argumentation. SAP, too, began to attempt to reconcile *valfrihet* with equality, indicating a further narrowing of ideological differences between the Liberals and SAP. Economic equality was a focus for this project. Income equality, for instance, could be thought of as forming the basis for "individual strivings" and "control over one's life choices."[55] Social policies aimed primarily at helping women enter the marketplace, too, were often justified with both equality and freedom of choice. SAP, for instance, argued that the new preschool law, which came into effect in 1973 and guaranteed access to preschool for all children of working mothers (or those actively seeking work), was "essential to ensure women's freedom of choice, and an expression of SAP's deep commitment to women's equality of opportunity."[56] This increasing use of both concepts to justify policy for women seems to have arisen in response to the increased influence of women within the party, many of whom framed their views on social policy with the principle of choice in mind, although it never became the sort of guiding principle that equality was.[57]

Secure, Equal, and Free Immigrants in the Welfare State

Both "equality" and "freedom of choice" became key guiding principles—constitutionally enshrined along with "cooperation" in the 1975 revision of the Swedish Basic Law—for Swedish immigration and integration. As the debate around immigration and integration principles and policy began to flourish in the late 1960s, it became clear that the consensus on welfare-state values could provide a useful framework for understanding how immigrants fit into the national community, economically, socially, and culturally. This debate was new and brought about a new way of thinking about the issue, but one which could, fairly neatly, be fit into the preexisting ideas of national community that social democracy provided.

It was a debate whose time had come. Immigration, after having subsided with the end of World War II, began to rise in the mid-1950s, reaching a high point in the late 1960s. In contrast to the earlier wave of postwar migration, the new immigrants were primarily labor migrants. As a consequence, the numbers of migrants coming to Sweden fluctuated largely in step with employment opportunities. By 1968, over 90,000 people born outside of the Nordic countries were living in Sweden, and an even larger number of Nordic migrants. Most of these, by far, were Finnish migrants, who used the Nordic open labor-market rules to take advantage of the higher wages and plentiful work opportunities that Sweden offered during the growth years of the late 1950s and 1960s. Immigrants from Denmark and

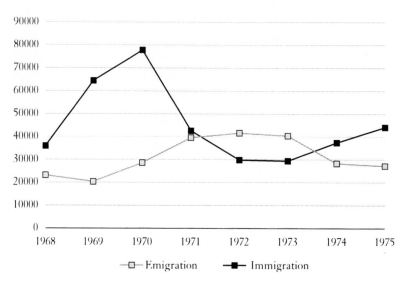

90000

80000

70000

60000

50000

40000

30000

20000

10000

0

1968   1969   1970   1971   1972   1973   1974   1975

—□— Emigration   —■— Immigration

Figure 2. Immigration and emigration, 1968–1975. Source: Statistiska Centralbyrån.

Norway, meanwhile, were relatively few, and most remained only temporarily. Western European (especially German), southern European (mostly Yugoslavian and Greek), and Turks made up the bulk of the rest of the migration.

Between 1968 and 1971, rules regarding immigration tightened and, increasingly, non-Nordic immigrants had to seek work permits before their arrival in Sweden. Despite this rule, immigration numbers reached record highs in 1969 and 1970 (see figure 2 for yearly immigration/emigration totals). When recession hit in 1971, continuing through the first half of 1973, however, the granting of work permits slowed to almost nothing. Sweden, in fact, experienced net *emigration* in both 1972 and 1973. Many of those leaving Sweden were noncitizens who had migrated to Sweden during the previous decade. As the economy rebounded, migration also rebounded, though the number of yearly migrants did not reach the 1969 and 1970 levels again until the 1990s. In addition to labor migration, several waves of refugees came to Sweden, most notably Czechoslovakian refugees in 1968 and Chilean refugees following Pinochet's 1973 coup. These groups were small in comparison to the labor migrants and, except in discussions of particular cases, newspaper reports failed to distinguish the two different types of migrants.[58] Immigration discourse in the 1960s and 1970s was considerably more general than the discourse following World War II. In other words, while almost all discussion of migrants in the immediate postwar period were ethnicized (i.e., about "Baltic refugees" or "Danish refugees," etc.), the discourse on immigration in the 1960s and 1970s was largely about "immigrants" without an ethnic qualifier. Discussions of particular groups were not completely absent; as the largest and most historically anchored group, Finnish immigrants were discussed frequently. However, there was a considerable decline in the use of ethnic qualifiers, and most debate occurred at a general level.

This debate reflects the greater recognition that Sweden actually needed a general immigrant (and immigration) policy. There was a growing acceptance that labor migration tended to be permanent and that immigrants, therefore, had to be integrated into the national community. One writer, for instance, declared that "it is no longer feasible for Sweden to simply assume immigrants will quietly work and then return home without making any impact on Swedish society. Immigration must become a central issue in the political debate."[59] Starting in the late 1960s, *DN*, in particular, published a great number of pieces addressing the "immigrant issue." These pieces were often written by immigrants and dealt with a large range of issues from the place of immigrants in individual workplaces to whether immigrants should be allowed to vote in Swedish elections.[60]

Because it could no longer be assumed that immigrants would simply assimilate or go home, commentators and political actors increasingly began to draw a line between immigration policy and immigrant (later "integration") policy.[61] The former had to do with who was allowed to immigrate, the latter with what policies would apply once within the borders of the country. This latter category included such varied things as citizenship policy, language instruction, and access to social insurance. Support for limiting the number of people coming into the country was seen in no way as incompatible with rather open and welcoming policies once foreign nationals had immigrated. This split is indicative of what had become the nature of this period's would-be crisis of closure. The question was no longer simply "who should we let in?" Rather, the question had become "do we let immigrants become full members of society once they are here?" The increasing separation of immigration and integration issues illustrated that migration actually presented two separate but related crises: one of entry and one of access to goods. The first was reflected in changes to entrance requirements noted previously; the second was primarily a definitional question: What did it mean to be or to become Swedish? To a large extent, the Swedes found their answer within the framework of social-democratic hegemony. To illustrate this point, I examine how the three social-democratic values outlined earlier in this chapter (security, equality and freedom of choice) extended to (or failed to extend to) immigrants.

Security for (and against) Immigrants

Trygghet was, of course, the most entrenched goal of the Swedish model. Did this "security" extend to immigrants? How was immigration thought to intersect with the security of native Swedes? Immigration was, at times, perceived as a threat to Swedes' economic security. Those who argued this point were generally concerned with immigrants as workers and, therefore, as additional potential stress on the labor market.[62] This attitude was most often found within the discourse on immigration, rather than integration, although there were some areas of overlap. The concern within the immigrant discourse was largely whether noncitizen immigrants had the same right to security as citizens and, if so, how was that right best guaranteed. Commentators considered immigrants not just as workers but as a potential members of society (*samhällsmedborgare*). The question within the integration discourse, then, was how far this membership extended.

Labor shortages in key Swedish industries, along with rising wages, were significant "pull" factors for immigrants to Sweden during the late 1960s. The low levels of unemployment experienced by all meant that there was a great deal of optimism regarding the Swedish labor market's ability to absorb labor migrants. "Many of our key industries are in need of labor, and there are many immigrants who wish to come here" wrote a commentator in a 1968 op-ed piece in *Arbetet*, continuing with the evaluation that "this can be nothing but a mutually beneficial situation."[63] Alongside this optimism, however, increasing attention was being paid to the regulation of immigration—understandably so, given the sheer number of immigrants seeking entry. As a result, starting in 1968, non-Nordic migrants needed to seek work permits before arriving in Sweden. This gave unions, especially the blue-collar LO unions, increased control over the process of immigration. Although the new regulations did not make an immediate impact in the overall number of immigrants arriving (see figure 2), the legislation did spark debate about what an acceptable level of immigration was for Sweden.

LO, with its new responsibilities, was deeply engaged in this debate. The LO's position, decidedly, was that immigration should generally be considered permanent. Immigrants were *not* to be thought of as "guest workers."[64] As such, while the LO was open to immigration in principle, they cautioned against "using immigrants as an economic tool in good times."[65] Ivar Lind, president of the large LO-affiliated Textile Worker's Union (Textil) explained this point of view: "We have taken advantage of foreign workers during the economic boom of the 1960s. When times start to toughen, we can't simply kick them out."[66] The concern was that, if recession set in, there would be an excess labor force that could not simply be sent out of the country. Consequently, LO took a restrictive stance toward immigration, arguing that immigration should be carefully regulated and that "other solutions" to labor shortages, such as the encouragement of internal migration, retraining programs, and targeted programs for underemployed populations (women, the handicapped, youths, and older workers), should be sought before importing workers. This position amounted to a voice in favor of merely intensifying active the labor-market policies pursued by SAP governments. The LO maintained this position through good and bad economic times. In fact, as Sweden recovered from the oil shock recession years, the LO argued this position even more forcefully. The LO's 1975 report on labor shortages and immigration, for instance argued that "to use immigration to regulate short-term unevenness in demand on the labor market is extremely problematic" and "is detrimental to the Swedish labor market, the labor markets of immigrants' countries of origin, and, indeed, the immigrants themselves."[67] The LO even went so far as to suggest that exporting capital to countries with surplus labor would be a better solution to labor shortages than importing workers.[68]

SAP also took a restrictive stance toward immigrants, but they were more directly protectionist in their reasoning. It was SAP that proposed and quietly put in to practice the new visa requirements in the late 1960s, although they did not publicly take a restrictive stance until the unemployment years of 1972–1973. During these years and especially during the 1973 election campaign, party leader Palme repeatedly spoke of the need to put the interests of unemployed Swedes before immigrants seeking entry and, therefore, to restrict entry into Sweden so long as unemployment remained high.[69]

Palme urged that every possible step be taken to get Swedes, with special concern for the aforementioned underemployed populations, into jobs before considering further labor migration.[70] Similarly, the LO argued that "we are of the opinion that, just as earlier, businesses should in the first place concentrate on employing unemployed Swedes, older people, the handicapped and other excluded groups."[71]

The immigration policy prescriptions (to restrict immigration, to get women into work, etc.) suggested by SAP and LO were, in fact, quite similar to those suggested in the post-WWII period. Yet while the arguments against labor imports from southern Europe in the late 1940s were largely cultural, cultural arguments are wholly absent from SAP's and LO's call for immigration restriction. Much of *ARB*'s coverage of immigrants stressed their ability to work harmoniously within Swedish workplaces.[72] And, although immigration law still privileged Nordic immigrants, the sources of immigration were rarely mentioned in Palme's call for restrictive policies. Of course, it was assumed that Finnish migration would continue unrestricted, but there was no longer an explicit division of Nordic from non-Nordic potential migrants in the discourse—a sign of, perhaps, decreasing saliency of ethnicity or, perhaps, increasing taboo on ethnicized speech.

Other actors, however, read something more sinister into LO's and SAP's (especially Palme's) restrictive stance. The Liberals—both through the mouthpiece of *DN* and in their electioneering—accused Palme of cultivating the "myth that immigrants have stolen jobs from decent Swedish workers"[73] and "speculating in prejudices":

> For years, [SAP] has downplayed unemployment and predicted good times ahead. When they finally acknowledge the problem, they make offhand comments that Swedes have to get jobs before foreigners: no immigration should be allowed until the employment situation improves.
>
> Is this Olof Palme speculating in prejudices? Oh no, every word has been weighed on golden scales: not a single gram upon close reading should tilt the scale in favor of hostile attitudes toward Swedish immigrants. The insinuations are subtle, so subtle. But they are not so subtle that they are not understood. The derogatory applause echoes.[74]

An unsigned *DN* editorial pointed out, further, that the "problem" of immigration during the high-unemployment years was actually not much of a "problem" at all:

What the Prime Minister is doing, in other words, is traveling around the country inciting anger against a risk of mass immigration that for all intents and purposes doesn't exist. If this is what Palme means in his call for national unity, we politely decline.[75]

SAP, they argued, was creating a bogeyman to explain their own lack of competence in dealing with the employment question. Implicit in this line of reasoning was that the market was able to deal with immigration effectively—that immigrants would come when jobs were available, and stay away when they were not.[76] A *DN* commentator noted, in support of this argument, that Finnish migration, even though open, was driven more by economic conditions in Sweden than in Finland. Finns did not come to Sweden when the labor market was bad in both Finland and Sweden, but they did come when both markets were good.[77] The Liberals were careful to note that they did not want to *encourage* mass migration, but they dismissed the idea that immigration was truly a threat to the economic security of Swedish citizens.[78]

At the same time as the LO and Palme were calling for restrictions on immigration, they were also praising the contributions immigrants had made to Swedish society. Palme called for increased striving toward a "societal solidarity" (*samhällssolidaritet*) that encompassed immigrants. In his May 1, 1971, speech, the prime minister stated the following:

> The hundreds of thousands of immigrants who have come to us since World War II have had a positive impact on Swedish society. Many of them are walking alongside us this first of May, especially in those industrial regions where such a large part of the Swedish welfare has been created.
>
> Of course, immigrants have problems and shortcomings—just like all of us. But this only underlines our commonalities, and our common responsibility to, together, create a better and more humane society.[79]

In his use of the phrase "common responsibility," Palme echoes his earlier description of Sweden's fundamental values and gestures toward the Swedish welfare state. This connection was more than gesture, too. Both LO and SAP were decidedly in favor of immigrants' equal access to the instruments of security available to Swedish citizens. Lars Alvarsson of SAP, for instance, argued that immigrants "should be given all the same opportunities for work, housing, education, social benefits etc. as any other Swede."[80] This position meant a thorough repudiation of the guest-worker model, both by SAP and by the LO. Social Democrat Eric Holmqvist opened the debate on immigrant policies with the following assertion:

> Those who come here should have the chance to become a part of Swedish society, to be able to feel secure here in the same measure as Swedish citizens. The system with so-called guest workers who are only offered temporary work is foreign to us.[81]

For LO, the guest-worker model meant necessarily excluding immigrants from equal treatment. The real fear was that this model might lead, eventually, to the erosion of protections and insurances already in place for all workers. Consequently, the LO argued against any social policy directed particularly at immigrants.[82] SAP and the LO were not alone in wanting to extend the same protections to immigrants as to Swedes. The middle parties and Communists joined SAP in asserting that, once in Sweden, immigrants had the same right to security as Swedish citizens. The Liberals, for instance, argued that "immigrants must be included in the general welfare if we are to avoid social splits"[83] and, later, that their inclusion was a matter of "justice and sound morals."[84]

The Conservatives alone argued that immigrants ought to be excluded from social insurances and general labor-market policies. In the Conservative *Svenska Dagbladet*, one reads during periods of low unemployment that immigrants were "living on the dole"[85] and during periods of high unemployment that they were "stealing jobs."[86] The Conservatives were not against immigration as such. In fact, they advocated for limited guest-worker programs that would ensure that immigrants would be able to fill specific needs in times of labor shortages, but which entailed little or no commitment to immigrants' economic or social needs should the work disappear. Despite their cooperation in elections, Center Party members and especially the Liberals denounced the Conservatives' position on immigration. SAP's prejudices may have inhered in "subtle insinuations," but the Conservatives were "reactionary" and "inhumane."[87] Conservative opinions seemed to have very little political traction. The party did not make immigration or immigrant policy a central part of their electoral strategy.

Including immigrants in the *general* solutions to insecurity that were aimed at all Swedes, rather than a separate set of "immigrant solutions," was seen as the best way to maintain national unity and, indeed, societal solidarity. This view is strikingly different from the immediate postwar period where migrants were offered "help" rather than "solidarity," which serves as a way to create symbolic distance between immigrants and native Swedes. By the 1970s, however, immigrants were to be thought of, first and foremost, as *samhällsmedborgare*—society members—not as "immigrants" or even, primarily as "workers."

Nevertheless, immigrants did face exclusion and discrimination in their day-to-day life. Nor does this analysis suggest in any way that the majority of Swedes saw new immigrants as their fellows. In fact, as with later periods, public opinion is considerably more negative toward immigrants and immigration than the political discourse would suggest. A 1969 survey, for instance, revealed that 76 percent of all Swedes would consider immigration only after all measures to get Swedes employed were exhausted and that 71 percent believed immigrants only came to Sweden to abuse social assistance. At the same time, the public mostly agreed (88%) that, once in Sweden, immigrants should be "secured the same standard of living" as native Swedes. Seventy-four percent, however, believed that immigrants should "become as like Swedes as possible," indicating little agreement with the "cultural pluralist" line of thinking.[88]

What is clear, though, is that the press and political discourse on *trygghet* suggested a growing acceptance by elite decision makers that immigrants could become society members, indicating a shift in political, if not public, culture and reducing the crisis of access to a noncrisis. Of course, this acceptance ought to be viewed alongside the crisis of entry that SAP's and LO's new restrictions on immigration indicated. Clearly, to some, there was a limit on the *quantity* of new members. However, the discourse on immigration, even the restrictive discourse, had loss much of its ethnic character. The dividing line seemed no longer to be, necessarily, between Nordic and non-Nordic, but between those already inside the country and those outside.

Bridging Difference: Equality and Immigrants

Giving immigrants access to the same instruments of security that Swedes had access to was also a way of ensuring some degree of equality. Yet, despite SAP's increasing focus on a kind of "bridging" equality, immigrants were not initially included in the broader equality discourse. This lack of inclusion can clearly be seen by examining the first SAP-LO joint report on equality from 1969. Alva Myrdal, in introducing the work in progress at an internal party meeting, stated that there was a need to take up the problems of inequality between groups and, in so doing, indicated a series of cleavages about which SAP should be concerned. These areas of concern included the cleavages between "low wage–high wage workers; rural–urban; men–women; ill and handicapped–healthy, etc."[89] The report, to a large extent, was organized around the measures necessary to create equality across these cleavages. "Swede–immigrant" or "majority–minority" did not make the list of key cleavages. Nor is it included in the "etc." that Myrdal appended to her list.[90] In the correspondence and minutes of the Committee on Equality, the first mention of immigration and immigrants occurs only after the release of the first report and, even then, is only a short notice that immigrant women may have "special needs and skills" that should be taken into account.[91] Immigrants, immigration, and minorities enter this seminal work on equality-as-social democracy only in two places—under "Equality on the Labor Market," where minorities are promised Swedish language instruction during work time,[92] and under the heading "Equality Before the Law," where there is a brief discussion of the need for a regulated immigration and for immigrants' equal rights within the justice system.[93] Immigrants' and minorities' positions in the labor market, in education, and within the domain of social policy is nowhere discussed. Equality between immigrant and nonimmigrant groups was simply not on the radar for the Social Democrats in 1969.

By the publication of SAP-LO's second report on equality, the position had changed somewhat. Two short, relatively contentless mentions of immigrant equality in the 1969 report were replaced with six mentions of immigrants and immigration in the considerably shorter 1972 report. Two of these were fairly simple statements that immigration had an effect on the overall size of the Swedish labor force. However, the remaining four mentions were meaningful attempts to understand how immigrants fit into the equal Swedish society. Three of these prescribed general policy directions: cultural policy to increase "contact and exchange" between different groups (including immigrants),[94] increased occupational training for immigrants,[95] and active recruitment of immigrants to unions and political activity.[96] The fourth acknowledged that "language and contact problems" led to difficulties in integration, which could lead to difficulties in maintaining "fellow-ship."[97] Six mentions may not seem significant, but the meaningful discussion of immigration found in the 1972 report represents a strong departure from the 1969 report. This departure is made even clearer when one considers that, while the first report was characterized by a systematic discussion of cleavages between groups, the second report de-emphasized such cleavages.

Two questions arise from the contrast between the two reports. The first is the question of how immigration got on the agenda at all. Simple numbers surely played a role; 1969 and 1970 were record years for immigration, despite the changes in visa laws that made it harder to immigrate to Sweden. Yet, such an explanation is overly simplistic. The rise in immigration numbers had steadily occurred since the mid-1950s without pushing immigration onto SAP's agenda. A more likely spark for the change can be found in the news coverage surrounding the wildcat strikes in the northern mining and metal towns of Kiruna, Luleå, Malmberg, and Sapavaara that occurred shortly after the release of the first report. These industries employed large number of immigrants at these locations, and many observers suggested that the immigrant workers' unfamiliarity with Swedish laws and customs, as well as their low rates of unionization, were to blame for the strikes.[98] In particular, the high rate of communism among northern Finns was cited as a potential cause of the strikes. Many speculated that this group was the organizing force behind them. In reality, immigrants seemed to play only a very small role in the strikes.[99] An investigation by LO representative Jalmar Rantanen found that the Finnish communists were too poorly organized to play any meaningful role in strike activities.[100] Nonetheless, the accusation that immigrants were poorly integrated into unions and the idea that there was a potential problem involved in ignoring the special situation of immigrants forced the issue onto the LO's agenda. The LO responded with an integration plan of its own, focused largely on language education and the provision of translated union information. Their participation in the writing of the second report on equality, furthermore, directly contributed to the changes in that document.[101]

The popular press also probably played a role in getting immigration on the agenda. As noted earlier, coverage of immigration in the popular press increased in the late 1960s and early 1970s. This trend is particularly evident in *DN*, which published a number of influential articles during the period under study. Many of the articles were written by the politically unaffiliated

Polish-Jewish immigrant David Schwarz, who became the leading expert on immigrant and integration issues in the 1970s.[102] *DN*'s increasing coverage appears to have driven other papers to pick up the issue of integration to a larger extent, though only *DN* published immigrant writers at such a high rate.[103] This press attention may have also worked to push SAP to take a position on integration.

The influence of Schwarz and other writers at *DN* may also help to answer the second question provoked by the juxtaposition of SAP's equality reports: Why an equality discourse specifically? Schwarz is perhaps best known for his arguments advocating cultural pluralism, but was also an impassioned defender of equality. He argued forcefully that immigrants should be given "equal opportunities and equal access to resources with Swedes."[104] It is difficult to assess how much influence Schwarz and those making the same claims had. However, it does appear that it is in this arena (*DN*) that immigration first appears as an issue, specifically, of equality.[105]

It appears, in addition, that the discourse on immigrants came to be an equality-focused discourse because of a Social Democratic interest in presenting a unified program. SAP heavyweights like Tage Erlander, Olof Palme, and Alva Myrdal all pushed the idea of equality as a "total concept" for Swedish society, applying it to both domestic issues and to international ones. Once SAP was forced (whether by the influence of LO or by the public debate) to take up the topic of immigration, the exclusion of this group from the "total organizing frame" of equality would have seemed an unacceptable internal inconsistency. Thus, while it is perhaps not true that SAP's use of an equality discourse was an "automatic" outcome of their social democratic ideology, it does appear to be likely that the overarching ideological direction that SAP was heading influenced immigration discourse to include egalitarian elements.[106]

In fact, it seems likely that the discourse on women, which was increasingly vocal and focused on equality, exerted a direct effect on the discourse on immigrants. That is, the success of the use of an equality frame for women (i.e., that the frame gained legitimacy for the women's movement, helped propel women to central positions within SAP, and formed a major part of SAP's new political equality direction) made it an attractive frame for writers in the popular press to pick up and use in regard to immigrants. Two factors speak to this "discursive co-optation" mechanism: First, the timing appears to be right. As discussed earlier, an egalitarian discourse on women's issues had been present in many ways since the first days of SAP's success. However, the efforts to push women's issues to the fore and, especially, the increasing commitment to design policies in order to bring reality in line with rhetoric only began to gather steam in the 1960s.[107] The appointment of several well-known feminist Social Democrats to SAP's Committee on Equality and Alva Myrdal's appointment to lead the committee are symbolic of the success of those efforts to put women's issues squarely at the center of SAP's politics by 1969. This coincides nicely with the beginning of the serious use of equality discourse in regard to immigrants.

Second, the two discourses are rhetorically similar. Both discourses, for instance, were focused on "equal access" to labor markets and to social benefits. Furthermore, the participants of both discourses recognized the "unique challenges" involved in providing equal access, although the solutions suggested often followed different logics (e.g., targeted vs. general solutions).[108] More importantly, for both groups equal access was not the only goal, but roughly equal outcomes as well. The removal of barriers to women's and immigrants' labor-market participation, in other words, was not enough: actual high levels of participation were sought. Thus equality came to be conceived of for immigrants in similar terms as for women: as indicating both equal access and equal outcomes. Immigrants were to be fully included in Swedish working life, public administration, and civil society on a footing equal to all Swedes.

Choice for Immigrants: The Freedom to Integrate (or Not)

When equality was enshrined as a goal for integration policy in the 1975 Basic Law, freedom of choice appeared alongside it. Although for women, freedom of choice often referred to the choice of whether or not to work outside the home, for immigrants it came to mean an immigrant's right to cultural self-determination. In other words, Swedish immigrants were to have the freedom to integrate, or not, to whatever extent they chose.[109] Either choice was to be supported by the state, with policies such as home-language education, state support for immigrant-language newspapers, and local and municipal voting rights for noncitizen permanent residents.

The lack of integration policy before the 1970s has been interpreted by many as the expression of an unspoken assimilationist ethos; immigrants were expected to either become Swedes or to go home, so no official set of objectives for integration was necessary.[110] SAP, in particular, seemed to support this laissez-faire approach to immigration that assumed assimilation as the final outcome.[111] As with the discourse on equality, however, the increased recognition of problems associated with immigration and immigrants necessitated an active position taking on these issues. There were, of course, those who argued actively for an assimilationist policy toward immigrants. Claes-Adam Wachmeister, a Conservative and member of the Swedish aristocracy, for instance, wrote in *DN* that assimilation was the "only realistic way to turn immigrants into full-fledged citizens,"[112] and the unaffiliated journalist Michael Wächter wrote that having a "double culture" was damaging to children psychologically, which would lead them to marginalization and crime. Therefore, for the sake of immigrant children, Sweden ought to pursue an assimilationist policy.[113]

Yet, counterposed to the demands for assimilation was a growing call for "cultural pluralism," a sort of proto-multiculturalism rooted in the same ideas of *valfrihet* that had come to characterize parts of the welfare-state debate. Unlike the welfare debate, however, and like the equality-focused part of the debate on immigration, the discourse on *valfrihet* for immigrants originated outside the political system. *DN*, with David Schwarz and a number of other writers with immigrant backgrounds again in the lead, pushed the "cultural-pluralist" line. The Liberal Party and, especially, SAP lagged behind. *DN*'s commentators, Schwarz among them, argued that freedom of choice for immigrants was best for both society and the individual immigrant. This freedom of choice, however, did not mean simply the removal of barriers to maintaining one's language, customs, and religion, but rather active support for those who chose to do so. Schwarz's main argument was that "the right to equality included the right to be different."[114] Schwarz and others, such as Voldemar Kivaed and Sven Alur Reinans, pointed to the success of schools that had been set up for the children of Estonian and Finnish migrants and taught in the children's home language as examples of "positive double cultures" wherein children came to see the value of both their parents' culture and Swedish culture. The possibility that they would become either rootless or negative toward Swedes and Swedish society was thereby reduced.[115] Such examples provided proof of the wisdom of what they called the "cultural-pluralist" model of integration, which was not only morally just (it prevented a "spiritual death" as Schwarz put it) but ultimately the most efficient way of integrating immigrants.[116]

SAP and, indeed, the LO took a more instrumental approach toward integration policies. The LO, especially, seemed more concerned with making sure that immigrants knew the "rules" (formal and informal) of Swedish working life than with any overriding principles of integration. This pragmatic approach is, perhaps, unsurprising. Many saw the integration of immigrants as the LO's responsibility, a view that the LO itself shared.[117] Trade unions, whether LO or not, were the first and most constant point of contact with Swedish society for many immigrants. The LO had a pressing need to find practical ways of dealing with its new members.[118] They had a complementary stake in making sure that immigrants became good—or at least compliant—union members, too. This goal came to be especially central to the LO's mission following the wildcat strikes discussed earlier. All of this added up to an LO position on integration that was not principally concerned with freedom of choice. Instead, the LO focused on efforts to provide information and training courses, especially on how Swedish unions and workplaces functioned and on what rights immigrants were accorded as workers and union members in Sweden. There was talk of providing broader information on Swedish society as a whole, but in practice such information was quite limited.[119]

The LO was committed to providing interpreters when necessary and to ensuring that employers provided the 240 hours of Swedish-language instruction the law required of them.[120] These requirements, too, were justified with the argument that a common language was necessary for immigrants' contacts with unions to be effective and for immigrants to become active union members.[121] In fact, LO attempted to pull immigrants into decision-making processes by creating a system of local and regional immigrant committees that would have an advisory role within the LO. In reality these immigrant committees were poorly organized and had little actual influence. Wuokko Knocke went so far as to call these committees "a way for LO to avoid thinking about the specific problems of their immigrant members."[122] In any case, this system of committees seems to have neutralized at least some of the concerns the LO had about immigrant incorporation by giving immigrant workers an illusion of influence.

SAP followed the LO in taking a pragmatic approach toward immigrant policy during late 1960s and early 1970s. Even many policies that later became bulwarks of the freedom of choice strategy of integration were justified with pragmatic reasoning at the beginning, acquiring a principled justification after the fact. Perhaps the best example of this type of policy is the provision for home-language education (*hemspråksundervisning*) that came into effect in 1968. This law specified that immigrants had a right to instruction in their home language, provided by the municipality in which they lived. In making the decision to provide this instruction, SAP relied on research that showed that children who were proficient (and literate) in their first language learned a second language better than those whose knowledge of their first language was incomplete. For instance, Lars Sköld, Social Democratic member of the Education Department, argued that "the evidence shows that if we insist on only Swedish instead of bilingualism, these children will end up with a double-half-lingualism (*dubbel-halvspråkighet*)" and that, therefore, "we must support home-language education as a step on the way to Swedish."[123] In other words, home-language education was primarily seen as a pathway to Swedish competence. Home-language education was a tool for integration—perhaps even assimilation—into Swedish society. This is a stark difference from the justification of home-language education as a way for immigrant children to maintain contact with the culture of their parents, a view that came to prominence toward the end of the decade. SAP's 1978 proposal for an immigration policy agenda clearly reasoned along cultural-pluralist lines in regard to home-language education:

> The 1975 immigrant policy decision meant that society was required to give immigrant children the chance to hold on to and strengthen their skills in their home languages. This is a necessary basis for their entire emotional and intellectual development. It is necessary so that immigrant children do not become a neglected group in society. Children must be able to experience their own cultural background and their own language as an advantage.[124]

Indeed, by the end of the period of study, Tage Erlander, by then retired, noted, that "people want more collective measures not just to advance the collective good but also to increase possibilities for individual self-realization," and that people ought to view "new demands from minority groups who want a more equitable division of welfare and influence" in light of this demand for individual choice.[125] By 1975, freedom of choice had become one of three core principles of immigrant/integration policy (equality, freedom of choice, and cooperation) that were enshrined in the new Swedish Basic Law.

So, what pushed SAP to redefine their stance as one that supported freedom of choice regarding integration? On the one hand, writers in the popular press seemed to exert some influence. While the role of any one person should not be overstated, the cultural-pluralist David Schwarz's reputation as *the* expert in the realm of immigrant and minority policy surely played some role in this shift. On the other hand, the desire to present a harmonious, unified policy may have also led SAP to adopt a stance that emphasized freedom of choice over assimilation or even the sort of pragmatic concerns that drove earlier integration discussions. The elevation of freedom of choice to a position equal with equality in other domains (women's and disability issues, especially) and the increasing recognition, more generally, that equality and freedom of choice could be mutually reinforcing may have made an assimilationist standpoint less tenable within a larger ideological framework for the Social Democrats. It is also true that there was increasing rebellion against treating Finns as special cases (for instance, the schools noted previously). Harmonizing the general policy toward integration with that applied to Finnish immigrants may have also been a driving force.

Yet, there remained unresolved tensions between equality and freedom of choice in the domain of integration/immigrant policy that went largely unrecognized by SAP and the writers in *DN* (and their counterparts in the Liberal party). Both suggested that immigrants ought to ascribe to a certain set of values that they felt were core to Swedish life. Most basically, the Liberals and SAP both expected that immigrants would respect the rule of law and abide by the basic tenets of democracy.[126] More pointedly, SAP was explicit in stating that they aimed not just to create equality but to teach people to value equality. This included immigrants. For example, the attempts to "actively recruit" immigrants into unions, the party, and working life were justified in part with a desire to "encourage immigrants to see the value in being part of a solidaristic community marked by equality."[127] Some values and norms were off the table when it came to freedom of choice.

It is also true that the LO, as stated earlier, made few references to freedom of choice for immigrants, despite their direct concern with the integration of immigrants. In fact, the LO's desire to make immigrants into good union members who valued democracy in the workplace, including the role of the LO as an organization, can be seen as a direct challenge to the principle of freedom of choice.[128] Given SAP's close institutional relationship with LO and their coauthorship of the reports on equality, it is unsurprising that LO's goal of recruiting immigrants into unions was explicitly stated, despite the contradiction with freedom of choice that this entailed. Perhaps this occurred out of a desire to paper over differences between the two organizations, although there is little evidence that the authors were concerned with (or even aware of) the apparent contradiction.

The more likely explanation is that such demands (valuing equality and democracy, participating in labor unions, etc.) were simply not seen as an encroachment on immigrants' freedom of choice. In practice, if not necessarily in principle, freedom of choice was mostly limited to such things as language, religion, and some cultural practices. A separate "cultural policy" with its own targeted programs was set up alongside the supposedly culture-free "economic policy" of the general welfare. In other words, what was on the surface a fairly radical statement of multiculturalism turned out to be considerably more limited, at least during the mid-1970s when it was first advanced. Demands for assimilation related to central features of the so-called Swedish model remained in full force; assimilation into the Swedish *welfare state*—accommodation to social-democratic hegemony—was considered a crucial aspect of successful integration into Sweden.

Conclusions: The Dog That Didn't Bark, and the Dog That Did

The story of the 1968–1975 period is really twofold: a story of a dog that didn't bark, and a story of one that did. The severe economic downturn of the mid-1970s did not provoke much of a crisis of closure-as-access to goods, even though one could argue that the increase in unemployment made those goods more scarce. This economic stability is largely attributable to social-democratic hegemony—a hegemony of values—that was firmly in place. In fact, when SAP finally lost control of the government in the 1976 election, it was mainly over the issue of nuclear power, not economics. The new government may not have been Social Democratic, but it certainly was social democratic, and there was no question of cutting benefits in the face of crisis. On the other hand, there was a crisis of closure-as-entry that had both political and policy consequences. LO and SAP had few problems in calling for restrictions on the number of immigrants entering the country, and new visa rules for potential migrants were enacted. Yet at the same time, the social-democratic hegemony set the limits for possible reactions to increasing immigration such that while entry into the nation could be disputed, the meaning of membership was not really renegotiated. The crisis of closure-as-entry did not provoke a crisis of closure-as-access to goods. The People's Home seemed to have more members, but the stuff that bound them continued to be welfare-statist values

A transformation had taken place, one that shifted the emphasis of nation building from *bonding* to *bridging*. In the 1940s, SAP was building a welfare state for Swedes and convincing Swedes that the welfare state was a defining feature of their national character. By the 1970s, SAP—and the newly social-democratic middle parties—was building a welfare state for immigrants, too. The welfare state had transitioned from being something that needed to be built up and defended to an institutional fact. It could, therefore, provide a useful framework for immigrant incorporation, particularly as the values that underlay it—security, equality, and freedom of choice—were clarified.

Chapter 4

1991–1995: People's Home No Longer?

The Breakdown of the Miraculous Welfare Machine

Although the 1976 election may not have been fought on welfare-statist grounds, social policy issues did not disappear from the agenda. The welfare-state consensus provided a basis for what was, according to some, one of the most disastrous policy initiatives the LO and SAP have ever jointly pursued: a profit-sharing scheme called the Meidner Model that would channel "excess" profits into worker-controlled investment funds used to create jobs and to raise wages. Essentially, the proposal called for the socialization of industrial profits. To the Swedish Employers Federation, this proposal was one step too far down the path to socialism. The massive backlash that the proposal engendered was, in some ways, the first major loss that SAP had suffered in terms of social policy since the 1950s.[1] Though the loss did not mean much for social-democratic hegemony, it did signal to SAP that they had, perhaps, reached the limit of reform. In practice, the late 1970's and 1980's saw few new reforms, though the public sector continued to grow and active labor market policies continued to be pursued.

Yet, the 1980s were a period of radical change, even as social-democratic hegemony persisted. Perhaps most consequential to the Swedish welfare machine—and its ultimate demise—was the problem of rising unemployment. Despite economic shakiness and slow (if steady) growth in the late 1970s and early 1980s, unemployment remained fairly steady. Soon, however, unemployment began to climb and, with it, public expenditures as the unemployed were cycled through the training programs, relocation programs, and unemployment insurances designed to maintain full employment. Faced with a choice to maintain this system or to fight increasing inflation, SAP chose the latter, a step away from Keynesian principles. Full employment was all but abandoned as a policy goal for the first time since the end of World War II. The consequence was that, as an international economic crisis hit, unemployment rose precipitously to reach over 10 percent by 1993, considerably higher than Sweden's previous postwar peak of 2.8 percent in 1984.[2] This development, accompanied by a high and rising state deficit, an aging population that placed ever more strain on Sweden's generous pension system, and a deep recession, meant that Sweden found itself in its worst economic crisis of the postwar period. This crisis led to SAP's catastrophic defeat in the 1991 parliamentary elections and ushered two new right-wing parties into parliament (the center-right Christian Democrats and far-right New Democracy).

At just about the same time, Europe was experiencing a refugee crisis. Sweden was particularly affected because more refugees per capita were accepted in Sweden than anywhere else in western Europe at this time. The new migration stood out from previous waves of migration. For one, the sheer number of asylum seekers was unprecedented. Although labor migration had fallen to almost nothing by this point, the number of asylum seekers skyrocketed, reaching a high point of 84,018 in 1992, driven in large part by the civil war in the former Yugoslavia. The number of asylum seekers granted asylum was also high, although this varied considerably from year to year. At its peak, the acceptance of asylum seekers reached 36,482 in 1993 and 44,875 in 1994, most of them Bosnians. A precipitous drop followed these figures in 1995, in part because 1994's record acceptances led to a partial clearing of the queue. Family-reunification migration followed refugee migration by a year or two, making the number of total immigrants to Sweden in these years consistently high, despite scant labor-market migration. In addition, the new migrants were increasingly non-European, nonwhite, and non-Christian. Besides former Yugoslavian migrants (most of whom were Bosnian Muslims), Iraqi Kurds, Iranians, and Somalians made up the largest groups of asylum seekers and family-reunification migrants.

Although neither the upswing in immigration nor the economic troubles of the previous period seemed to have provoked a broad crisis of closure, the 1990s' troubles certainly did. In this period, both kinds of crisis of closure were closely entangled. Essentially, the economic crisis and the refugee crisis resulted in a loss of confidence in the state's capacity to effectively regulate Swedish society to the benefit of all. The long-standing consensus around a generous, universalist welfare state began to dissolve. However, this erosion of consensus did not mean a total abandonment of the Swedish model—with the exception of a major overhaul of the pension system, few major changes to the institutions of the welfare state were made. What it did mean was increasing acceptance of opposition to the welfare state. At the same time, policymakers and pundits began to argue that there was a limit to the number of new members the nation could absorb and, indeed, that simply giving these new members access to the general solutions of the Swedish welfare state was an ineffective strategy for integration. In other words, just as a highly vulnerable population of refugees was entering Sweden, much of the support system previously available to them was coming under heavy fire. The discourse on the welfare state and the discourse on immigration became more closely entwined than before, both in terms of what immigration meant for the welfare state in general and of whether the welfare state was good for immigrants themselves.

The two crises of closure—of entry in regard to the question of immigration and of access to goods in regard to questions of the future of the welfare state—too, were closely entwined. They represented processes that were mutually reinforcing. The faltering of the welfare-state consensus contributed to growing anti-immigrant sentiment, and conversely, this sentiment contributed to the breakdown of social-democratic hegemony. This mutual relation was highlighted particularly by the way in which it became widely acknowledged that a social-democratic welfare state that did not make special provisions for immigrants was failing to do the work of integration that politicians in the earlier periods had expected it to do. This failure to manage integration was an illustration of the welfare state's limits as an engine for progress, but also, for many, a sign that the new refugees were somehow different, harder to integrate, and less desirable than the labor migrants who had come before them. Neither of these crises works in isolation.

This chapter elaborates the breakdown of consensus on both these points, focusing first on the welfare state alone. I examine three general orientations to the welfare state: (1) an anti-Swedish model view, most clearly expressed by the newly successful Conservative party that called for sweeping privatization and drastic cuts in the public sector; (2) a reformist view that accepted the basic values and goals of the Swedish model, but which demanded far-ranging changes, including a reduction in the public sector, a greater focus on economic stimulus, and, most importantly, a switch to a "basic security" over the "income-maintenance model" that had thus far prevailed (this view was most common within the Center Party, the Liberal party, and Christian Democrats, but had many influential backers within SAP as well); and (3) a preservationist view, which wished to maintain the Swedish model in its current form, making only superficial changes. By the end of this period, we see that the Swedish model continued, despite challenges, to provide a source of identity for Swedes, an identity consistent with previous periods.

Immigration discourse in the 1990s presents perhaps the clearest case of a crisis of closure-as-entry in the entire twentieth century. Immigration/immigrants began to be considered by some to be a direct threat, both to culture and to the welfare state. Both of these threats are framed as a manifestation of Sweden's failure to successfully integrate immigrants, a framing that makes clear the growing doubts about the state's ability to "handle" immigrant issues, especially through the "general solutions" of the welfare state.[3]

Welfare State under Fire: Dissolving Consensus, Persisting Institutions

In 1995, Conservative Frederik Reinfeldt compared the impending collapse of the Swedish model to the fall of the Berlin Wall:

> The Swedish welfare state has grown up together with our Swedish traditions and is based on Swedish customs. It's because of this that the welfare state is so strongly rooted in Swedish consciousness. When this Swedish dream—because that is how we understand it—is now headed for collapse,

it is an isolated Swedish system collapse of almost the same magnitude as the fall of the Berlin Wall.[4]

Earlier, when the nonsocialist parties ruled in coalition in 1976, they were more or less social democrats with nonsocialist party affiliations. They ran on mostly welfare state–preservationist (indeed, expansionist) platforms and did little to change the Swedish model.[5] But the 1991 election was different: the coalition of nonsocialist parties (Conservatives, Liberals, and Center Party) that stood for elections posed serious questions about both the economic wisdom and moral basis of the social-democratic welfare state. Deep economic recession, coupled with an increasingly complacent and incoherent SAP, led to victory for this set of parties—the so-called 1991 "earthquake election." This earthquake was not merely party political. It was fundamental, sparking an intense debate about what Swedish society should look like.

In the conclusion to a retrospective collection of essays about the 1991 election, editor Björn Fryklund wrote that "all the authors agree that 1991 spelled the end of the *folkhem* as a hegemonic way of thinking about Swedish politics," adding that "however, nothing new has come to take its place."[6] The election was a catastrophic loss for SAP, whose support dipped below 40 percent (to 37.7%) for the first time since 1928. Furthermore, the election ushered two new parties into parliament and brought to power a center-right coalition more united than any previous nonsocialist collaboration. The reaction to this earthquake election was one of shock: it had not only thrown Europe's strongest social-democratic party out of power, but it had also destabilized one of Europe's most stable party systems.

The idea that Sweden's 1991 election was a vote for or against the People's Home became a central interpretation in both the popular press[7] and among academics.[8] Some argued that SAP had lost its way, abandoning the "workers' politics" that had brought them to power and pointed toward the abandonment of full employment as an example.[9] In this interpretation, SAP had changed, shifting to a more market-oriented position, while the voters had remained committed to the "old" *folkhem* model.[10] Other observers saw a much broader shift away from a welfare ideology altogether. For this group, the 1991 election represented a "system change" that was reflective of a confluence of economic, political, and cultural changes that worked against the People's Home model among voters.[11] It was SAP's association with this model, in fact, that led to their defeat. Still others saw the election less as an indictment of social democracy and more as a reaction against "bad times." In this view, both the voters and SAP remained essentially aligned, but the economic crisis and high unemployment led to a nonideological "protest" vote.[12] All agreed, however, that SAP could no longer count on reigning uninterrupted and that, unlike the nonsocialist victories of the 1970s, there were likely to be lasting reverberations from this election.

Instead of a universal welfare consensus, then, three general orientations to the Swedish model became clear during the period under study: an anti-welfare-state orientation, a reformist welfare-state orientation, and a preservationist welfare-state orientation. The most radical critics of the welfare state suggested a complete overhaul, suggesting that the welfare state was no longer tenable:

> The last 20 years' catastrophic economic development has made it so that we're now headed toward the collapse of the traditional welfare state. . . . Everything points to the fact that it's already too late to reconstruct the welfare state, one of history's greatest and most interesting projects.[13]

This attitude was reflective of a broader neoliberal trend in international politics, one that in the previous decade had ushered in anti-welfare-state conservatives such as Margaret Thatcher and Ronald Reagan. Many in the popular press declared that the "right-wing wave has finally reached Sweden."[14] Like Thatcherites and Reaganites, welfare-state critics argued for vast reductions in the size of the public sector, privatization of public services and insurances, reduction in taxes and expenditures, and severe cuts in benefits. The most extreme anti-welfare-state critics came from outside the party system, although neoliberal ideas had a prominent place in the Conservative party, too. The most concrete manifestation of the right-wing swing in Sweden was the 1992 Lindbeck Commission—a commission put together by the center-right government to propose solutions to the economic crisis. The result was a report that called for sweeping macroeconomic reform, including corrections for "distorted markets" and "inappropriate and outdated institutions." The report doubted the effectiveness of active labor-market policies in a situation of crisis and decried the rapid growth of the public sector since the 1970s.[15] The report was nothing short of a condemnation of the Swedish model in the modern economic climate.[16]

Such a position was unthinkable even as late as the mid-1980s. Harsh critics of the welfare state, of course, had existed throughout the twentieth century. These critics, however, had rarely been given space in major newspapers, and certainly not on the floor of the parliament. Yet, by 1993, Bo Södersten could write in Sweden's most popular daily newspaper that taxes were "confiscatory," that, speaking of the public sector, the welfare state had created a large class of people who were "taking" (*tärande*) without "making" (*närande*),[17] and that those who now supported the welfare state were merely a "left-over and completely intellectually degenerate leftist mafia."[18] While Södersten's rhetoric was more extreme than most, his conclusion that "the thought that we can manage our welfare in the future through just marginal changes in the public sector and the social security system is, and will remain, an illusion" was shared by many.[19]

Journalist Anders Isaksson, for instance, pointed to the fundamental insolvency of the welfare system given the new climate of instability in the international market, saying that "quite simply, the money has run out. The only thing that is growing in our country today is the public sector."[20] He argued that Sweden ought to reduce benefit levels so that "they were enough to survive on, but not enough to live on if one isn't a fakir."[21] Isaksson's arguments against the welfare state were primarily economic and were characteristic of a broad group of Conservatives, both within and outside the party system. This group often saw the value of a system that had equality as a goal, but argued that such a system was unsustainable in the modern economic climate. The crisis of the 1990s, in this interpretation, was largely a result of that system's inflexibility and cost.[22] Others argued that the insolvency of the system made it fundamentally irresponsible not to overhaul it.[23]

Others, however, saw the welfare state as *immoral*, both in the way that it redistributed goods and in the consequences it had for people living within the system. Part of their argument was that the welfare state unfairly redistributed goods from productive to unproductive parts of the population. The problem was that the redistribution benefited not just those who were unproductive because of old age or sickness, but those who were unproductive because they were unwilling to take responsibility for their own lives.

> The problem is, our welfare system does not just support those who are unwillingly weak, but also those who are unnecessarily weak—who through active choice or simple passivity choose not to participate in the productive society.[24]

In fact, the system, they argued, *encouraged* dishonesty and abuse, a critique launched particularly toward sickness insurance. Critics pointed to the anomaly that Sweden with its high standard of living still had the highest rate of sickness leave in the world.[25] They concluded that this high rate must be a result of fraud. They pointed especially to the large number of less verifiable maladies such as "burnout" as particularly suspect. People defrauded the system not because they were dishonest in character, necessarily, but because the incentives to do so were too high.[26]

More fundamentally, however, Conservative critics argued that the welfare state was immoral because it pacified citizens, who came to expect the state to solve all their problems. Frederik Reinfeldt, then president of the Conservative Youth Association, called Swedes a "sleeping people" who had been "pacified and made dependent on benefits."[27] Conservative Carl-Frederik Jaensson placed the blame for this solely on "politicians who mean well but do everything wrong anyway" going on to say that "the political system has grown over the heads of citizens."[28] Conservative parliamentarian My Persson, furthermore, argued that the welfare state "was beneficial so long as it was just a guarantee of basic security. But as the safety net has became finer, it has tended to smother the individual."[29]

This view of Swedes as "passive" and "dependent" was, of course, subject to challenge. Left activist Göran Grejder, for instance, wrote that, rather than putting people to sleep, the "welfare state is a long waking up from a sleeping state. It has made us more aware than any other known system."[30] Walter Korpi and Joakim Palme, furthermore, marshaled evidence to show that Swedes are neither work-shy nor inactive in politics and social life.[31] Nonetheless, the perception that Swedes were passive and welfare dependent—and, therefore, that the welfare state was immoral—persisted among many Conservatives.

Both those with economic objections and those with moral objections had the same remedy for the "problem" of the welfare state: a radical turn toward "market solutions" with mechanisms of competition that would iron out the inefficiencies that the large public sector, heavy regulation, and perverse work incentives had created. For instance, Ulf Laurin, president of the Swedish Employers Association, argued that the market needed a freer rein in order to increase the productivity of the Swedish state. He asked several questions:

> Security!? But what if there is nothing to distribute? Where is "security" then? Where did production go? Shouldn't someone first produce that which

is to be distributed? ... But that [production] which is well-being itself can never be created with political decisions. The capacity is quite simply missing. Politicians are a bit like eunuchs that way. Maybe they want to, but they can't. Dynamic development will be found instead in the market.[32]

This solution to a troubled economy was, of course, what the Lindbeck Commission suggested as well: to strengthen the market, weaken the state and overhaul centralized collective bargaining. This approach would move Sweden toward a continental, or even American, style of economic governance. It is worthwhile to point out that Laurin uses a central Swedish concern with security (*trygghet*) in an almost mocking way—something that would have been unthinkable in the previous period.

There were others, however, who assessed Sweden's economic dilemmas similarly but disagreed that the best solution was to scrap the welfare state. This "welfare-reform" group encompassed most of the members of the middle parties, and the Christian Democrats as well as many Social Democrats. These reformers suggested a significant, but not drastic, reduction in the size of the public sector; increased emphasis on macroeconomic stimulus; and the renewal of traditional employment measures. For the most part, reformers saw themselves as preserving the ideals behind the welfare state, especially the ideal of "general welfare" (*generell välfärden*). Yet, they realized that the policies that had previously sufficed to reach these ideals needed to be adapted to the realities of the modern international economic system. Economist Jan Bröms, for instance, wrote that "the fundamental ideas behind welfare policy need to be brought to life. This includes not only the security those policies can provide, but also what they cannot be expected to provide."[33] Bröms preferred a far-reaching reform to the entire social insurance system that would introduce blended private/public insurances. He had formally proposed this reform several years earlier to the SAP government. Bröms's solution was typical of the reformist perspective that aimed to maintain a welfare-state core while bringing certain radical new principles to bear.

One of these new principles was "basic security" (*grundtrygghet*) rather than "income security" (*standardtrygghet*) for social insurances. This principle was not exactly new. In fact, a debate over basic versus income security had divided SAP earlier in the twentieth century and had been a fundamental part of the welfare state's early formation. This debate, however, had fallen into the background after the victory of the income-security principle in the early 1950s. In the 1990s, the concept of basic security made a major comeback, backed especially by the Center Party. Party leader Andreas Carlgren put it this way:

> Center wishes to take the lead in creating basic security in Sweden during the 1990s. The current system does not create a just distribution of wealth. It's time to seriously question how long the state can give the most to those who already have the most.[34]

Carlgren further emphasized that his party's plan was not a "patchwork plan," but a program for a "unified system" of social insurances that would provide 80 percent of income up to a "normal industrial worker's income" in case of sickness or unemployment. Those who made more than a "normal industrial worker's income" would be advised to get private insurances if they wanted to maintain their current standard of living.

Indeed, allowing for private options that complemented public solutions was part of the nonsocialist parties' renewed commitment to freedom of choice, something they believed SAP had abandoned. Liberal Bo Könberg, for instance, wrote the following:

> It's a banal, but also true observation that the great majority of people strive for both freedom and security. Democracy and market economy answer to the first of these. The general welfare system to the second. For social liberals, this means welfare with choice. For some years right around 1990, it looked like many Social Democrats were on their way to accepting our perspective on the value of freedom of choice and competition even within those areas where we pay collectively through taxation. But now this whole belief in choice and competition has been destroyed.[35]

The Liberals were perhaps overstating things when they declared choice abandoned by SAP. However, just as in the previous period, choice remained contentious, and what SAP meant by the value of freedom of choice did not always align with what the Liberals meant by freedom of choice, either as a value or as an institutional feature. SAP argued for individual choice supported by and solely within a framework of the state. This concept of choice primarily had to do with the way people organized their lives (e.g., what kind of family to have), not with what services they would use.[36] The nonsocialist parties, on the other hand, argued for increased choice between state and private options, an argument that rested on the positive benefits of competition.[37] Note that for this group, too, the solution was the market—though a market tempered with, not embedded in, a reformed and reduced welfare state.

The Center Party and the Liberals both saw the problem with the current welfare state as a direct result of a self-satisfied left that, according to Carlgren, "simply counted up rights" without looking at the costs or obligations attached to these rights.[38] Liberal leader Bengt Westerberg argued that SAP "pretends that solidarity is just making promises of help and support without demanding anything in return."[39] The Liberals, in general, were considerably less radical in their suggestions for reform than the Center Party, standing behind both the "general welfare" and the principle of income-replacement in social insurances. In fact, many within not only the Liberals themselves but also within SAP saw social minister Bengt Westerberg as a "defender of welfare," though he himself was careful to point out that he was neither a "defender of institutions" nor a "system preserver" (*systembevarare*).[40] Westerberg, for instance, supported a thoroughgoing reform of the workmen's compensation legislation, one that resulted in the decreasing of claims significantly.[41] Furthermore, Westerberg was in support of the cuts to benefit levels that were made to social insurances, though he also fought to keep their basic structures intact.

Even within SAP, many saw the need to fundamentally reform the welfare system in order to preserve the values behind that system. SAP member of parliament Birgitta Dahl, for instance, recognized the problems in the system of social insurances, but called for preservation:

> We, the Swedish people, have everything to win if SAP and the Liberals cooperate to stop those who want to use this crisis as an excuse to tear down welfare and equality instead of actually dealing with the real problems—unemployment and structural problems in social insurances.[42]

Most of SAP, however, sought to keep the welfare state largely intact. They were joined in this effort by the Left Party and the "welfare-chauvinist" wing of New Democracy. The pro-welfare-state group argued that the Swedish model remained a viable and efficient economic system that was strong enough to weather the current crisis with only minor changes. Sociologists Walter Korpi and Joakim Palme argued in a *DN* op-ed that "we can choose to tear down the |Swedish| model. But there are no unambiguous facts that say that economic reasons are forcing us to do it."[43] Journalist Maria-Pia Boethius and political scientist Bo Rothstein contended that increasing efficiency within the public sector could save, conservatively calculated, 25 billion kronor without any decrease in the level of service provided.[44] Others argued that small cuts were permissible (such as the move to cut supplementary pensions from 100% to 95% of income), so long as the basic structure of such programs was retained. Ingrid Carlberg, for instance, contended that "the advantages with the basic structure of our welfare institutions are clear. It is possible, despite this, to make significant cuts without sacrificing the humanity of the general system."[45] The basic belief, carried over from earlier periods, that equality was a contributory factor to a strong economy remained intact: "We must take measures to ensure that our economy's greatest strength, the equal division of incomes, remains."[46]

Defenders of the welfare state made a moral argument analogous to the one made by welfare-state critics, as well. It was immoral, they argued, to abandon the welfare state, especially in times of crisis. Boethius, for instance, wrote in favor of the welfare state:

> We in Sweden must realize that it is more important than ever to hold onto the Swedish model, whatever the economists and opinion page writers and other gullible people try to say. It is important that there are alternatives to the dictates of capitalists, alternatives that continue to insist on every person's equal worth.[47]

This argument rested on the obligations to fellow citizens that the welfare state entailed, obligations that were partly based on ideals of citizenship and partly on the "fairness" of removing welfare protections from those who had for so long paid into them.[48] This group, too, engaged in the promotion of "social-democratic values—*trygghet* in particular—but unlike the reformists, they believed the only way to realize those values was to keep the welfare state in essentially its same form, even if it meant some financial sacrifices.[49]

So what, given this debate, was the actual impact on welfare-state institutions? The answer is, despite the newly legitimized hostility toward the welfare state, much of the institutional shape of the Swedish model remained. Generous unemployment, parental and sickness insurances based on income-replacement models, and universal child allowance and day-care policies remained in effect at the end of the period of nonsocialist governance. In part this continued maintenance of existing institutions was due to the ineffectiveness of the center-right parties. They had a hard time working together and, in 1993, were forced to reorganize and regroup following a no-confidence vote that left many with doubts that the nonsocialist parties would *ever* be able to cooperate. That institutional persistence was at least partially attributable to this inability to work together is evinced by the fact that cuts to benefit levels were actually carried out in the 1990s—but not until the center-right left office. Cuts to benefit levels were carried out by a SAP-led government and included a one-day waiting period for sickness insurance, a reduction in replacement rates for sickness insurance (from 100% to 80%), and reduction in parental and unemployment insurance (from 90% to 80%). However, replacement rates remained high by international standards, and the basic structure of the programs were not altered.[50]

The major exception to institutional persistence was the complete overhaul of the pension system, again, carried out by a Social Democratic, not a center-right government. A small "guaranteed pension" continued to be available to those with short or nonexistent work histories. It was a replacement for the old *folkpension* and was similar in generosity, but it had the character of a targeted policy rather than the universalist *folkpension*. The new guaranteed pension was conceived mostly as a "safety net" for those who fell through the cracks of the regular system, not a universalist foundation on which an income-replacement pension could be built. The *folkpension* had been accompanied by a "general complimentary pension" (*allmänna tjänstepension*, ATP), which was based on an income-replacement model that provided 100 percent of the average of the fifteen best-paid years for anyone with a work history of thirty years or longer. This was abolished and replaced with two parts: (1) an income-replacement pension (*inkomstpension*), based on lifetime income, and (2) individual retirement earnings accounts (*premiepension*), which individuals may opt to place in privately managed financial accounts or to allow the state to manage.[51] This system was the result of a compromise between five of the seven parties, covering nearly 80 percent of all members of parliament, all of whom described themselves as "satisfied" with the new system,[52] although critique of the new system from civil society was widespread.[53] Both the Communist and the newly elected Green Party saw the new system as breaking fundamentally with the principles of the social-democratic welfare state. Meanwhile, SAP and the other parties saw it as a way to maintain these principles in the face of economic threats.

The debate that went into this reform mirrored the broader debate on the welfare state, in that reform was seen as necessary to increase both financial solvency and "fairness."[54] The new pension system also represented a set of compromises between the old way of doing things and the new reformist strains of debate. It had, for instance, a blend of public and private management schemes that reduced some of the state's responsibility, but involved the state to the extent that it acted as a guarantor of the system. Furthermore, the new system retained both universal coverage and redistribution as goals (achieved largely through the guarantee pension and revisions in the ways in which pensions are taxed), but was more transparent in the way it rewarded long working histories and high preretirement wages.[55] The system furthermore represented a compromise of the principle of choice in the way that it handled individual retirement accounts, as well as more flexible retirement ages, but also had a component that ensured equality through standardization.

Thus, anti-welfare-state critics actually made very little real impact on policies in the period under study. However, the fact that cuts were made at all and that the welfare state was as hotly debated as it was is significant. Public opinion remained fairly reliably positive when asked about maintaining or expanding specific policies throughout the 1990s.[56] However, the late 1980s and early 1990s do show dwindling support for "social reforms" when questions were asked in the abstract.[57] This ambivalence about the "welfare state" as an idea while support for its institutions continued closely mirrors the public and political debate. This newfound skepticism represented nothing less than a breakdown of social-democratic hegemony. Yet this breakdown did not mean that no one any longer viewed the welfare state as an enduring feature of Swedish identity:

> For Sweden especially, the idea of the good welfare society has been more than just an overriding ideology: it has given us a sort of national identity and feeling of home. Yet this central feature of Swedish society is now facing harsh judgment from an opportunistic media that knows all the right reactionary moves.[58]

For SAP and the Left Party, social democracy as a Swedish identity was being threatened by the nonsocialist parties, the Conservatives especially. They saw this part of Swedish identity as worthwhile and valuable and in need of preservation, indeed, that the welfare state was "worth fighting for"—either through preserving the welfare state as is or through reform.[59]

For some in New Democracy, on the other hand, the primary threat to the welfare state was to be found in immigration. Although some in the party pursued neoliberalism, a significant faction pursued a welfare-chauvinist line that depicted immigrants as "stealing our welfare." Immigration was seen not just as an economic threat but an attack on the very identity of Sweden:

> It has become all too clear that, in the face of mass immigration, Sweden will not be able to preserve that which has been its best feature, that which makes Sweden Swedish: our welfare state, and the national community that goes with it.[60]

Thus, in the area of immigration, the same preservationist argument was made: social democracy is key to national identity and therefore must be preserved. What was different was the source of the danger. Indeed, migration was increasingly identified as just that: a threat.

Refugee Crisis: Migration as Threat, Opportunity, and Test Case for the Swedish Model

The coincidence of Sweden's most severe economic crisis since the 1930s with the arrival of large numbers of refugees, especially refugees from new, less familiar places and cultures, contributed to an increasingly critical debate on the place of migrants within Swedish society. This debate coincided with and was deeply entwined with the debate on the welfare state, both in terms of how immigration affected the welfare state and how the welfare state affected immigrants. Indeed, because the welfare state had become the framework through which an effective economic and cultural integration could be pursued, it was precisely through a welfare frame that the new refugee crisis *had* to be understood. Migration was framed as both a threat and an opportunity. Integration of immigrants also formed a sort of "test case" for welfare-state effectiveness, providing a perfect example of the ways in which the two crises of this period, of entry and of access, worked together.

Many commented that the debate on immigration was wholly inadequate and thus unlikely to stimulate any real solutions to the "refugee problem." The debate was seen as inadequate in two related ways. On the one hand, the debate was said to be taboo-laden, with many fearing being labeled "racist"/"xenophobic" if they suggested restricting immigration or pursuing assimilationist policies. Jörgen Westerståhl, for instance, wrote in *DN* about "silence" on the topic and the risk of taking a restrictive position in the debate:

> Immigration policy is largely a taboo area in Swedish public debate. . . . This silence is not based in the fact that differing opinions and interpretations of immigration don't exist. The silence is based in the opinion-climate: As soon as someone gives an opinion that can be interpreted as restrictive, or gives reasons for and against in general, they run the risk of being labeled racist. And then all discussion ends.[61]

On the other hand, the debate was also criticized for relying all too often on moral instead of rational (e.g., economic) or factual claims.

The first of these accusations was generally leveled not so much at the press itself, but at elected officials. Indeed, the press debate was considerably more conflictual and critical than that found within parliament. With only a few notable exceptions, members of parliament avoided restrictionist and assimilationist discourse to an astounding extent. All parties, except New Democracy, argued for a "generous" interpretation of the Geneva Convention definition of refugees, and all officially stuck to more or less multiculturalist integration policies, or were silent on the issue. Table 4 illustrates the range of immigration policy positions expressed in the party platforms of all parties represented in parliament during the late 1980s through 1995 (plus the Greens, who were in parliament from 1987 to 1991 and 1994 on). Note that all parties were relatively positive toward both accepting migrants and toward multiculturalist policies, or alternatively silent on the issue.

Both the Left Party and the Christian Democrats called for "regulated" immigration, though they were careful to note that this term did not mean closing the borders or turning away anyone in need of help. Both parties argued that regulated immigration was for the protection of the migrants

Table 4. Immigration/integration positions in party platforms

IMMIGRATION	Free immigration	Pursue generous refugee policy	Shorten time-to-asylum decision	Special policy for children	Don't split families in refugee decisions	Regulated immigration
Left Party						
1987		x				x
1993		x				x
SAP						
1990		x	x			
Greens						
1993	x	x	x	x		
Christian Dems						
1987		x	x			x
1993		x	x		x	x
Center						
1990		x		x		
Liberals						
1982		x	x	x		
Conservatives						
1984					x	
1993		x				x

INTEGRATION	Support multi-cultural	Info on Sweden refugee language	Trans-lation of foreign cre-dentials	Support home-language education	Voting rights: Local	Voting rights: National	Fight racism	Improve Swedish courses	Reduce immigration unemployment	Support immigration organizations
Left Party										
1987	x						x			
1993	x			x	x	x	x			
SAP										
1990	x	x	x	x	x	x	x	x		x
Greens										
1993	x	x	x	x	x	x	x			
Christian Dems										
1987	x			x			x	x		
1993	x			x	x	x	x	x	x	
Center										
1990	x						x			
Liberals										
1982	x			x			x			
Conservatives										
1984	x						x			
1993	x									

themselves, so that the process of immigration remained "humane,"[62] and so that migrants could attain a standard of living similar to native Swedes.[63] Not surprisingly, the Conservatives took the hardest restrictionist line in their party program. They warned against the "unacceptable consequences"—including "uncontrollable" social tensions—of policies, which allow "free entrance" to the industrialized countries.[64] However, the Conservatives emphasized Sweden's responsibility to people in need of protection and called for a generous interpretation of the Geneva Convention.[65] This small range of views is largely echoed in the parliamentary debates.[66]

The only truly restrictive, anti-immigrant voice in parliament in the 1990s, however, was New Democracy. New Democracy was a far-right populist party that received 6.7 percent of the vote in the 1991 election, becoming only the second new party to enter Swedish parliament for over seventy years. The party, led by entertainment mogul Bert Karlsson and eccentric aristocrat Ian Wachmeister, entered parliament on primarily a tax-revolt protest vote, but turned to immigration as a major issue once elected. Their attack on immigration was two-pronged: They argued that the agencies set up to deal with immigration were corrupt, inefficient, and incompetent,[67] but also, more fundamentally, that immigration was a threat to the fabric of Swedish society—both culturally and economically. New Democracy's participation in the debate, however, was not long lasting. Within a few years, internal ideological splits between those who favored neoliberal solutions (led by Wachmeister) and those who took a more welfare-chauvinist line (led by Karlsson) led to a series of defections and a loss of electoral support. They failed to repeat their successes in the 1994 election, and by 1998 their support fell to 1.2 percent. By 2002 the party no longer existed.[68]

This lack of support for far-right parties, however, does not mean that the Swedish people were universally in favor of relatively open immigration policies and multiculturalist integration policies. In fact, opinion on both of these issues was sharply divided. For instance, by 1993, over half of respondents to a national survey agreed either "completely" or "largely" with the statement that "there are too many foreigners in Sweden."[69] Indeed, between 55 percent (in 1994) and 64 percent (in 1992) of respondents thought that the proposition that Sweden should accept fewer refugees was a "good suggestion" throughout the course of the time period under study.[70] As regards integration, a full 26 percent "disagreed completely" that "immigrants in Sweden should be able to freely practice their religion," and a further

33 percent "neither agreed nor disagreed" with that statement.[71] However, studies also have shown that immigration was not a primary concern for voters. Relatively few listed it among the top three social problems of concern in Sweden (between 12% in 1994 and 25% in 1993 listed it as such),[72] and even fewer gave it as a reason for their voting decisions.[73] Thus the problem was not a lack of diversity of views among the Swedish people, as such, but a constricted debate among officials.

Writers pointed out two possible problems with such lack of debate. On the one hand, it was seen as constricting the possible range of solutions to the problems that accompanied refugee migration. Anders Åslund, for instance, wrote the following:

> My conclusion is that immigrant and refugee problems are to the greatest degree caused by state actions. If we are going to solve these problems, we must be able to discuss them openly without hypocrisy, and all options must be on the table.[74]

On the other hand, an artificial consensus on migrants/migration, especially given that the public did not always see eye to eye with politicians, was seen as potentially contributing to racism and xenophobia. Excluding certain types of discourse might radicalize those groups who were critical of open and generous refugee policies. Many pointed to the constriction of the debate as a factor in New Democracy's 1991 victory. The extent to which New Democracy voters were responding to immigration issues, rather than using their vote as a protest against an establishment that was seen as ineffective, is highly debatable.[75]

Party officials, despite their rhetoric, did take restrictionist actions. Such moves generally were, however, made by high-level appointees, not elected officials per se. SAP, for instance, in 1989 decreed that it was restricting refugee status to only those who met the strict Geneva Convention definition. This pronouncement was thought by many to signal a shift toward more restrictive policies, but such a shift never materialized.[76] Large numbers of asylum seekers continued to be granted permanent resident permits under the heading of "exceptional need of protection."[77] The nonsocialist government, headed by the Liberals, overturned this decision in 1991 just as the refugee crisis was intensifying. Liberals themselves, however, took restrictionist actions once in government, as well, introducing visa requirements for residents of the former Yugoslavian states in 1993, drastically slowing down the flow of potential refugees from, especially, Bosnia-Herzegovina. All the while the Liberals maintained that they were, in principle, continuing a "generous" refugee policy and that the new visa requirements were simply a necessary response to an imminent crisis.[78] There was some truth to this contention—the nonsocialist government they were a part of granted resident permits to nearly 40,000 Bosnians already in the country at the same time the new visa requirements were passed, over objections from SAP who favored offering support to refugees to repatriate. In 1995, too, SAP suggested that state-supported repatriation was a "right" for refugees, a move that could be read as either restrictionist or not depending on one's perspective.[79]

The second accusation, that the debate was "overly moral," was espoused both by those who wished to place greater restrictions on immigration and immigrants as well as those who wanted to loosen those restrictions. Most agreed that Sweden had an obligation to help those who were truly in need, even if the definition of who was in need varied greatly. Jabar Amin, writing in *DN*, for instance, wrote "the most important thing is that we give people protection when they need it. Giving protection to people in need must remain independent of economic conditions."[80] Even New Democracy party member Henning Sjöström called for a "a just and fair system of help for those who truly need it."[81] Yet such broad moralizing claims were seen as inadequate if they did not lead to "real" action. Birgitta Albons, for instance, wrote that "the only thing we stand together for is to make a reality everything that Sweden boasts about: Solidarity and human rights. But these should not be empty words."[82] It was not enough to "feel sorry" for immigrants, but rather there must be a realistic and informed debate over both the cost of immigration and its utility:

> We have never really admitted that we need immigrants. We motivate our refugee acceptance with noble solidarity, tolerance and a general "feel sorry for" attitude. Because we've never admitted that we need immigrants, we've never been able to demand anything of them.[83]

Similarly, in *ARB*, Karen Söderberg writes that:

> Swedes rarely talk about the utility of refugees, immigrants and foreigners who work in Sweden. People gladly admit that there is a need for cheap baby-

sitters, cheap cleaning and cheap lunches. . . . It's amusing that people show so much enthusiasm for the free market, but so little for the free movement of people that supports it and has much the same effect.[84]

Likewise, there was a demand for "real" figures regarding the costs of migration, both in terms of the cost of the asylum process and the cost/benefit analysis of immigrants participating in the labor market and welfare state long term.[85]

It was also argued that an overly "moral" debate, especially with one side having a "moral monopoly," was damaging to public opinion about immigration.[86] SAP member Bo Göransson, for instance, responding to a controversial anti-immigration article in the paper *Expressen,* put it this way:

> *Expressen* got their facts wrong. . . . But the critique against them was mainly moralizing. I am convinced that the majority of the Swedish people believe that *Expressen* was right, but that they weren't "allowed" to be right: that the moral establishment kept *Expressen* from formulating their "truths."[87]

Indeed, many criticized Sweden for trying to appear to be, as Anders Fogelkou put it, a "moral great power" (*moralisk stormakt*), instead of addressing the problem of immigration rationally.[88]

The absence of real conflict among elected officials (with the small exceptions noted earlier) and the strong moral taboos placed on the immigration debate led to a situation where it was difficult to associate any one party or political views with a particular migration standpoint. The Liberals attempted, in 1991, to brand themselves as the party with the most generous and humane refugee policy but, once coming to power, were split over what that brand might mean in practice. Immigration did not feature prominently in their next campaign. Perhaps this lack of connection between parties and migration views explains why voters did not list immigration issues as a major reason for their votes, even as concerns about immigration became more pronounced in the media.[89]

At the same time that the official debate was under fire for its one-sidedness and moralizing, the press debate encompasses views that were increasingly critical of Sweden's immigration and integration policies and of the idea of Sweden as a country of immigration. For the first time since the immediate postwar period, the Swedish press contained open discussion of whether immigration was a "threat" or an "opportunity," a debate which focused both on Swedish culture and the Swedish welfare state. Jesus Alcala, writing in *DN*, described this debate in stark terms, writing that "some day we will have to face the question of what would be most devastating for us to lose, both as individuals and as a society: our material welfare or our morals?"[90]

The discussion of culture, identity, and immigrants in the 1960s and 1970s focused mostly on what effect Swedish society ought to have on immigrants' culture and identity. Although this concern continued, by the 1990's, it was complemented by a concern with what effect immigration, especially immigration from outside of western Europe, would have on Swedish culture and identity. This concern was framed primarily as a "loss" of something valuable, though what was lost was rarely specified. Widar Andersson argued that "the rapid increase of asylum seekers, together with the internationalization of information, places enormous strain on national cohesion," asking finally, "Where is Swedishness heading in Sweden?," while Social Democrat Mauricio Rojas called for a "necessary grieving process" over Swedish homogeneity:[91]

> The number one most important factor [in Swedes' discontent with immigration policy] is the very meaning of immigration for Sweden as a nation. In a few decades, the country's ethnic makeup has changed in a drastic way. Mass immigration has consigned Sweden's ethnic homogeneity, the country's most characteristic feature, to history.... The meaning of this has not yet been understood or dealt with in an adequate way. A necessary grieving process has in practice been made taboo and removed from the public conversation.[92]

Many also feared that the increased pace of immigration (and changing sources) would lead to an increase in racism and xenophobia among the native population. Although many were concerned primarily about the prevalence of discrimination, the physical and psychological well-being of immigrants, or the potential for violence, some were also concerned that this rise in racism was a blow to certain core Swedish values of democracy, tolerance, and equal value of all people (*alla människors lika värde*). Ana Maria Narti, for instance, wrote that "the biggest threat to peace is not refugees, but xenophobia, which uses the crises of our time to spread aggression with the aim to replace democracy with new or old types of totalitarian governance."[93] Birgitta Albons, similarly, wrote that Sweden's *reaction* to immigrants and refugees has meant that "not all people are seen as equally valuable" and that this was a "loss of a core value of the Swedish people."[94] For some, racism was to be combated through economic reforms, as well as information campaigns, rallies, and more stringent laws on hate speech. Journalist and public intellectual Pierre Schorri wrote the following:

> If our foundations have been shaken through unemployment, through alien-
> ation and isolation, then we can no longer think rationally. Instead, a fer-
> tile soil for simple solutions and incitement to hatred, gang formation and
> subcultures arise. Therefore campaigns against unemployment, against
> marginalization and for social solidarity and cooperation, for education
> and knowledge, become synonymous with and indispensable to the fight
> against intolerance, xenophobia and racism.[95]

For others, however, restricting the number of immigrants (particularly non-European immigrants) was vital to protecting Sweden's culture of tolerance and equal worth:

> Of course we should accept refugees from the terribly affected Bosnia—
> but this should happen only in cooperation with those who live near the
> acceptance places, not against their will. If Sweden is to accept so many
> migrants that they need to commandeer locales for refugee camps, then
> New Democracy and the [far-right xenophobic party] Sweden Democrats
> would be the only winners.[96]

The debate on immigration was also re-ethnicized by the 1990s. Immigrants were no longer simply "immigrants" but rather referred to by specific ethnic groups (i.e., "Kurds," "Kosovar Albanians" etc.), or, more often, simply "non-European."[97] That these immigrants were refugees and not labor migrants was also highlighted. "Immigration policy has gone from being labor-market policy to being refugee policy, something much more based in morals and culture."[98] Indeed, many focused on culture, pointing out that refugees were increasingly "different" culturally than previous waves of immigration. Westerståhl, for instance, argued that the new refugees were more "difficult" to integrate because they are "farther away, especially culturally," from Sweden, though he does not suggest that they should not be accepted nor that they should be treated differently.[99] In emphasizing that the newer immigrants are more "difficult," however, the discourse tended to both trivialize the experience of integration of previous groups of immigrants and to exaggerate the distance between Swedes and the new immigrants. In other words, it was not necessarily simply immigration that represented a "threat" to Swedish culture, but immigration from places that were non-Western and hence "alien."

Immigration, further, was increasingly framed as a threat to the welfare state itself. Immigrants and immigration were sometimes framed as a direct threat to state financing, both because of the high cost in processing and housing asylum seekers and because of the large number of social assistance (*socialbidrag*) recipients among the immigrant population. These arguments framed refugees solely as a "cost" contributing to the increasing national debt and the insolvency of the welfare state. Those using the first frame pointed to the inefficiencies in the asylum process and, especially, to the large number of asylum seekers without legitimate reasons for asylum. These "economic refugees," a term which had a strong negative connotation, were framed as dishonest, manipulative and opportunistic, and "not real refugees."[100] Critics claimed that these nonrefugee refugees not only cost the state directly, but indirectly increased the cost for the entire system by creating an increased need for both scrutiny and supervision, even for those refugees with legitimate reasons for asylum.[101]

Those who pointed to the high proportion of social-assistant recipients among refugees made a much more direct statement of threat: immigrants were "takers" (*tärande*), not "makers" (*närande*). While the percentage of the welfare-state budget that went to social assistance was quite small, many pointed out that immigrants, especially refugees, tended to be "permanent" social-assistance recipients, and therefore *only* a cost.[102] These permanent recipients were in contrast to most unemployed Swedes who received unemployment insurance that they had spent many years paying payroll contributions to support. It should be noted that few ascribed this difference to either individual or culturally predicated work shyness. Most blamed a combination of discrimination, a poor economy, and an overly generous Swedish state for making immigrants passive welfare dependents.[103] Despite a potential realization that it was the system, not necessarily the migrants themselves, who were the problem, the message continued to be one of immigrant-as-threat:

Swedish society has not succeeded in integrating immigrants in either social or working life, which has led to many of them becoming dependent on social assistance (*bidragsberoende*). They are the new underclass, and that status makes them a threat to our social solidarity.[104]

Essentially, it was considered inevitable, given the background of immigrants and the shape of the Swedish state, that immigrants would become welfare dependents. Thus, it was the immigrants themselves who formed a threat.

Further, because social assistance is means-tested and, therefore, a "social net of last resort," it is among the least favorably viewed social programs. Many argued that the large number of immigrants using this program both sharpened dislike for social assistance and widened the gulf between immigrants and Swedes. Ingrid Björkman, for instance, wrote that "when ethnicity coincides with other differences—especially the economic differences that lead to immigrants' high rates of social-assistance claiming—group differences are greatly heightened" and can lead to "decreased confidence in the institutions of the welfare state."[105] In other words, the high level of "welfare dependence" (*bidragsberoende*) among immigrants was detrimental to the solidaristic welfare state. There is some degree of truth to this—living in a neighborhood with a higher number of immigrants on public assistance is a good predictor for negative attitudes about the welfare state in Sweden.[106]

Immigrants were posited as a threat to solidarity in a few other ways, as well. This line of argument repeats many of the tropes discussed earlier in terms of immigrants as a cultural threat. On the one hand, the argument was that (nonwestern European) refugees were simply too different from Swedes to inspire trust and solidarity. Therefore, the argument goes, the large number of new migrants is eroding support for redistribution:

> Refugee policy is the greatest challenge of human solidarity. Solidarity, in the first hand, is directed toward friends, toward one's own group, village, class, guild or union. Solidarity with deviants and strangers is considerably weaker and more vulnerable. The People's Home and Swedish welfare exclude strangers.[107]

On the other hand, some argued that immigrants did not share the same social-democratic values as Swedes and that we must demand that they do. Widar Andersson, for instance, writes that respect for democracy, equality, regulation of the labor market, and solidarity must be the "limits of Swedish culture which everyone in Sweden must live within."[108] Such lack of shared values was framed as a threat to the welfare state, as something that undermined solidarity between Swedes and immigrants. It was, in some ways, a remnant of the welfare-state method of immigrant integration that had developed in the 1960s and 1970s. The LO and SAP of the 1960s tried to use the welfare state to make immigrants into good trade unionists and social democrats. Many in 1990 thought that such was impossible with the new immigrants.

However, neither in the realm of economics nor culture was immigration framed solely as a threat. The Liberals (and *Dagens Nyheter*) were at the forefront of the campaign to paint immigration as an opportunity and immigrants as contributors to Swedish society. Mats Lundegård, for instance, pointed out that immigrants are often used as scapegoats in times of economic crisis, and that 1990s Sweden is no different:

> "It's the immigrants who are undermining the welfare state and taking over the labor market," the rawest rhetoric says. This is not now nor has it ever been true. All of Europe's economies have benefited from immigration since the end of World War Two.[109]

Some even link problems with welfare-state financing with the scapegoating of immigrants:

> With a conservative regime, our security system will fall. The campaign against the public sector hits people right in the gut with words like "wasteful." It's a problem with Sweden's economy, and no one can say where the problem lies. . . . It's typical that we would then risk opportunities for a party like New Democracy that says "It's because we give too much money to immigrants. We take in too many refugees."[110]

Furthermore, it was argued, immigration did not actually "cost" as much as critics believed. Liberal immigration minister Birgit Friggebo provided a rundown of the financial costs and benefits of immigrants. She pointed out that the majority of immigrants are, indeed, employed and that they contribute both through being consumers and taxpayers. On the whole, she argued, immigrants are more "benefit" than "cost."[111] Furthermore, it is often pointed out that because most immigrants come as working-age adults, they tend to be net contributors to the welfare state.[112] An economist writing in the business newspaper *Affärsvärlden* even went so far as to argue that immigrants benefited native Swedes *especially* in times of unemployment by acting as a "shock absorber." He argued that employment levels are largely set by macroeconomic factors and that because immigrants are more likely to become unemployed, they would take the place of native Swedes who would have otherwise become unemployed during recessions.[113]

It was, furthermore, frequently noted that immigrants started small businesses at a high rate and often in sectors that Swedes avoided because of the long hours or unpleasant work.[114] Though this choice of work was taken to be a sign of the difficulties immigrants faced in entering labor markets, it was also pointed out that their efforts were a benefit to the Swedish economy, and a resource:

> Immigrants are an important source of entrepreneurship and new businesses.... Many immigrants come from countries where small businesses are much more common than here in Scandinavia. They have a tradition and competence which we must take advantage of and develop.[115]

Immigrants were praised for both their initiative and their innovation, and support for potential and actual immigrant entrepreneurs was sought from the state.[116]

Countering the idea that immigrants might be a cultural threat, many on both the left and the right spoke of the value of multiculturalism. Mostly this discussion amounted to nonspecific statements that contact with other cultures had gone on for centuries[117] and was "enriching":

> We must convince the Swedish people that difference does not lead to division, but to change and development. Contact with other cultures is not always a "culture clash" (*kulturkrock*), but can be beneficial to all.[118]

Few noted what about contact with other cultures was enriching, and when they did, they most often pointed to superficial characteristics of culture, such as food or dress.[119] Nonetheless, multiculturalism was framed by many as not only good for the immigrant but good for the host society as well. Stefan Jonsson went so far as to write, in support of multiculturalism, that "the Western World has no legitimate right to defend and protect their own national, cultural or European identity."[120] The world, he argued, was moving toward a multicultural world, and Sweden ought to embrace that—not defend what was just one among many equal cultures.

Not everyone was quite so positive about multiculturalism as a mode of integration, however. As discussed in the chapter 3, the adoption of equality and freedom of choice as the fundamental goals for Sweden's immigrant/integration program meant that immigrants were to have the choice of how and to what extent to integrate into Swedish society. Yet, by the 1990s, it became increasingly clear that a passive statement that immigrants were to "choose" was no longer sufficient. In fact, that immigration was a threat to both Swedish culture and the Swedish welfare model was attributed by many to Sweden's failure to integrate immigrants. Given the welfare state's central role in integration, this failure was essentially a failure of state capacity. It was not that discrimination within private industry and civil society were absent or that they were considered unimportant as mechanisms for marginalization. Rather, most believed it was within the Swedish state's purview to prevent or to remedy discrimination and marginalization. Failure to integrate was indicated, among other things, by high levels of unemployment among immigrants, high levels of social-assistance usage and residential segregation, problems that were (and are) well documented.[121]

That Sweden was failing to integrate immigrants, and that it was the fault of the state (either through not doing enough or not doing the "right" things) was a view that was widely shared by proponents of both increased restrictions on migration and those who wanted to apply a more "generous" migration policy. Yet this discussion of "generous" versus "restrictive" refugee policy became a part of the discussion on why Sweden was failing to integrate migrants. One of the most commonly cited justifications for introducing stricter rules for asylum, bringing Sweden into line with the rest of Europe, was that Sweden had a "structurally limited integration potential" and that "a country can only take in so many immigrants without creating imbalances in the economic system, society and social relations."[122] Political scientist Jose Alberto Diaz linked this limit to the possibility of multiculturalism, saying:

> A country has a structurally limited integration potential. There are limits to how many people we can take in in a short time if they are to become equals (but still remain different) with the majority population.[123]

According to many, Sweden had exceeded that limit by accepting so many refugees so quickly. Ingrid Björkman pointed to both the cultural and economic effects of accepting too many immigrants, concluding that "to, under the mantle of morality, ignore the fact that the country's integration potential has been exceeded belies a grave irresponsibility."[124] This group, then, argued for a *restrictive* solution to the refugee crisis of the 1990s, and both cultural and welfare preservation was, at times, part of this argument. This argument, it should be noted, had considerably more proponents within the media (and, indeed, within public opinion) than within the political parties.

A related argument was that it was not so much the number of accepted migrants that mattered, but what "kinds" of migrants. They argued that Sweden's resources were strained by having to sort through so many asylum seekers without "real" reasons for asylum. Those in this camp often argued for reinstating a regulated, but relatively open system for labor migration in order to reduce the number of so-called "economic refugees" who cost the state in terms of administrative and material assistance:

> Our borders should always be open for those people who are forced to flee to save their own lives. But we should also create alternatives for people who lack cause for asylum. Those who don't have cause cost Sweden enormous sums in the form of investigations and living arrangements. In addition, their presence means that many of those who actually have real cause for asylum risk not being believed because so many people lie.[125]

They also wished to change the makeup of the migrant streams, arguing that this adjustment would ease the burden of integration because such migrants would be assured a job on arrival, eliminating one of the key factors in lack of integration.[126] Employment alone, however, was not the only benefit to this system. Employment served, as well, as a key to the "good" parts of the welfare state—sickness and unemployment insurance—and provided an alternative to consigning migrants to social assistance, which ought to have been temporary, but was becoming a "permanent support system for many."[127] Proponents of this perspective, such as the restrictionists, saw little wrong with the general mechanisms of the welfare state and labor market as tools for integration, but instead pointed to a poorly regulated system for immigration that kept out precisely those "types" of immigrants who were easiest to integrate. They argued, then, for a *selective* response to the crises of the 1990s, one that selected primarily along skill/educational lines.

Finally, there were those who argued that Sweden had a moral duty to continue to pursue a generous refugee policy. On the surface (as noted previously), this group included all elected officials, with the exception of New Democracy and small number of Conservatives. Yet even those who suggested continued migration at the same or higher levels largely agreed that Sweden was failing to integrate its immigrants, citing many of the factors listed earlier.[128] It was this camp that most strongly questioned the efficacy of simply offering access to the general welfare state to new (potential) members. Instead, this camp argued for recognition that Sweden's problem was in *integration*, not in *immigration*, and that the state had to pursue an integration policy that was suited in particular to the former, not the latter issue.

In other words, much like in the general welfare debate discussed previously, the belief in the miraculous welfare machine alone to "fix" the potential problems of migration faltered in the face of the 1990s crisis. SAP politician Bo Göransson put it this way:

> The welfare state has not helped immigrants.... Unemployment is higher than among Swedes. Many immigrant children have difficulty finding security and a foothold in society, with broken homes and identity problems and unemployed parents leading to isolation, rootlessness and criminality among the youth. Immigrants as a group have worse health, worse economics and shorter life expectancies than Swedes. They live in the physically and socially worst parts of town. They feel less and less like participants in Swedish society.[129]

A minority of critics, many of whom were not directly associated with a political party (though most had some ties to Conservatives or New Democracy), pointed toward a free-market solution to integration:

> In the building of [a diverse] society, it is not just tolerance, well-wishing and an open debate about culture clashes. We need concrete ideas about how the newly arrived groups' economic integration in society will work.... The new government needs to decisively abandon those measures which unnecessarily make clients out of immigrants and seek market solutions to immigrants' problems.[130]

They suggested that immigrants' access to the welfare state, including not just means-tested social assistance, but more universal programs such as child allowances and parental insurance, should be restricted, even for those who were given permanent resident permits. Suggested policies varied, but most suggested a temporary restriction aimed at preventing welfare dependency from developing in the early years of residence:

> Immigrants must be freed from a degrading begging journey through different institutions. . . . This means, concretely, that assistance-politics and such must stop. We must accept that immigrants under the first adjustment period should not have access to our welfare institutions and transfer systems. And this, primarily, is for their own good.[131]

The majority, however, argued for *more* state intervention, though intervention that was increasingly targeted at immigrants. Of course, targeted policies dated back to the 1960s, such as both state-funded Swedish and home-language education. Support for immigrants' cultural organizations had also long been provided by the state, and work-place "introductions" for immigrants had been carried out by LO. However, when it came to many of the key areas of life (work, health care, education, etc.), immigrants were simply given equal access to the same institutions as Swedes. By the mid-1990s, the ethos behind integration policy had shifted away from simple access (though access was not restricted) and toward active intervention. The measures that generally worked for native Swedes were seen as insufficient for immigrants:

> The mass unemployment among immigrants and refugees is unsustainable and unreasonable. Many of these thousands of people are young and well-educated. . . . Much of what is being done to combat unemployment generally is good. Unfortunately, you can't say the same thing when it comes to unemployment among immigrants and refugees.[132]

Those who supported targeted policies suggested such measures as increased support to immigrant and antiracism organizations, special measures and money for the education of immigrants, rationalization of and increased resources for the translation of foreign qualifications, and "positive special treatment" (*positiv särbehandling*) of immigrants on the labor market, ranging from incentives to hire workers with immigrant backgrounds to separate employment services for migrants:

> Many measures have been taken recently to improve the livelihoods of immigrants: language training, use of introductions and 'introduction stipends,'

employment measures and immigrant internships. This is, however, far from
sufficient. We need new, powerful measures directed at immigrants and a
faster implementation of already passed measures.[133]

Perhaps the most concrete result of this shift to a belief in targeted solutions, however, was the creation of a new "integration minister" alongside
the "immigration minister" in 1995 (first filled by Leif Blomberg in 1996).
Although this minister was "housed" first in the Department of the Inte-
rior, and later in several other departments (Culture, Justice, briefly in its
own "Integration Department," and finally in the Department of Labor), the
creation of a post solely devoted to integration indicated the special attention
this area was seen to entail. Like the major changes to pensions and the
major changes to immigration policy, this restructuring of the bureaucracy
responsible for integration was carried out not by the nonsocialist government, but by the reelected Social Democratic government. Social Democrat
Juan Fonseca, for instance, argued that an integration minister could "spend
all his or her time and energy on integration issues, that is to say, all that has
to do with the multicultural society and how immigrants are to be integrated."[134] This new orientation, already supported by the policy changes
noted previously, was additionally codified in the SAP-authored 1997 proposition "Sverige, framtiden och mångfalden: Från invandrarpolitik till integrationspolitik" (Sweden, the Future and Diversity: From Immigration to
Integration Politics), which sought to collect integration policies under a unified integration politics.[135] This unified politics did emphasize, on the one
hand, the goal of bringing immigrants into the general "societal community"
(samhällsgemenskap) and thus warned against any policies that would create
permanent "special measures" for immigrants.[136] On the other hand, the
document emphasized the need to recognize the particular issues that immigrants faced and, therefore, the need to create policies directed toward
them, at least for the "first years."[137] Much of the document was devoted to
these targeted policies.[138]

   The discourse on how and how much to integrate, too, became a discussion about whether or not freedom of choice (and hence, multiculturalism)
was even the right goal to be pursuing in integration policy. An increasingly
vocal group argued that it was not and, in fact, that "multiculturalism is a
utopia."[139] Critics of multiculturalism argued that pursuing multicultural-

ism would result only in creating a fragmented society, with immigrant groups isolated not only from native Swedes but from the labor market, social services, and, in general, the high standard of living that had become the norm in Swedish society. Conservative Gustaf von Essen, for instance, linked multiculturalism to "divisions," in saying,

> We should not divide the cultures and let them live separate lives [as multiculturalism promotes.] There should be interaction that will develop Swedishness, but we have norms, values, laws and rules that should be generally accepted and not questioned.[140]

This division would, in turn, lead to a number of social ills for all of society: increased poverty, crime, poor health, and so on.[141] Many argued, essentially, that one could not simultaneously pursue both equality and freedom of choice in the way that these had come to be understood and that, as one observer put it, equality "was the only goal worth taking seriously in the 1975 declaration of immigration policy."[142]

Others argued precisely the opposite: that without freedom of choice, equality was meaningless. Bo Göransson, for instance, wrote, echoing David Schwarz, that "the right to equality *includes* the right to equal treatment despite differences."[143] It is interesting to note that many of those who argued for freedom of choice in the case of immigrants were in the same ideological camp (indeed, sometimes the same people) who argued against freedom of choice in terms of welfare services. Göransson, who promoted multiculturalism and freedom of choice for immigrants, argued,

> In today's Sweden, market forces, which always work in a segregating direction, have gotten help from a politics that under the name of "freedom of choice" gives the middle class possibilities to make things better for themselves, to arrange their own lives.[144]

In many ways, this seeming internal contradiction was a manifestation of a growing skepticism about the People's Home model as a cultural model and a realization of some of the unrecognized tensions between "freedom of choice" and "equality" that had been present ever since the words came to characterize Swedish minority policy.

Conclusion: The Inflexible, Outmoded, and Persistent People's Home

In the face of these crises in the 1990s, the very idea of the People's Home came under fire. There was a rash of popular press publications that declared the concept of the *folkhem* dead with titles such as *Break-Up Times: An Exchange about the Split Folkhem*[145] and *System Change: Four Folkhem Debates*.[146] In *DN*, Mauricio Rojas described the crisis:

> In the true spirit of the *folkhem*, the state has taken responsibility for immigrants' integration in society. . . . But, oh! what great toil and spending of resources for such a disastrous result![147]

Critics wondered whether the concept of a People's Home was something that "belonged in the past" as an organizing concept for society, both as an economic and cultural model.[148]

As an economic model, many came to associate the People's Home concept (*folkhemstanken*) specifically with many of the negative aspects of the Swedish welfare model. The *folkhem* became a symbol for the old system: inflexible in an increasingly contingent labor market, unable to deal with the repercussions of an international crisis, unsuited to an economy that relied less and less on manufacturing, and unable, indeed, to deal with the economic difficulties experienced by immigrants. In many ways, the *goals* of the People's Home as an economic model (income equality, full employment, etc.) continued to be seen as valuable, but the means necessary to achieve these goals no longer seemed feasible.

Despite these economic associations, however, the *folkhem* was, and had always been, primarily a *cultural* model, one which prized community, solidarity, equality and cooperation above all. On the cultural front, consequently, the debate was even more intense. The bases of community had shattered or shifted or come under threat, depending on whom you asked, and the goals of equality and cooperation had come to be more elusive with the abandonment of full employment. Many came to see the People's Home as an oppressive cultural model that left little or no room for difference. "Difference" for these critics applied to a whole range of domains: lifestyle, family structure, religion, education, and working life. Critics also wondered whether there was any room for immigrants within this cultural model.

> It is perhaps true that, for all of its benefits, the *folkhem* is not the best system for immigrants in Sweden. Perhaps a system with greater flexibility, greater allowance for and respect for difference built-in, would most benefit these newcomers.[149]

From this perspective, it was not immigrants who threatened the *folkhem*, but the *folkhem* that threatened immigrant identities. Critics began to wonder if the *folkhem* was not, perhaps, fundamentally incompatible with a multicultural society.

Yet despite these critiques, the idea that Sweden was the good People's Home, that Sweden, fundamentally, was a society that had solidarity, community, cooperation, and equality at its core continued to have resonance. SAP and others, especially some Liberals, continued to search for ways in which diversity (of many types) and the *folkhem* were compatible:

> If the *folkhem* does not allow for freedom of choice or promote individual initiative, then perhaps we need to reconstruct the *folkhem*. It doesn't benefit anyone to simply discard a model that, for so many years, provided solidarity and security to the large majority of people.[150]

Lotta Gröning, editor of *Norrländska Social-Demokraten* (*NSD*), argued that although the *folkhem*-ideology was not only a valuable, but a necessary, part of the "labor movement's soul," it was in need of a "renewal" that

> entailed new ways of thinking about both methods and, especially, people, and primarily the individual. Social Democracy must do away with that part of the People's Home ideology that, though with a paternal hand, took away people's initiative and let the state and society do everything.[151]

Thus, there was a call for a model of Swedish society that allowed membership despite "difference," yet there were few ideas for how to actually achieve that ideal. The welfare state was no longer a miraculous machine that could solve all problems and integrate all people. Refugees and immigrants, as well, ill-served by the general policies of welfare and perceived as increasingly different, were being, discursively, pushed out of the nation as a membership body. These two things are deeply intertwined. The need to reform, in part or in whole, the welfare state seemed to go hand in hand with the need for new solutions to immigration. In both cases, inflexibility, lack of personalization, and a fear of creating passive rather than active citizens drove reform desires from both ends of the political spectrum, though how far either system needed to be reformed was an object of debate. What this debate represented, in many ways, was a dissolving of the previous hegemony of social-democratic values. The result was not that everyone, or even a majority, gave up on these values—merely that dissent was now possible. Yet welfare-state institutions remained largely intact during this period. In the case of immigration policy, too, the basic structure of policies remained the same, although restrictive decisions for particular groups were sometimes taken. What was missing, in fact, in both cases, was a cohesive set of alternative guiding values. In short, although the Social Democratic hegemony had broken down, there was no counterhegemony to replace it.

Interlude 2

Is There Room for Difference in Social Democracy?

Increased ethnic heterogeneity in the 1960s and 1970s, perhaps unexpectedly, did not initially have much effect on the societal solidarity supporting the welfare state. The miraculous welfare machine was already, to a large extent, built. It only had to be tweaked a bit to handle the new population. SAP and the other parties, operating under a set of hegemonic social-democratic values, acted in ways that were largely expansive toward migrants within their borders, even as immigration regulation increased. Immigrants were included with equality, security, and freedom of choice as the guiding values for this inclusion. The use of such an expansive strategy toward immigrants in this period represents a sharp break from the previous ethnically delimited definitions of the nation (and by extension, the welfare state). However, in many ways, the ability to pursue an expansive strategy is a result of the remarkable success of SAP in attaching a particular set of civic characteristics (i.e., social-democratic values) to the Swedish nation. The focus on social-democratic values, equality especially, provided a way to incorporate immigrants that was internally consistent for SAP.

The welfare state itself was to act as a mechanism for pulling immigrants into the Swedish national community, even as immigrants' rights to cultural autonomy were affirmed. Such rights to cultural autonomy did not include the right to go against the hegemonic (social-democratic) values of Swedish society, though. In other words, immigrants had to ascribe to the civic definition of nation that was ascendant by the late 1960s.

When economic crises became more acute, and the sources of migration shifted away from Europe, things changed. The breakdown of the social-democratic hegemony, hastened, in part, by the actions of SAP itself, went hand in hand with increasingly negative reactions to diversity. The miraculous welfare machine that had been able to manage new populations before began, suddenly, to look like a failure as an integration machine. That the welfare state had failed to integrate immigrants became an indictment of the system as a whole. Combined with the SAP's own moves toward the middle and an international economic crisis that sent Sweden's unemployment rate soaring near to 10 percent, the result was a victory for nonsocialist parties that, unlike their victory in 1976, truly signaled a departure from the Swedish model. The relationship between immigration and the welfare state in this period went both ways. On the one hand, the failure of the welfare state to integrate immigrants called into question the wisdom of accepting so many immigrants. On the other hand, the welfare state's inability to act as an integrating mechanism for immigrants caused many to question the efficacy of the system more generally.

Social-democratic values had lost much of the hegemonic quality they had in earlier eras. Nonetheless, those values and the institutional arrangements they supported persisted among a significant portion of the population. When SAP came back to power in 1994, it was with record support. In some ways, despite their moderation, SAP continued to promote the values they always had. It was in the name of those values that the pension system was overhauled. SAP's particular claims to social-democratic values, in fact, may have allowed them the leeway necessary to make such a radical reform. The important takeaway message from this analysis, however, is this: dissent had become possible. The social-democratic welfare state was no longer the self-evident best system for immigrants or for Sweden. The miraculous welfare machine's blueprints were open for corrections.

One particular and powerful reason for the persistence of social-democratic values is that there was no cohesive ideology that could take the place of the now-defunct social-democratic hegemony. The nonsocialist parties were in agreement that the system could not continue forever, but they did not present a unified front. They did very little to convince the Swedish electorate that the types of reforms they were making were going to help everyone. Rather, they argued that their reforms were apolitical "economics" that would keep Sweden's economy afloat in the international arena. Some, the Liberals in particular, made claims to a set of universal values (individual freedom, in particular), but it was never clear that this was an *alternative* to social democracy. Individual freedom, after all, had come to have its own place under the rubric of *valfrihet* among Social Democrats, too. In other words, by the 1990s, no counterhegemony had developed that could guide and support a true revolution in the Swedish system. Recent events in Swedish politics, however, indicate that this may no longer be the case.

Chapter 5

THE END OF SOCIAL-
DEMOCRATIC HEGEMONY

If the 1991 "earthquake election" opened the door for challenges to
the social-democratic hegemony, the 2006 parliamentary election sent the
right wing crashing right through that open door. Between SAP's re-
sumption of power in 1994 and their loss in 2006, the nonsocialist parties
had some difficulty presenting a united front. This was perhaps most dra-
matically illustrated in the election of 2002, when the Conservatives received only a paltry 15.2 percent of the vote. Much of the loss of votes had
been to the other parties of the right—the Liberals in particular regis-
tered 13.3 percent of the vote. This loss was an indication of a deep split in
the nonsocialist parties, as well as of dissatisfaction with the party that
had been, since the 1990s in particular, the leading light for the center-
right. The failure of the 1991–1994 government to do much of anything
lent credence to SAP's insistence that voters did not know what they were
getting with any potential "bourgeois" government. Because the nonsocialist parties were incapable of articulating a clear program for government
before elections, little hope was to be had for a postelection cooperation.

The parties of the center-right, however, were, as a whole, more popular than ever.

At the same time, back in power and dealing with the new realities of a Europeanized, globalized, and marketized Sweden, SAP was busy trying to adjust itself, in both policy (especially the pension overhaul discussed in chapter 4) and principle. The party congress of 2001 marked a watershed in the development of SAP. Although SAP had, as the first chapters of this book lay out, given up the idea of a socialist revolution long ago, it had retained in both principle and practice, the goal—crucial to social democracy as an ideology—that the state and party had a unique mission to "reshape society" and to subject economic production to democratic political control. In 2001, a new program was released that marked a drastic reversal from this point. Instead, in the new program, citizen control in the market was reduced to "influence," the stated aim to "reshape society" was removed.[1] Democracy was still asserted as a key principle, but it was the democracy of the market and of negative, not positive, liberty. SAP had laid its emphasis on "democracy" to the detriment of the "social." Not only was social democracy no longer hegemonic, but the party itself had lost much of its social-democratic color.

These two developments: a more popular, but poorly organized, right and a less social-democratic left, set the stage for an ill-defined, slow-rolling crisis of closure that has characterized the last seven years of Swedish politics. In some ways, the years from 2006 to 2014 described in this chapter present the polar opposite of the period described in chapter 3. The late 1960s and early 1970s represented a period of crisis conditions without, necessarily, much crisis itself. The 2006–2014 period, on the other hand, presents a period where crisis—both of closure-as-access to goods and closure-as-entry seems near constant, but the underlying economic and social conditions do not, on their face, seem likely to produce crisis. These crises are framed by a series of three hotly contested, difficult-to-predict elections and party political machinations in between. As such, this chapter is organized primarily around these three elections and chronicles two clear trends. The first of these is a newly stable and consistent support for the center-right which has had material consequences for the way goods are distributed in an increasingly marketized Swedish economy, pushing individual responsibility and freedom of choice over community and solidarity. The second of these is the rise of the anti-immigrant far right, manifested most clearly in the electoral successes of the Sweden Democrats. This success can be seen as an indicator that there is a crisis of closure-as-entry as questions of belonging have become increasingly acute. It is not only among the xenophobic right that the discourse of belonging has shifted. Increasingly, too, the left has been concerned primarily with an individualistic "antiracism" over structural concerns about integration, a concern that brings into sharp focus the idea that the welfare state is no longer the machine for integration, even for the left.

Election 2006

The Rise of the New Moderates and the Alliance for Sweden

In 2004 a new, united center-right coalition, Alliansen för Sverige, was formed.[2] Rather than attempt to build a nonsocialist government after elections, Alliansen was built *before* the 2006 election with the express purpose of forming a center-right government. The cohesion of Alliansen as both a pre- and postelection coalition has ushered in an era of a more strongly divided "block politics" that has persisted through the three elections discussed in this chapter. In fact, some commentators speculate that Sweden is beginning to look increasingly like a two-party system.[3] The Conservative party, led by the media-friendly, well-liked Frederik Reinfeldt, emerged as the heart and soul of this new coalition. In allying itself with the other nonsocialist parties, the Conservatives also underwent a transformation of their 'brand.' Like the shift to the middle that many left parties underwent in the 1980s—the example of "New Labour" in Britain is particularly apt and one the Conservatives drew themselves[4]—the Conservatives claimed a shift leftward, labeling themselves informally as the Nya Moderaterna (literally, the New Moderates).[5]

In 2006 Sweden's economy was doing fairly well, even on the metrics that the right prefers—gross domestic product (GDP) growth, for instance. Sweden's economy posted a remarkable 4.3 percent GDP growth, its highest since the 1970s. By all rights, the party that oversaw this growth, SAP, should have reaped its electoral benefits. Instead, the right parties hammered away at the incumbent party on the issue of "hidden" unemployment. Alliansen argued that the "true" unemployment rate was not the reasonable 6 percent that SAP claimed it was, but, after taking into account early employment and long-term disability, was actually closer to 25 percent.[6] This was a frightening number—and the unemployment numbers among the youth that Alliansen quoted were even more dramatic. Göran Persson and his SAP colleagues, meanwhile, were convinced that unemployment, which was relatively low and falling by SAP's reckoning, would not be an important election question; thus they adhered to their position, saying that the numbers indicate "that issue is solved."[7]

Alliansen, Reinfeldt, and his New Moderates managed, however, to control the discourse on unemployment. Replacing the party's classic focus on economic growth with a closer focus on work, specifically getting more Swedes into productive labor, was a major piece in the "softening" of the Conservative party. The Conservatives went so far as to argue that theirs was the "worker's party" for the twenty-first century, and the party branded itself in welfare-statist terms. The Conservatives' election campaign was entitled "More people in work—more to share," linking employment to the redistributive goals of the welfare state, a tactic adopted by Alliansen as a whole. This is a traditional social-democratic economic (and rhetorical) tactic, but Alliansen accused SAP of focusing so much on the transfers of the welfare state, that they had lost sight of the necessity for productive employment in order to have "shared welfare." Lars Leijonborg, Liberal party leader, for instance, argued that "while SAP gives notice that they will raise unemployment insurances, we say "a new jobs program so that more can work."[8] Alliansen positioned itself, in other words, rather successfully, as guarantors of a reformed welfare state, one built to withstand the new political and economic conditions of a globalized (and Europeanized) world.

Yet, on closer examination, Alliansen approached the problem of work differently from SAP and the traditional left. For Alliansen, there was little emphasis on creating "good" or "equal" jobs. Putting more people to work meant reducing absenteeism caused by what Alliansen, and the Conservatives in particular, labeled overly generous sick benefits and early retirement provisions that unfairly reward those with shorter working lives.[9] Anders Borg, then head economic adviser for the party and later finance minister, for instance, argued that "it is not reasonable that a civil servant who goes into early retirement at age 30 has a better pension than a blue-collar worker who has worked their whole lives" and further that "all politics that reduces unemployment, especially hidden unemployment, will decrease economic differences."[10] The proposal regarding early retirement was to put in place a more rigorous testing system to ensure that those who could work did. SAP argued in response that such attempts to push early retirees and long-term sickness insurance recipients back into work were merely an attempt to create new low-wage labor markets favorable to employers.[11]

Because these features of Alliansen's goals were hidden behind a desire to create "more to share," the coalition has managed to come across as less extreme and less of a threat to the social-democratic way of life than the previous right coalition of the 1990s.[12] Combining a rebranding with a newly cohesive coalition proved a recipe for electoral success. Alliansen won, combined, 48.24 percent of the vote. The Conservatives themselves were the primary beneficiaries of the center-right's unity, with 26.23 percent of the vote. Sweden had, once again, a center-right government. This government was put in place much less as a "protest" against the status quo, and much more as a result of the realignments in both the parties and in the electorate. The Conservatives, for instance, had little success in convincing industrial and low-wage workers that the party was "the new worker's party," but middle class voters increasingly moved to support that party. Support for Alliansen, but not the Conservatives, however, could be found increasingly among the working class. It became—and has remained—more difficult for SAP to claim to be the only working class party.[13]

Voting the previous conservative government in was a protest, but few were really ready to listen to an openly anti-welfare-statist coalition when it came to policymaking. As noted in chapter 4, the only real changes to the welfare state in the 1990s came after SAP had returned to power. Alliansen has had a much bigger impact, almost immediately starting the work of drastically changing the landscape of the Swedish social economy. For instance, in 2008 the coalition changed rules around sick-leave, limiting the number of days workers could receive sick pay for inability to perform one's "usual" duties, and allowing employers to eventually, after 180 days, terminate employees on sick leave if the Swedish Social Insurance Agency declares that they are able to perform work elsewhere on the labor market. Similar reforms have created increased incentives to work through the reactivation of early retirees,[14] reduced replacement rates in unemployment insurance, and imposed tough requirements to be considered "actively seeking a job."[15] All these changes were justified under the new government's "work-first principle" (*arbetslinjen*). *Svenska Dagbladet* wrote regarding stricter rules about unemployment for recently graduated students: "The fact that 74% of students take a year and a half before they get their first job sounds shocking. But why not call for reforms that produce more jobs, not more unemployment insurance?"[16]

In addition, several previously state-controlled sectors (pharmacies, some transportation functions) moved toward privatization, and others were slated to do the same (alcohol sales). These reforms were largely instituted in the name of, on the one hand, increasing consumer choice and freedom; for instance, in the case of breaking up the government pharmacy monopoly, so "that Swedes should be able to soothe a cold, headache and other small ailments even after 6 PM."[17] On the other hand, they were based on the belief that competition would improve the efficiencies of the market. New tax deductions, too, were introduced or expanded, including the highly controversial ROT and RUT that offer deductions for home renovations and home services (babysitters, maids, etc.), respectively.[18] These were justified at least partly with the new jobs they would produce. For instance, Pernilla Ström argued in favor of RUT: "Labor intensive services aimed at the household . . . had, in fact, an untapped employment potential. If full employment is the general norm—shouldn't one then make it easier for these jobs to be created?"[19] Objections to the new tax deductions, more strongly articulated in regard to household services than to renovations, centered around the buyers of services—largely, critics argued, the rich and near rich—rather than the new jobs created, although some pointed out that such jobs were poor-quality jobs.[20]

The reforms have had actual concrete results. Most clearly, Reinfeldt's work-first principle has been successful in reducing absenteeism—many would say to the point of forcing many who ought to have been long-term disabled back into work. The overall effect is that Sweden no longer occupies the top spot when it comes to the replacement rates of social insurances, nor when it comes to income inequality. Sweden is becoming a less equal place, unless, as Conservative prime minister Frederik Reinfeldt's press secretary, Sebastian Carlsson, suggested people do, we "ignore the top and bottom tenths."[21] Though the increases in inequality began under social-democratic governments, they have accelerated under Alliansen. In May 2013, the Organisation for Economic Co-operation and Development (OECD) listed Sweden, along with the other Nordic countries, as the country where income inequality has grown fastest in the last decade.[22] Further, while absenteeism was reduced, unemployment, largely, was not.

Yet these changes did not result in political suicide because the nonsocialist block of the 1990s—in concert with economic crises, the policy decisions of SAP itself, and globalization—had already done much of the difficult cultural demolition work. The main shock was the destruction of the social-democratic hegemony, which, as we have seen in the previous chapters, had already been largely accomplished. Alliansen has been able to fill some of that empty space with new potential counterhegemonies based on ideals of negative liberty, personal responsibility—created with "incentives" and "individual risk"—and an emphasis of the duties of citizenship over the social rights associated with them.[23] The focus of Swedish conservatives in the press on these particular values—not new, but retooled for the modern world—points to a more consistent and coherent conservatism than that of the protest parties of the 1990s. The softening of the image of the Conservative party in particular, had its effect, as did the concept of "economic pragmatism" that served as the rationale for many of the changes.[24] Anders Borg, Conservative finance minister, for instance, argued consistently in this period that "taxes should not be lowered for ideological reasons, but only to the extent that our welfare tolerates and because it will move more into jobs. State-owned businesses should not be privatized for ideological reasons either, but when the time is right and the utility is greatest for citizens."[25]

As much as these results were a result of a politically and ideologically cohesive right, they were also a result of crisis in Sweden's left, especially the traditional left made up of SAP and the Left Party. In part, this is a crisis of ideology. SAP has made several moves to the middle over the last twenty years. As ruling party, their decision to abandon full employment in the 1980s and their own benefit-level cuts in the 1990s (both discussed in chapter 4) belie a shift toward economic pragmatism that has led them to occupy an ideological position somewhat nearer the Conservatives than is, perhaps, comfortable to their traditional base. Further attempts at moderation have weakened their political message (and their electoral returns) in the 2000s.[26] Many have begun to see SAP as somewhat indistinct from Alliansen—as a party for, primarily the "upper class."[27] SAP's share of the working-class vote fell about 5 percent between 2002 and 2006, part of a general long-term downward trend. As a result, SAP comes off as a party that is not able to adapt its core (social-democratic) values and its commitments to core constituencies to new situations. To borrow T. H. Marshall's phraseology, SAP is finally feeling the "indigestion" of the contradictions inherent in social democracy in a global economy, and they show no signs of being able to find an effective antacid.[28]

On Diversity: The Discourse Begins to Loosen

The second slow-rolling crisis—that of closure-as-entry—makes less of an appearance in the 2006 election. Through 2006, most party-political platforms maintained a commitment to relatively open refugee policies and a general positivity toward the multicultural society. Alliansen did not make immigration or refugee issues a major part of their electoral campaigns. Many of the same themes as were present in the 1990s discourse continued in the 2000s. For instance, the idea that the welfare state—social assistance in particular—was smothering the potential of immigrants continued. This idea was, however, in line with Alliansen's focus on the importance of work, increasingly coupled with the idea that work was the key to integration: "Work for everyone," Malin Åkesson wrote in *DN*, continuing that "social assistance and all of these courses [about Swedish life/culture] only increases resentment. Too much benevolence becomes in the end a kind of oppression."[29] Yet even studies that focus on Sweden's relative success in getting immigrants into jobs comes under fire, much in line with the critique in previous periods.[30] In this area, the critique focuses on the difference between refugees, especially those who are constructed as especially different, such as Iraqis and Somalis, and other types of migrants, including large number of Nordic migrants, who are supposedly easier to integrate. Thus the Swedish Integration Agency is accused by the Liberals, in particular, of whitewashing by not considering separate groups.[31] Further accusations accuse the authors of this agency's reports of ignoring experiences of interpersonal racism in favor of other measures like employment. These accusations, likely, represent a correct view of the issue—whatever the discourse on diversity, immigrants' everyday experiences are still colored by racism and xenophobia in both covert and overt, including violent, forms.[32]

These accusations are part and parcel of the beginnings of the loosening up of discourses on diversity. Consider, for instance, that the idea that Sweden had to do more to take into account the "cultural dimension" of immigration and integration beyond simply liberal values of democracy and equality, was espoused by Andreas Carlgren, a Center Party official who took a break from politics to head up the Swedish Integration Agency from 2000 to 2006.[33] This position was considerably stronger than the previous ones that looked to structural solutions even for the "cultural" threats identified in the 1990s. The year 2006 marked the beginning of a move away from a structural discourse of "integration" and toward a more cultural and individualistic discourse of antiracism, law and order, and personal responsibility that I chronicle later in this chapter. Such elements were not particularly common in the 2006 election, however.

Although the center-right was working in a liberalizing direction when it came to immigration (but not necessary integration; see later discussion in this chapter), other forces were at work in the extraparliamentary right. In particular, the Sweden Democrats experienced a steady growth in popularity. The Sweden Democrats, a party with roots in the openly and unapologetically racist Bevara Sverige Svensk (Keep Sweden Swedish) movement, has only recently and only tenuously convinced Swedes that it is not a neo-Nazi organization.[34] The party has advocated stopping immigration from Muslim countries and forbidding the building of mosques on Swedish territory. Individual candidates went even further, including at least one elected municipal politician who expressed the opinion that Muslims who do not celebrate "Swedish holidays"—clarified later in the interview as "Christian holidays"—should not be allowed to receive Swedish citizenship.[35] Considering this extreme position, it is unsurprising that the party was long considered an unlikely candidate for success.[36]

Despite their extremism, the Sweden Democrats gained over 2 percent of the vote in the 2006 election, making it the largest extraparliamentary party. This election result was a surprise to many. Regarding the Sweden Democrats good election results in local and national elections, political scientists Anders Hellström, Tom Nilsson, and Pauline Stoltz, for instance, wrote that "the belief that Sweden is a land that is spared from xenophobia is not just a sign of peculiar smugness, but also positively misleading. The Sweden Democrat's success in local elections in Skåne and Blekinge shows that it's time to revise our self-image."[37] They continue by pointing out that it is disproportionate media attention on things such as street violence, the war on terror, and problems in schools that lay the ground for these victories, but that the party should be dealt with in a democratic way, not shut out and made "martyrs." This question of whether dealing with the Sweden Democrats as any one would with any other party or shutting them out of governance altogether was the better option for Sweden's politics and culture, in fact, became a recurring theme as the Sweden Democrats grew in power, particularly after the election of 2010.

Election 2010

Confirming the Counterhegemony

Alliansen's 2010 victory was just as decisive as their 2006 victory. Partially, that victory can be explained by the state of the economy. Alliansen saw Sweden through the worldwide economic crisis that rippled toward Europe from the 2007 U.S. mortgage collapse. By all accounts, Sweden has weathered the storm well. Although the country did not avoid recession, its recession was comparatively shallow and short. Unemployment has remained a problem, but not much more of a problem than it was before the recession. Whether Sweden's relative success has anything to do with Alliansen's welfare reforms is doubtful. It is equally—perhaps more—plausible that the underlying intact social-democratic institutions Alliansen inherited have provided a bulwark against the worst of the long-term unemployment and slow growth that the current crisis has brought. States whose recession lasted longest, or are still ongoing are either those that have adopted strong austerity measures or those with relatively low effective taxation levels.[38] Nonetheless, it is probably true that Sweden's relatively successful weathering of economic crisis had something to do with Alliansen's resounding electoral victory.

On the other hand, if Alliansen won in 2006 because its claim to be the savior of the welfare state was plausible, then its attempts at retrenchment should have cost the coalition the 2010 election. SAP and its party leader Mona Sahlin, in fact, hammered on the increased divisions in society that had arisen through Alliansen's tenure, connecting them to differing attitudes toward the welfare state. "The Conservatives," Sahlin argued, "want to make Sweden into a tax paradise. I want to make it into a welfare paradise."[39] One would expect that, had the social-democratic hegemony remained fully intact in 2010, this message would be highly successful; there would have been serious backlash to Alliansen's successful welfare-state cutbacks. Instead, surveys show that Swedes, on the whole, have shifted considerably toward conservatism in the past ten years, particularly during the years that Alliansen has been in office.[40] Many of the gospel truths of Swedish elections seem not to hold. It is, for instance, certainly no longer true that promising tax cuts is an ineffective electoral strategy in Swedish politics. It is also no longer true that SAP sets the tone and agenda for Swedish elections, whether in power or not.

SAP itself was at least partially to blame for this. The party was often maligned as complacent and inflexible, a line of critique best illustrated by the party's choice of leader following 2006's loss. Göran Persson, who oversaw SAP's rightward shift in the 1990s, left the party shortly after its 2006 defeat. Persson's clear successor was Mona Sahlin, a SAP stalwart who had held several ministerial posts throughout the 1990s. Sahlin, however, was not a popular leader, either as leader of the opposition or as the head of SAP's disastrous 2010 election. Sahlin was closely associated with both Persson himself and the moderate part of SAP more generally. She was seen by many as a status-quo candidate ill-equipped to transform the party into a truly twenty-first-century party. Jenny Wennberg, editor for the Social Democratic paper *Arbetarbladet*, writing in *NSD* called for Sahlin's resignation following the election: "It's time for a new Social Democracy. And it cannot be led by the old guard which has twice led SAP to electoral defeat. It's enough. Give the party over."[41] Polls showed that voters were even less keen on Sahlin than they were on SAP more generally.[42] She stepped down shortly after the election, at the time the only SAP party leader to never serve as prime minister.

SAP's crisis, coupled with Alliansen's success, has meant that the new logic of Swedish elections, set in 2010 and later confirmed in 2014, is essentially that of a two-block system.[43] The Red-Green block (SAP, Greens, and the Left Party) presented themselves as a left coalition in the same vein as Alliansen starting already in 2008. The Greens, who announced their full intention of being a party of government, seem to have received a boost from this realignment. The Greens represent a younger, fresher, less materialist, and more radically democratic party, while maintaining a politics that was more centrist than leftist in regard to a number of issues.[44] The Greens have seen their share of the vote rise from 4.6 percent in the last SAP-won parliamentary election in 2002 to 5.24 percent in 2006 and 7.36 percent in 2010.[45] On the one hand, this growth in Green Party votes means that the left as a whole is not in as bad a shape as the numbers for the Left Party and SAP alone might indicate. Assuming that most Green voters were drawn from the traditional left, the loss of votes between 2006 and 2010 is a much less striking 2.48 percent. The Red-Green alliance effectively broke down in October 2010, but was reformed for the 2014 elections.

The idea of a semipermanent Red-Green coalition is not as straightforward as it might seem. Despite the oft-used comparison of the Green Party to a watermelon (green on the outside, red on the inside), the Greens and SAP are not two versions of the same party. For one, the Greens have a considerably more open position toward potential labor migrants—a characteristic that makes them more like the center-right than SAP. In fact, the Greens cooperated with Alliansen on migration policy and have been occasionally open to a more formal cooperation in government. This cooperation was partly a way of blocking the participation of the far-right Sweden Democrats, but also a decision consistent with their political preferences.[46] The Greens are consistently and centrally interested in nonmaterialist issues like the environment, as their party name indicates. This orientation means when it comes to welfare that, at least from an ideological standpoint, the Greens are more interested in quality of life than in economic growth per se. Since the Greens have never formed a government, it is difficult to say how this commitment might translate into actual policy, but the difference in emphasis from SAP is worth noting. The Greens are, as well, more interested in radical, grassroots democracy—and in economic democracy that puts small and cooperatively owned enterprises in the center. To a certain extent, this outlook fits well with SAP's increasing focus on the *democratic* over the *social* in social democracy, but it betrays an even more fundamental break with the corporatist, embedded-markets model of old social democracy.

Such block politics, however, did not solve SAP's problems of renewal, and the 2010 election, too, was lost, provoking a new series of leadership scandals. With no obvious successor to Sahlin, the process of picking a new leader revealed deep internal conflicts over the direction SAP ought to take—back to a more radical twentieth-century Social Democracy continuing along the moderate path or transformation into a new Social Democracy. In the end, Håkan Juholt was chosen. Juholt was the son of a union printer and a left-wing social democrat with extensive experience in the Social Democratic Youth Organization and local government. Juholt's selection signaled to some that SAP was, perhaps necessarily, going "back to its roots." Tommy Möller, for instance, wrote,

> Around the world for quite a while now, a shift of values has taken place. Material welfare has grown, and people have become more individualistic. How should the Social Democrats' fundamental ideology be translated in this society? That's the party's critical question these days. That the party would choose a leader [like Juholt] who makes clear gestures to the left is logical. Polling shows that an overwhelming majority of parliamentary candidates want a traditional social-democratic politics.[47]

But the choice of Juholt was controversial precisely because of his reputation as a traditional, pre-1990s Social Democrat. Although he represented a clear departure from Persson and Sahlin, many doubted his ability to lead the Social Democrats toward "renewal." In fact, his tenure as party leader was short-lived, and he never really had the confidence of the party as a whole.[48] Embroiled in a scandal over housing allowances, company cars, and eventually incompetence in foreign affairs, Juholt resigned after less than a year as party leader.

Juholt was replaced by the almost completely unknown Stefan Löfven, a former president of the metalworkers union, IF-Metall, and current SAP executive board member. Löfven's main qualification seems to have been that no one could really object to him. Many speculated that he was selected in order to solve the internal problems of SAP and to bring the party back together around shared social-democratic goals, rather than to focus on electoral success. Political scientist Jonas Hinnfors, for instance, wrote,

> Party political research shows that poor handling of crises and inability to create consensus around political direction are important factors as to why party leaders are forced to step down. Seen from this perspective, SAP is in desperate need of peace and quiet. In the short run, therefore, Löfven is an excellent choice. As a union leader, he is well-suited to negotiation and compromises; that is to say, the central parts of the Swedish model. In many areas where the party is in crisis he has been measured and tentative. His focus has been on pragmatic issues rather than big ideological gambits.[49]

His reputation, in other words, was quietly, pragmatically welfare statist and social democratic. Löfven's leadership in the months following his selection were anything but radical, focusing mostly on job creation and improving "industrial relations." However, he did manage to lead the Social Democrats to a successful election in 2014—if a somewhat ambiguous one, as discussed in the following section.

The Sweden Democrats' Breakthrough and a Shift in the Integration Discourse

The 2006–2010 period contained a clear notice from the Conservatives that they did not see immigration merely as a threat. In 2008, Alliansen, with the Conservatives in the lead, reformed labor migration in an increasingly open way. Most important in this reform was that the "need" for the importation of workers was considered best judged by individual employers, not by the state's employment agency, and that work and residence permits for labor migrants were extended to four years and could lead to a permanent residence permit.[50] It also became easier for refugees who had been denied asylum to receive work permits. Like other parts of Alliansen's politics, work was connected to welfare and, in particular, the greying of the population. Conservative politician Mikael Cederbratt asked in the context of the reform, "We can look at Sweden and see how it will be for us in terms of securing our welfare. How will it be in the future when our population ages and we'll have fewer people who actually work?"[51] The Greens, but neither the Left nor SAP, supported the reform. Regarding the opposition, Center MP Frederick Federley accused the two parties of speaking out of both sides of their mouths, echoing much of the rhetoric on immigration during the 1960s and 1970s:

> The two red parties in the opposition talk about openness and solidarity and welcoming during their speeches and during the first of May. But when it comes to actual politics, to really opening Sweden, they're critical. It's possible that they, in their rhetoric, are insisting that they're still positive to labor migration and making it easier for more people to come to Sweden, but when it comes to debates in the chambers of parliament and to decisions, they're not at all positive.[52]

We see in this debate a strong difference between the Greens and the other parties in opposition: SAP and Left both maintained a somewhat restrictivist position, whereas the Greens sided with the nonsocialist parties. It is telling, however, that this debate was primarily over *entry* (immigration) and not *access to goods* (integration).

If social-democratic hegemony—both as a culture and as a set of policy preferences—provided a framework for understanding the place of immigrants and minorities, then the demolition of that hegemony should create new dilemmas for closure, particularly in the sense of access to goods, material and symbolic, in the Swedish nation. There is certainly evidence from the period leading up to and immediately following the 2010 election that something fundamental has changed in Swedish ethnic relations. This is clear less in the violent demonstrations that have popped up intermittently in immigrant neighborhoods in Stockholm and Malmö, unsettling though these may have been, and more in the sustained, introspective discussion of race, racism, and belonging that has permeated the Swedish press of late. The high-profile exchange between Justice Minister Beatrice Ask and author and playwright Jonas Hassein Khemiri provides a particularly telling example.

In March 2013, an open letter to Minister Ask went viral in a big way. Within a day, it had become the most shared article from *Dagens Nyheter* ever, shared by over 600,000 people.[53] The letter was about racial profiling within REVA, a cooperative program of the Swedish police, the Migration Board, and the prison system that aims to find and repatriate undocumented migrants. Racial profiling is a relatively new topic in Sweden, compared to the United States, and REVA has been highly controversial. Minister Ask, when questioned about the experience that dark-skinned or dark-haired Swedes had of being constantly targeted by police and migration officials to prove their citizenship, stated that this was just a "personal experience" and a matter of paranoia.[54]

In his response, Khemiri, a Swedish-born citizen with a Swedish mother and Tunisian father invites Ask to live in his skin for a bit. He asks her to experience the Swedish *folkhem* as a person who is only ever questionably a member of the *folk*. Relating a story of when he was young and thrown in the back of a police vehicle without explanation, Khemiri writes: "It is impossible to be a part of the community when Power always assumes you are an Other."[55] In so doing Khemiri connected the personal, bodily experience of Swedes who don't look Swedish with those who do. Given the discourse on diversity in Sweden, this is a radical thing to do. The letter shoves differential experiences into the forefront and invites Beatrice Ask—and, therefore, white, ethnic Swedes—to consider how, despite the universality of the welfare state, they are not, in fact, universal subjects. In a way, it is an article that questions the very basis of the social-democratic *folkhem*. At the same time, it questions the conservatism that replaces it as well.

Alliansen has been, in general, more willing to openly espouse policies like the one Beatrice Ask was defending, despite openness to allowing immigrants to enter the country *to work*. These are policies that go beyond just seeking "special solutions" for unintegrated immigrants and that target immigrants and refugees as always-suspect foreigners. Alliansen's Minister of Integration from 2006 to 2010, Nyamko Sabuni (Liberal), for instance, openly advocated assimilatory policies, such as a hijab ban for girls under fifteen. Sabuni went so far as to suggest subjecting Muslim girls to gynecological exams to prevent female genital cutting.[56] If we are to follow the logic of the preceding chapters, we can link the shift in discourse on immigration and integration to the processes of erosion and outright retrenchment of the welfare state and social-democratic hegemony noted earlier. The *folkhem* idea provided a workable, cohesive framework to immigrant integration. As the *folkhem* idea lost its hegemonic character, the questions of the role of the state in integration, the proper goals for integration, and what to expect from immigrants themselves became more open. There was more space for new ideas about diversity. More attention was suddenly given to fears about permanent exclusion of immigrants, potential violence both from and toward immigrants, and the sustainability, in particular, of high levels of Muslim immigration. Public opinion has reflected this attention. Although most Swedes remain comfortably in the moderate middle, there has been polarization at the edges of opinions. The extremists on either side seem to be getting more extreme.[57]

Partially, this polarization has resulted in a move toward xenophobia, suspicion, and fear. The Sweden Democrats' success in 2010 is part and parcel of this shift. The party flew over the 4 percent bar for entry into parliament with 5.7 percent of the vote, placing it just above the Christian Democrats and the Left Party in popularity. The policy influence of the Sweden Democrats between the election of 2010 and 2014 was marginal. Although cooperating with the Sweden Democrats would have given Alliansen an absolute majority in parliament, the coalition refused to do so. However, the parliamentary stage brought new legitimacy and attention to the party and its ideas. Given the party's questionable ties to violent nationalists, one consequence of this new attention has been frequent high-profile scandals involving its members, such as when a video surfaced showing high-ranking party members threatening Kurdish-Swedish comic Soran Ismail with iron pipes.[58]

The Sweden Democrats' 2010 election has also, however, contributed to the broadening of the debate on diversity in Sweden. On the one hand, it made the positions Alliansen takes seem more moderate and, therefore, more legitimate. The REVA legislation Ask was supporting pales in comparison to calls to deport immigrants simply because they are Muslim. The addition of extremist views has widened the space for legitimate debate in a restrictionist direction. However, it has also widened the debate in other, superficially paradoxical ways. Sweden's report card on integration, as reported by the EU Migrant Integration Policy Index, has been consistently good over the last decade.[59] Headlines declaring that Sweden is "Best in Integration" in Europe have recurred. These indices, however, largely look only at whether or not certain "best practices" policies are in place, without actually measuring outcomes. In fact, Sweden has relatively high and enduring levels of residential and occupational segregation.[60] Swedish immigrants report discrimination and other forms of interpersonal racism at rates that seem surprising given these "top marks."

This contradiction is perhaps explained, in part, by the long history of welfare statism in Sweden: the focus in Sweden has been on addressing "structural" problems, focusing on economic integration, and remedying institutions. Relatively little attention has been given to interpersonal racism until fairly recently. Now the focus seems to have changed—the attention of the state has certainly shifted toward a more individualistic understanding of race and racism (and its intersection with class).[61] Public discourse has followed suit. The Ask-Khemiri exchange is one example. Another is a set of back-and-forth op-eds in *Svenska Dagbladet* that directly problematizes the issue of immigrant individuals with personal agency within racist structures; as one writer puts it, that "racist structures exist—but they are not insurmountable,"[62] arguing that to understand the latter, we also have to focus on the former.[63] Essentially, the debate has moved even further away from the idea of the welfare state as an integration machine. In fact, the debate has moved away even from the idea of immigrants as needing "targeted solutions" and toward the idea that fixing "immigrant problems" means fixing individual immigrant's "problems." This new view includes increasing accountability and personal responsibility for those on the right and fixing interpersonal racism for those on the left.

It is notable, too, that the Sweden Democrats are not a neoliberal party, but a welfare-chauvinist party seeking to protect Sweden's welfare state against an "invasion" of potential (perhaps imagined) benefit parasites and wage depressants. Their election slogan, for instance, is "Security and Tradition" (*Trygghet och tradition*). In this context, it is worth pointing out that this makes the party seem less like the Conservatives of today, who are remarkably open to labor migration, in particular, and to a lesser extent to refugee migration. The Conservatives, starting in 2010, after all, worked together with the Sweden Democrat's arch-enemy, the Greens, on migration policy. Rather, the Sweden Democrats are actually much more like the Social Democrats of the pre–World War II era and, perhaps, even closer to the long-standing positions of the Social Democrats and the Left than any other party on certain of their positions. This likeness, of course, does not hold true when it comes to *closure-as-access to goods*, and only when it comes to *closure-as-entry*. This realignment of parties over migration and integration issues says a great deal about how social democracy has evolved and, even more fundamentally, how ideas of the meaning of Swedishness have evolved.

Election 2014: The Return of SAP, but Not of Politics as Usual

The year 2014 and early 2015 provided yet another shock to Sweden's political system. The election was characterized, if anything, by an increasing feeling of "block politics"—with SAP in coalition with the Greens in one block and Alliansen in the other. The Sweden Democrats, given an extra measure of visibility and influence, played a greater role than ever in the 2014 election campaign, but because the other parties continued to disavow them, they did little to realign the blocks. The most important issue of the election, according to voters, was that of education, where the differences between the parties were actually quite slim, with the major exception that Alliansen was generally in favor of more choice and private influence in the schools.[64] The Red-Green coalition has remained steadfastly welfare statist, and the bulk of the noneducation-related election rhetoric focused on traditional welfare-state issues. However, it was, in a way, a kind of quiet and pragmatic

welfarism that inhered in opposing privatization of "welfare institutions"
such as health care and schools, focusing on active labor-market policies to
produce jobs, and seeking to swing unemployment insurance and sickness
insurance back toward generosity.[65] SAP, however, continued to lack "big
ideas" to reform the welfare state, and their campaign was largely one against
Alliansen's politics rather than one for any particularly ambitious program.

Regarding immigration and integration, the left has evolved to an extent
on issues surrounding closure as access-to-goods, though not on issues of
closure-as-entry. In part, it seems that much of the left is increasingly concerned with antiracism rather than integration. The two, of course, are related,
but they are not the same. The Swedish left seems to be much more concerned
these days with, on the one hand, countering the forces on the extreme
right. Much energy is taken up in fighting against the Sweden Democrats.
On the other hand, the left itself has also moved toward a more individualistic understanding of discrimination, "social exclusion," and, indeed, integration.[66] Within the immigration debate as within the welfare debate, the
shift away from institutional, whole-society solutions, and the increased
focus on individual experiences of immigrants means, essentially, that Sweden is becoming less exceptional.

Alliansen chose to continue as a united front in the election campaign,
and their electoral strategy was largely to continue to point to their successes
in getting Sweden through economic crisis. They argued, against the claims
of SAP, that their jobs programs, in particular, were working. Conservative
journalist Per Gudmundson, for instance, wrote that "under Alliansen,
more than a quarter of a million jobs have been created in Sweden, despite
the global crisis," and that the increase in unemployment *rates* is merely
demographic—that immigration had increased the working-age population, and that those who had been falsely retired early were now seeking
work.[67] Further, Alliansen's election campaign showed that they continued
to stand for privatizations (especially in the schools) and continued "activation"
policies for those who were on sick leave or retired early. Alliansen toned
down their call for tax breaks from earlier elections, declaring that enough
had been done on those fronts already. They promised only that "no new
taxes would be placed on work or entrepreneurship."[68]

Perhaps more importantly, however, we find during this period the strongest expression of an open—even expanded—refugee policy from the Conservative party, even if that meant that some reforms could not be carried

out. Frederik Reinfeldt, in a heartfelt speech at the beginning of the election campaign, asked that

> the Swedish people . . . have patience and open up their hearts for the vulnerable people we see around the world. When many people flee in such a short time, it creates tensions in the Swedish society. But we have learned that the people who come here build Sweden together with us.[69]

Reinfeldt's "open-hearts" comment became one of the most-quoted statements of the election cycle. Reinfeldt's increased attention to refugee issues was attributed by friends to an "inner journey" that pushed him to greater engagement against racism and intolerance.[70]

His position, however, likely sent some voters to the Sweden Democrats, who reacted with statements against this position. Though the Sweden Democrats continued to maintain that they were not racist, but that the policies Reinfeldt was suggesting show that "welfare has to take a step back. And I don't believe that's the right priority," as Sweden Democrats' party leader Jimmie Åkesson put it.[71] The Sweden Democrats continued to profile themselves as welfare chauvinists and as "protecting Swedish values," but also, increasingly, as political martyrs. The established parties' refusal to cooperate with the Sweden Democrats, despite their place in parliament, had a prominent place in the Sweden Democrats' election rhetoric, as did the supposed "unfairness" of the media which painted them as extremists and racists.[72] Whether or not the party members actually are extremists, as they seem to be, the latter characterization of the media coverage is true. Articles attacked Sweden Democrats for racism, even at times calling for the banning of the Sweden Democrats as a hate organization.[73]

The outcome of block politics in the election was inconclusive—the vote share between the two blocks was close to evenly split. The SAP-Green coalition saw almost no change in their election results, either in terms of total vote counts or in the way they were divided up between the parties. The coalition won 39 percent of the seats in parliament. The Left Party, not part of the preelection coalition, joined together with SAP-Green on a budget package, bringing the Red-Green block to 45 percent of seats. Alliansen, on the other hand, suffered a decline of about 10 points, winning only 39.5 percent of the vote (41% of the seats in parliament). It was Alliansen, now, who faced a crisis—one primarily concerning the wisdom of continuing the alliance itself—especially in regards to the Christian Democrats' future participation, although the resignation of popular leader Frederik Reinfeldt may also be a sign of this new, as-of-yet unresolved, crisis.[74] Alliansen's loss is, more importantly, directly related to the success of the Sweden Democrats, who captured a remarkable 13 percent of the vote, making it the third-largest party in parliament. Rapid election studies show that the Sweden Democrats gained votes from all parties, but drew by far the most from the Conservatives.[75] Both blocks continued their policy of noncooperation with the Sweden Democrats, which meant that Löfven, as party leader, was able to form a minority government.

Minority governments have been the rule rather than the exception in Swedish politics, and both rules and unwritten conventions have allowed them to govern effectively, for the most part. However, a combination of factors made this particular minority government fragile. It is relatively small by historical standards, for one. More importantly, Alliansen promised to submit to parliament its own budget in competition with the government's budget. Most expected that the Red-Green budget would still be passed—they have more votes than Alliansen, and the Sweden Democrats, by convention, should have abstained from the voting. The Sweden Democrats, however, refused to support the budget, even passively. To block the Red-Green budget, they declared their intention to vote for Alliansen's budget. It was the first time in modern Sweden that a government's budget had been entirely voted down. The Sweden Democrats had thrown Swedish politics into chaos.

Löfven declared that he would not govern under Alliansen's budget, and his last-minute efforts to court active support from the smaller of Alliansen's parties (the Liberals, especially) were unsuccessful. Löfven surprised most commentators by announcing that he would call a new election as soon as he was legally allowed, on December 29. Only three times before in Sweden's history had a new election been called, two of them predating universal suffrage. Löfven promised that SAP would campaign with the Red-Green budget proposal as the party's election manifesto, although without the Greens themselves, who planned to campaign on their own. Löfven highlighted, especially, the redistributive aspects of it: reduced taxation for pensioners, a higher ceiling on unemployment insurance, and increased tax for those in the highest income classes.[76] Yet, the budget offered very little in the way of new, big reforms. Instead, the initial election campaign fit Löfven's profile—cautious and quietly welfare statist rather than revolutionary:

> Of course neither the manifesto nor the budget lacks priorities and efforts, but, for example, strengthening unemployment and sickness pay are more like attempts to reset fifty-year-old reforms than any new type of effort. Nowhere in either the manifesto or budget that has just been defeated in the parliament, is there any reform with economic priority of that kind that made SAP the dominating party in Swedish political life for fifty years.[77]

As in the 2014 election, it became clear that, although SAP's internal crisis had, perhaps, abated, their party had not undergone the kind of renewal that would be necessary for success in the future.

Notably, SAP did very little to address the issue that had sparked the crisis. The Sweden Democrats made it clear from the beginning that their actions were motivated by migration politics and very little else. The Sweden Democrats promised to "bring down any government which would give the Greens decisive influence on migration policy."[78] The choice the Sweden Democrats presented was either to allow the party to act as a pivot party, giving them a role comparable to their support in the election, which they would use to slow immigration, or, alternatively, to fail in governing. Mattias Karlsson, temporary party leader of the Sweden Democrats, declared that "the only demand we made before the budget vote was that Sweden's extreme immigration policy should not be allowed to become still more extreme, and that the other parties should talk with parliament's third-largest party," adding that the party "planned to make the new election in March a referendum for or against increased immigration."[79] Their minimum demand was that refugee and family reunification migration would not increase further, and they believed the upcoming election would show that they could go even further in their demands. The Sweden Democrats used the crisis to air their views that immigrants were a drain on resources and a cultural threat, but also to lament their exclusion from formal channels of politics.

In the end, however, an agreement was reached between all parties except the Left and the Sweden Democrats, which prevented the new election from ever being called. The so-called December Agreement aimed to make governing from a minority position easier by allowing the block with a plurality—not a majority—to insist on their own budget as a whole, though they would be required to make concessions on individual points. This procedure is not a change in hard-and-fast rules, but rather a change in conventions. The agreement was praised for preventing the new election, but was criticized as "undemocratic" by a handful of high-level politicians from most of the parties. As expected, the Sweden Democrats were sharply critical and called out the established parties for continuing to make martyrs of them.

As of May 2015, there is some evidence that Alliansen's voters—especially Conservative and Center voters—are beginning to see cooperation with Sweden Democrats as a better alternative than allowing a small Red-Green plurality to govern under the new December Agreement. In fact, a plurality, 46 percent, of all Alliansen voters desire just such a thing, at least on those issues where the parties are generally in agreement, that is, not on refugee issues.[80] Whether the Sweden Democrats would accept a collaboration without concessions to their position on migration, given their statements during the budget struggles, however, is doubtful. It is worth noting that this pattern of opinion looks quite similar to the pattern of opinion that brought right-wing extremist parties into the heart of government in Norway and Denmark, and it is not unreasonable to believe that the same may happen in Sweden eventually.

Conclusions: Modern Sweden in International Context

After eight years of crisis and nonsocialist governance, where does social democracy stand—and what does that standing mean for "belonging" in the Swedish nation? The first thing that needs to be emphasized is that, whatever Sweden is, it is neither a neoliberal paradise nor (any longer) a social-democratic one. If anything sweeping can be said about Sweden in the twenty-first century, it is that the multiple pressures of globalization, internal and external crises, and changing demographics have made Sweden less exceptional than it once was. Much of the institutional framework of the welfare state remains in place, even as it is eroded by cuts to benefits, waiting days, and new restrictions and requirements. But these erosions have made the Swedish welfare state look more and more like the European countries that lay to the south.

Sweden, for instance, is more like Europe in that its process of government building and the outcomes of elections are considerably less predictable than they once were. SAP's period of long-term dominance is well and truly ended, and no party can reliably count on passive support, making minority governance more difficult in the future. This brings Sweden into line with most of the rest of Europe,[81] which seems likely to make large reforms like the 1990s pension reform, more difficult. Swedish social democracy, too, has undergone the same shift rightward and the same loss of purpose that many other European social-democratic parties have experienced.[82] Alliansen's election and, more important, reelection, has also shown that Sweden's right is no longer exceptional. Although they outwardly espouse welfare-statist positions, their policies have shown them to look much like a slightly less extreme version of the parties of austerity that have done well in most of continental Europe since the crisis. Unlike those parties, however, they did not suffer major backlashes in the most recent election. The debate on immigration, likewise, is starting to look more like the debate elsewhere. The extreme anti-immigrant message of the Sweden Democrats finds its counterpart in parties not just in the Norwegian Progress Party or Danish People's Party, but also further south in the Vlaams Belang in Belgium, the Front National in France, and the Golden Dawn in Greece, who share the Sweden Democrats' neo-Nazi roots. Alliansen's strong positivity toward immigration and refugee migration, even in times of economic recession, however, does remain exceptional. Likewise, Sweden has held on to its beliefs—and its policies—regarding gender equality, perhaps a sign of some lingering exceptionality.

Regardless of all the ways in which Sweden has become less exceptional, much of the welfare-statist culture remains. Swedes still value equality, and certain ideas that lay behind the Swedish left's drive for equality still hold strong. In general, it seems that some of the meanings ascribed to "equality," "security," and "freedom" have changed drastically from the radical social-democratic conceptions descended from SAP's 1960s and 1970s equality reports. The belief that equality is an "engine for growth" no longer unites the traditional economic concerns of the nonsocialist parties with the social concerns of the traditional left. Instead, equality has come to be much more an object of political debate, and "equality of opportunity" rather than "equality of outcome" more often the focus. Gender equality and racial/ethnic equality have become much more about removing barriers rather than taking purposive action to ensure equality, as the social-democratic welfare state attempted to do. All of this speaks to the view that the counter-hegemony that has arisen in counterbalance to the social-democratic hegemony is most accurately a reassertion of *individualism* as the central value for Swedish culture and politics. It is a philosophy that has a certain kinship with neoliberalism, but it is not the straightforward neoliberalism of, say, the United Kingdom or the United States.

In line with this new emphasis on individualism, "belonging" has become much more tenuous a proposition. Cultural assimilation has become a much more legitimate position to take, but many Swedes, outside of the far right, have a hard time articulating what that "culture" is. There is less of a core of social-democratic ideals to integrate into than there once was. To complicate the matter, many Swedes continue, perhaps as a legacy of the radical egalitarianism of the 1960s and 1970s, to see themselves as "beyond nationalism" (and all the better for it).[83] If there is no Swedish nation to speak of, how are immigrants supposed to come to belong? On this point, too, Sweden is no longer exceptional, as Carl Schierup and Alexandra Ålund have so eloquently and forcefully argued.[84] Instead, the same debates about multiculturalism, assimilation, integration, and racism that are being played out elsewhere are being played out in Sweden as well. The "miraculous welfare machine" is no longer so miraculous—and integration no longer assumed to be automatic or relatively unproblematic.

The welfare machine itself works on, but it is showing all the signs of aging. Some of its parts have worn out and have had to be jury-rigged. Others have been replaced—perhaps unnecessarily. Its blueprints have been altered in places, such that the relatively straightforward goal of transforming human capital into human *welfare* in its most abstract sense—the goal that used to be the unquestioned purpose of the Swedish state—has been replaced by a machine that is increasingly designed to turn human capital into economic capital (measured, crudely, by GDP). The results of these modifications and "repairs" are becoming evident. For those who would like to see a shift to individual responsibility, as opposed to collective responsibility, and those who see competition and private initiative as the basis for sound economics, things may be looking up. Yet, for those who lionized the Swedish welfare state as a paradigm of equality, tolerance, and, indeed, sound economics, the results may be disheartening.

Conclusions

Who Belongs in the Swedish People's Home?

From the launch of the social-democratic *folkhem* ideology in 1928 through the premature declaration of its death in 1991, and its final demise in the 2010 elections, the concept as an economic and cultural model represented a focal point for the Swedish nation. The ideas behind the Swedish *folkhem*—security, equality, and solidarity—provided a persistent blueprint for the miraculous welfare machine, even as the complex of policies that provided the machinery for realizing that design shifted and grew. In the end, the image of the community itself—who was to benefit from the welfare machine—shifted as well: from a newly integrated union of classes, united in common ethnicity in 1932 to a community of "brothers" where the key ethnic qualifier was more precisely "Nordic" than "Swedish" and where inclusion began to be entangled with a nascent welfare state in the late 1940s, to a suddenly diverse nation where ethnicity was pushed into the background, but assimilation to a set of social-democratic values became key, to, finally, a community in flux where ethnicity was once again visible, but taboo laden, and where the welfare state was under both conceptual and institutional threat. The blueprint, of course, still exists, and many parts of the miraculous welfare machine rattle on, but repairs to the machine no longer follow the old blueprint religiously, and even the purpose of machine is no longer quite as clear-cut as it once was.

The social-democratic hegemony that provided that blueprint for the welfare state has also provided the terms for closure. Most straightforwardly, the hegemony affects closure-as-access to goods, as social democracy is fundamentally about issues of how goods are to be created and distributed in a society to produce security, equality, and freedom, precisely the goods to which members of the state ought to have access. But it has also, at times, set the terms for closure-as-entry, as a broad-based social-democratic equality sometimes pushed in favor of more open borders, but also as more narrowly construed ideas of solidarity may have pushed against them. Both forms of closure were, of course, closely related, though they did not always vary together in predictable ways.

Who belongs in the Swedish "people's home" was subject to change even as the People's Home model persisted for much of the twentieth century. This took the character of expansion at times: in 1928–1932, SAP sought to include the working class in an integrated whole, expanding the definition of the nation, perhaps paradoxically, through the use of a definition of nation with strong ethnic elements. In 1945–1950, SAP sought to redefine the nation in a way that squared with its own policies and values and in so doing sought a universalist national definition that equated Swedishness with social democracy. SAP strengthened the civic part of the definition of "Swedishness," invoking a decidedly social-democratic civic identity. In the 1960s and 1970s, it became clear that immigrants, at least theoretically, could be considered full members without the loss of their "cultural particularity," so long as they ascribed to the basic values of democracy and the welfare state. By this time, in other words, shared civic values came to eclipse ethnic belonging almost entirely as a defining feature of Swedishness, if perhaps, only momentarily. Immigrants were treated with a similar logic as that applied to the inclusion of underrepresented groups (especially women), who were to be brought into the welfare state by way of the labor market and therefore embraced by the "equal" *folkhem*. In a way, too, the particular brand of Swedish individualism that presented, at last, a counterhegemony to social democracy also presented a kind of expansiveness. Alliansen and the Greens' openness to immigration (closure-as-entry), coupled with a shift toward individualism in integration, represented the idea that anyone could potentially become a member of the Swedish society if the conditions were right and they just worked hard enough at it (closure-as-access to goods).

These "expansive" strategies included both bonding and bridging. Those which sought to consolidate the welfare state by emphasizing sameness (in the first two time periods) were prime examples of "bonding." It was only necessary to emphasize that Swedes were all the "same people" (with some necessary adjustment for Nordic brothers and sisters) in order to have a base to build on. By the 1970s, however, "bridging" strategies that sought to bring new members in, despite their difference, became the order of the day. Of course, there was, to a certain extent, a searching for a *civic* and *social-democratic* "sameness" even here, something evident in the requirement to adopt certain core welfare-statist values. By and large, however, this inclusive strategy was framed as bridging across difference—that there was, at times, room for at least a conditional sort of diversity in the Swedish People's Home. The diversity of the last time is something different. To a certain extent, the recognition that it is individual effort on the part of both integrator and integratee is a kind of bridging, but one that has less to do with the open-hearted extension of a culture seen as unproblematically "good" like that in the 1960s and 1970s.

At other times, however, the reconfiguration of the terms of membership in the Swedish nation entailed restriction. Even adopting the largely inclusive ethnic definition of the "people" in 1928–1932 entailed restriction at the margins. The Sami were pushed, symbolically, out of the nation more by neglect than anything else. The Tattare were targeted for sterilization. Finnish-speakers, conversely, forced to assimilate and "become Swedes" in large measure in order to be fully included in the nation. In the immediate postwar period, restriction as a strategy was even more pronounced: refugees from outside the Nordic areas were to held at a distance, both physically through deportation and symbolically through being made the object of charity instead of solidarity. In the 1960s the inclusive bridging strategies undertook by SAP and the LO were coupled with the simultaneous introduction of stricter border controls. In 1991–1994, a large number of refugees were let in, and formally/legally made into full members rather quickly. However, in the cultural-symbolic dimension important here, the renewed emphasis on ethnic difference, immigrants' "outsiderness" (including welfare dependence), and the construction of refugees as a "problem" served as a *restrictive* strategy. In recent years, party politics seems to have opened the door to restrictionism in a way that was unacceptable given the opinion climate in 1991–1994, with Alliansen aligning itself on the side of openness with Greens, and both SAP and the Sweden Democrats practicing a kind of restrictionism, though to very different degrees and, to an extent, with different goals.

Finally, a *selective* strategy that picked out Nordic migrants as already practically members and non-Nordic migrants as unable to even become members operated explicitly in the period 1945–1950. While this strategy was not explicit in the other time periods, the same selective split between Nordic and non-Nordic migrants (and in the 1990s, between "Western" and "non-Western") continued under the surface in the later time periods. For one, a free labor market between the Nordic countries, and quick and generous provisions for citizenship continued. That this strategy was largely unremarked on does not mean that it did not have an effect on the shape of the nation. Rather, its unspoken nature meant that such a selective strategy was seen as natural and correct. Finns, meanwhile, were singled out for special treatment, evidenced in their ability to form Finnish-language schools in the 1960s. The wisdom of this selective strategy, however, *was* remarked on, and this "special treatment" deeply questioned in the bridging era of the 1970s. Finally, in the 1990s it was the prospect, specifically, of "nonwestern" migrants that commentators found so threatening. Underlying this was the assumption that both Nordic and western European migration would be perfectly acceptable, although not stated explicitly. In fact, when Sweden joined the European Union in 1994, little fear was expressed about EU migration. The mechanism for selection in the final period seems to have shifted toward willingness to work, at least for Alliansen and the Greens who have worked to make it easier for labor migrants to come to Sweden and for refugees to "convert" to labor-market refugees.

Three Propositions about National Closure

This set of crises (and noncrises) and responses helps us to consider the three propositions made in the introduction to this book: (1) national closure, rather than being a unidirectional process, is subject to periodic "crises of closure," encompassing both closure-as-entry and closure-as-access to goods.

Examining these crises give us insight into the ways in which membership is defined and redefined; (2) political elites can and do act strategically to manage crises, though the strategies available to them are conditioned by the economic and political conditions of a certain time period; and (3) elites are constrained by culture, but they can also create new constraints that affect the potential "solutions" to future crises of closure. Indeed, these new constraints may affect whether crisis even occurs. Each of these three propositions is examined in here in light of the empirical evidence presented in the previous chapters.

National Closure Is Subject to Crisis

Sweden's status as a unified nation is considered "unproblematic" in much of the literature on nations and nationalism.[1] This makes it an especially good test case for the idea that national closure is neither permanent, nor does it develop unidirectionally. The general arc of "national" history just described provides evidence that the Swedish nation has not always been self-evident. In fact, the terms of national closure have not even been particularly stable, even in the Swedish case. Sweden underwent, as Wimmer predicts,[2] concurrent processes of state building and national closure. Closure-as-entry became increasingly more fraught and subject to political control as closure-as-access to goods became more important. Neither state building nor national closure entailed ever-increasing closure, however. Rather, even as the geographic boundaries remained unchanged, the terms of closure were in constant flux. The shape of the nation was deeply affected by various shocks originating both within and outside the previously established boundaries of the nation. We can see evidence of these shocks in many places—the demand to integrate the working class into the Swedish nation, the challenge of refugees, both culturally "near" and "far," and in the "problems," real or imagined, of labor migrants who did not understand what it meant to be a Swedish (union) worker.

It is unlikely that Sweden is a special case in this regard. On the one hand, processes that have affected Sweden—increased mobility across borders, increased sensitivity to the international economy, and (for Europe) Europeanization—are global phenomena. In the Western world, especially, many of the debates on migration and the welfare state have played out using a similar vocabulary, if not always with similar results. It seems unlikely that the processes that provoked crisis in the case of the highly "settled" Swedish nation would not have provoked crisis in other nations. We can look just south to Denmark to see the way that the politics of the far-right anti-immigrant People's Party irrevocably changed the terms of closure for that country sometime in the 1990s. On the other hand, the internal mechanisms of party competition and policy building that have allowed political elites to shape Swedish responses to crisis are present in all modern states, though they take different forms. That these elites, in part, defined changes in conditions sometimes as "crises" and sometimes not in Sweden suggests that many do the same in other places. Indeed, this may be true not only in the obvious instances where parties make "closure" a central feature of their ideology, but even in the few remaining places where such parties have been unsuccessful.

Political Elites Act Strategically to Manage Crises

Sweden's periodic twentieth-century crises of closure, then, were not simply the result of changing economic or social conditions. Rather, crises were manufactured by actors through their interpretations of events and conditions, perhaps at times something more akin to "moral panics"[3] than crises, per se. There was certainly no guarantee that the nation would be reformulated at every juncture noted in this book. SAP recognized early that their preferred policy positions, determined not only by working-class demands, but by concerns for "buy-in" from the middle classes and designs to be considered a national party, required a base of solidarity that was best built on national grounds. It was not simply in choosing among strategies for managing crisis that SAP and other political elites had power, but in the creation of crises in the first place.

Of course, some crises seem, on the surface, much less "manufactured" than others. There are a set of obvious and concrete issues involved in managing the over 80,000 asylum seekers who landed on Swedish soil in 1992, for instance. Yet, the refugee crisis did not necessarily have to become a crisis of closure. The magnitude of this occurrence as a "crisis" and the ways in which such crises would be managed were crucially determined by political (and, increasingly, cultural) elites. The managing of asylum seekers could have been framed merely as a "technical" or "logistical" problem instead of as the more fundamental "threat" or "opportunity" for the nation that it was framed as.

Indeed, rising immigration in the 1960s and 1970s was often treated in just that technical, logistical, pragmatic way. In general, we see in the "noncrises " of the 1960s and 1970s that the definition of a situation as a crisis of *closure* was heavily dependent on the interest of political elites, especially SAP elites, in reformulating the nation. The economic downturn was genuine, and it was perceived as a real crisis. Likewise, there was genuine concern—even at times panic—about the number of immigrants and their level of integration, especially into Swedish working life. Yet neither of these things, even simultaneous as they were, produced a genuine crisis of closure. Crucial to the differences between the 1990s and the 1960s and 1970s were the actions of political and cultural elites. A social-democratic hegemony that determined the terms for inclusion was, by then, well ensconced. Neither the economic nor the immigrant crisis challenged these terms. The oppositional parties could have used these crises to challenge that hegemony, but they did not. It was simply not politically profitable to do so. Change occurred, but it was largely to extend the social-democratic hegemony to new populations. The final period, too, shows that "crises" may arise out of conditions that are not objectively "crisis conditions." Alliansen took power and began to renegotiate closure before the economic crash of 2008, successfully manufacturing a crisis out of thin air.

The resolution of these crises, too, rested heavily on the actions of political and cultural elites, not just in policymaking but in the way elites came to discursively act to include or to exclude potential members of the national community. In the case of Sweden, elites employed the three strategies noted throughout the text: expansive, restrictive, and selective strategies. To take one example, the "selective strategy" applied to Nordic versus non-Nordic migrants in the late 1940s inhered in both the set of policy choices taken by political actors that gave Nordic migrants easier access to jobs and citizenship, as well as the choices by both cultural and political elites to refer to this group as "brothers" while referring to refugees from elsewhere as "refugee" or simply "human beings." Perhaps even more central to the story being told here, the attempt to make social democracy into a characteristic of being

Swedish was a purposeful strategy of SAP aimed at expanding, redefining, and solidifying the national community in a way that privileged social-democratic politics. Yet the end result was not only a social-democratic welfare state, but a new set of "cultural limits" for Swedishness.

Whether changes in closure-as-access spark changes in closure-as-entry or vice versa is too highly dependent on elite actions and the availability of various strategies to such elites. The two exist separately sometimes—as in the 1960s and 1970s where access-to-goods was relatively uncontroversial, while entry was highly controversial. However, they can be closely intertwined, such as in the 1990s, where the two types of crises symbiotically produced a breakdown in social-democratic hegemony.

The three strategies used by Swedish elites in the twentieth century appear to be the universal set of strategies available for managing crises of closure. The choice of strategies is clearly a function of both actors' interests and the economic, social, and cultural conditions under which those actors operate. The examples in this book illustrate, too, that elites are able to pursue multiple strategies simultaneously. There is little evidence that actors had these broad strategies in mind when formulating their course of action; the strategies were negotiated under particular local conditions as solutions for particular local problems. Yet the smaller actions and stratagems taken seem to have worked in concert to add up to considerably broader strategies. In any case, what is clear is that what elites did and said mattered concerning how economic, social, and cultural conditions became crises of closure and how these crises were resolved into new terms for national community.

Elites Are Constrained by Culture and Create New Constraints

Elites do not have an unlimited set of choices when faced with crisis. As noted previously, economic and social conditions limit the choices elites can make. Elites are also constrained by the current constellation of political power. SAP's electoral dominance is a cause and not just a consequence of their ability to shape the national community. More fundamentally, elites are constrained by the symbolic and cultural frameworks within which they act. SAP benefited from immense popularity, but even they could not create a new basis for national community completely independently from the ways in which the nation had been conceived before. Certain policy options, too, were completely off the table because of cultural constraints. Deporting foreign labor when unemployment rose in 1971, for instance, was simply not an option given the preference for inclusion reinforced by the social-democratic culture as it functioned at the time.

Yet, SAP did have more latitude than most actors to take strategic action because, over the course of the twentieth century, SAP itself had come to re-define the constraints within which they acted. SAP parlayed electoral sup-port and a successful claim to the "national party" status into a new cultural hegemony wherein social democracy set the terms for legitimate debate. The *folkhem*, a social-democratic project from the start, came to be synony-mous with the "good society" across the political spectrum. It thus became the starting point for evaluation of policies and the end goal for policy out-comes. It should be noted, of course, that SAP was not acting alone in build-ing the *folkhem*. Though they later tended to exaggerate their influence, both the Liberals and Center Party were important partners in the early stages. The broad organizing ideas for the *folkhem* however, were provided by SAP. In this way, by the 1960s, SAP exercised a great deal of control over the interpretation of crises, both regarding how to resolve crises and whether events or conditions even constituted a crisis at all. Responses to crises be-came were constrained in ways that privileged social-democratic solutions, even when the actors proposing them did not carry the Social Democratic label. This was true even when SAP was not a particularly active partici-pant in the migration debate, ceding that role, especially, to the Liberals.

SAP's party political difficulties, beginning in the 1990s and continuing through today, has reduced SAP's ability to set the terms of the debate. These party political losses in the 1990s undermined, but did not destroy the cul-tural hegemony SAP had built around social democracy. A new cohesive counterhegemony centered around a particular Swedish brand of individu-alistic neoliberalism has allowed the center-right to assert their political power, and their electoral successes have, in turn, allowed this alternative cultural and institutional model to thrive. Whether it will become truly he-gemonic in the end, setting new strict limits for the terms of closure in Swe-den, or whether there will continue to be a back and forth between the two competing organizing principles remains yet to be seen.

The narrative of SAP's development and its cultural effects look very much like Gramsci says hegemony building should look. SAP first trans-formed their party from a class to a national party, building interclass hegemony. This was followed by an elaboration of the content and form of that hegemony; SAP designed and built the welfare state, and the welfare-statist culture. By the 1960s, we observe that all parties hold the same basic assumptions and goals regarding the welfare state and, indeed, the nation. Furthermore, as Gramsci predicts, neither SAP's nor the other parties' positions can be entirely explained by economic interests. The effects of SAP's hegemony are social, political, and cultural in addition to economic.

Other states, of course, have their own hegemonies. One form of democracy or another acts as a hegemonic culture for much of the developed world. Yet, what is remarkable about the Swedish case, however, is the narrowness of this hegemony. It is a specifically *social-democratic* hegemony, not simply a democratic one. The absence of a viable counterhegemony for so long—even as the social-democratic hegemony began to crumble—is also remarkable. That a single political party could represent this social democracy—that is, that the intellectuals who created and maintained this hegemony for so long were remarkably cohesive and well formalized—is what made it possible for SAP to be able to dictate the boundaries of the nation to the extent that they did. In other words, SAP did not merely become the party of the nation, but came to dictate the very shape of that nation.

As noted earlier, although the occurrence of crises of closure and the importance of actors are likely to be general phenomena, neither these crises nor their responses are likely to look just like the Swedish ones. This is true even when the same general processes—refugee migration, globalization, recession, and depression—are at work. Others have suggested the same thing in regards to globalization: that the same "global" processes have different "local" consequences given the differences in the cultures of nations and other localities.[4] It is expected that, in regard to responses to "crises of culture," the cultural constraints will be different and will therefore result in different types of responses, even if the broad strategy (selection, restriction, expansion) is the same. Thus, no nation is expected to take the same path as Sweden. There is little reason to expect that increasing heterogeneity will have or has had exactly the same effect even in the other Nordic states.[5] However, the analysis carried out in this work provides useful tools for describing and explaining how crises of closure are managed and how homogeneity and heterogeneity come to matter or not.

The Complicated Story of the Homogenous Welfare State

We ought, now, to return to the question that motivated the writing of this book in the first place. How *does* diversity affect the welfare state? How does *nationalism* matter for the welfare state? The answer, of course, is a complicated one. The relationship between ethnicity, migration, nation, and the welfare state is anything but straightforward. It can be emphatically stated, however, from the evidence presented here that there *is* a relationship. The growth of the welfare state was conditioned by homogeneity. The advent of heterogeneity occasioned changes in the welfare state. In turn, the welfare state conditioned how increased ethnic heterogeneity was received. This is not a trivial finding. Much of the literature on the welfare state either assumes a relationship between homogeneity and the welfare state without giving much evidence or offers explanations that focus on other factors— class mobilization, heavy bureaucratization, etc.—to the exclusion of concerns about homogeneity and heterogeneity.[6]

Nevertheless, homogeneity does not *automatically* lead to a welfare state. The emphasis on an ethnically defined nation was a strategic choice by SAP. Conversely, heterogeneity does not *automatically* lead to a decline in that welfare state. In fact, in the face of labor migration in the 1960s, the welfare state was reaffirmed, even under conditions of economic uncertainty. Simply put, homogeneity and heterogeneity mattered to the extent that *political actors made it matter*. In the case of the early welfare state, this meant that homogeneity (with some wiggle room for other Nordics) became a key feature of the Swedish welfare state. Heterogeneity, on the other hand, had a much more ambiguous effect, working to reaffirm the welfare state in the 1960s and 1970s, but to present a threat both symbolically and materially to the welfare state since the 1990s. These differences are largely a result of the features of elite discourse, including most crucially, the ways in which SAP came to tie its own ideology to Swedishness. Diversity—potential or actual—was for most of the twentieth century filtered through a social-democratic hegemony that was controlled in large part by SAP elites and is now the subject of a tug-of-war between the competing hegemony and counterhegemony.

The very success of the promotion of social-democratic hegemony contributed to the ways in which economic and refugee crises became intertwined in the last period. The welfare state had become so bound up with Swedish identity, that the economic crisis challenging the welfare state became a crisis of Swedishness itself. As such, Swedishness became open to reinterpretation, allowing for a resurgence in ethnic conceptions of nation, on the one hand, and a new legitimacy for neoliberalism, on the other hand. In this way, it was the crisis in the welfare state that led to an increased salience of ethnic divisions, which then fed back into concerns about the effectiveness of the welfare state. Given the persistence of institutions, it is clear that these concerns did not translate into actual welfare-state rollbacks by the end of the twentieth century, but are beginning to in the twenty-first, although not in a straightforward way. The argument that immigrants presented a direct threat to the welfare state can, and is, channeled into a preservationist "welfare-chauvinist" position, and expanding access for labor migrants also has given legitimacy to the idea that immigrants may provide support for the welfare state. However, the increasing legitimacy of the idea that immigration had negative economic and cultural effects does seem to have hastened the decline of social-democratic hegemony.

What this suggests is that the power-resources model of welfare-state development is in need of reconstruction. The model's focus on political actors, especially on labor movements and working-class parties is reaffirmed here. SAP, backed in part by an influential labor movement, set the tone for political debate. They did not, however, do this through class—either working class or middle class—mobilization. Rather, this was achieved through the building of a wide-reaching consensus that not only entailed agreement on the shape of institutions but agreement on the terms of national closure—a national closure that was dictated by social-democratic values. Just as the analysis of welfare-state origins calls into question some popular explanations for the development of the Swedish welfare state, the analysis of 1990s politics gives the lie to certain influential explanations for retrenchment. Neither explanations that point to international trends toward austerity nor the power-resources approach can fully explain welfare retrenchment or, indeed, persistence when retrenchment might be expected. Austerity-focused explanations do an admirable job of identifying the potential sources of crisis, but in downplaying the role of political actors, they ignores one of the most powerful sources not only of retrenchment but of persistence. That the 1991–1994 period did not provoke significant structural change in the welfare state is perhaps best explained *not* by institutional inertia, but rather by the nonsocialist parties' inability to put forth a legitimate alternative to social-democratic hegemony.

Since the victory of the center-right Alliansen in 2006, however, this may have changed. Although certain features of the welfare state are likely more or less permanent (especially generous family policies), the deep cuts and, indeed, structural changes to policies such as sickness insurance and health care in combination with sweeping privatizations in a number of sectors, signal a significant change in Swedish politics. A particular Swedish version of neoliberalism has finally become the powerful counterhegemony necessary for a revolution. Indeed, while the statement that the *folkhem* was dead did not ring true in the 1990s, it has a certain face validity today. The breakdown of the old hegemony in 1990s may have been the starting point for a long, slow death. Alliansen remains divided on the question of immigration, but the Swedish brand of neoliberalism provides little direction for a new "common sense" regarding immigration and integration policy that centers on the duty to work and individualistic notions of antiracism, personal responsibility, and choice. However, the continued uncertain grounds for Swedishness, combined with a new legitimacy for restrictive immigration discourse, may have paved the way for an increased importance of ethnicity in Swedish politics.

Yet all is not lost for the miraculous machine, either as a creator of human welfare in general, or as an engine for humane integration of immigrants and refugees. The international economic climate seems to be beginning to swing away from "austerity" as the saving grace of stagnant European economies and back toward at least a theoretical re-embrace of good and equal jobs as the key to the good society. Such a pendulum swing can, if harnessed and deployed correctly, be good for social democrats. Yet any gains that are to be made for social democracy—in Sweden alone and in Europe more broadly—will only come with a political fight. SAP itself is still dealing with the shock of their loss of hegemonic position. Although the accusations on the right of "complacency" among Social Democrats may have been overstated, it is true that SAP seems to have lost the ability they had in the early twentieth century for making a case for equality. A reintroduction of a distinctly twenty-first-century social democracy—one that is clearly a fighting creed—is necessary. Whether it comes from a new generation of rising Social Democrats or from those who vote for the Greens, the Left, or the Feminist Initiative, who all represent a less materialistic left.

Such a reintroduction will have to take into account not just the changed political landscape but also the changed global and demographic landscape. It may be wise for the left to seek to make immigrants and refugees into 'good leftists' as they sought in the 1960s. They cannot, however, try to do so in a way that simply turns them into traditional, acquiescent SAP-voting trade unionists, but rather takes into account their unique experiences, needs, and capacities. If the fall of the miraculous machine was deeply intertwined with the crises of closure brought on by increased diversity, it stands to reason that its repair must be likewise intertwined. A new social democracy must be dynamic and worldly so that it is powerful enough to speak back, not just to neoliberalism—and the particular brand of suspicion and racism this ideology brings—but to welfare chauvinism as well.

Notes

Introduction

1. E.g., Alesina and Glaeser 2004; Offe 1996.

2. E.g., Goul Andersen and Bjorklund 2000; Kitschelt and McGann 1995; Freeman 1986.

3. Markus Crepaz's (2008) extended study of immigration, trust, and the welfare state is perhaps the best example, discussed later in this introduction.

4. Freeman 1986, 61–62.

5. Alesina and Glaeser 2004; Wilensky 1975.

6. Offe 1996; Bergmark, Thorslund, and Lindberg 2002; Hjerm 2005; Myrdal 1960.

7. Quadagno 1994; Goldberg 2007; Gilens 1995; Fox 2012.

8. Sears and Jessor 1996; Sears and Citrin 1985; Gilens 1995; Virtanen and Huddy 1998.

9. Quadagno 1994 on "unfinished democracy"; Voss 1993; Fox 2012.

10. Esping-Andersen 1990.

11. Xu 2007.

12. Hjerm 2005; Hansen and Lofstrom 2009.

13. Bergmark and Backman 2004.

14. Brett 1997; Byrne 1999; Vasta 2004.

15. Crepaz 2008.

16. Svanberg and Tydén 1992.

17. Olson 2006; Marshall 1964.

18. Wimmer 2002, 62.

19. Faist 1996; Van der Waal et al. 2010.

20. Anderson 1983.

21. Bosniak 2000.

22. Billig 1995; Sutherland 2005; Brubaker 1992.

23. Weber 1978.

24. Brubaker 1992, 21–33.

25. Wimmer 2002, 212.

26. Ibid., 61.

27. Ibid.

28. Cohen 1972.

29. Trägårdh 2002.

30. The literature on social capital uses "bridging" and "bonding" to discuss different types of capital within a group (e.g., Putnam 2007), but the concept can logically be used more broadly to discuss the relationships between people in a group.

31. Swidler 1986.

32. Sewell 1980; Skocpol 1985b.

33. Brubaker 1992. See also Schall 2012; R. Smith 2003.

34. Löfgren 1989, 1993; Hobsbawm 1983. Anthony D. Smith (1986) also makes this point.

35. Heilbroner and Milberg 1995; Berman 1998.

36. Kjaer and Pedersen 2001.

37. Gramsci 1971.

38. Laitin 1986.

39. Riley 2010, 14–15.

40. See Adamson 1980, chap. 4.

41. Gramsci 1971, 18, 460.

42. R. Smith 2003, 40.

43. Gramsci 1971, 144.

44. E.g., Mann 2001.

45. Gramsci 1971, 5–6. Anne Showstack Sassoon (2000) points out that Gramsci actually leaves more room for "citizen" involvement than many give him credit for. This involvement, however, is predicted to come in during the last stages of the development of "true" democracy (implicitly socialist democracy) as the state withers in its traditional functions. It seems to me that a social-democratic hegemony is not conducive to the "withering" of the state in *any* of its functions.

46. Polanyi 2001.

47. Brandal, Bratberg, and Thorsen 2013.

48. Esping-Anderson 1990; Schumpeter 2010.

49. Brandal, Bratberg, and Thorsen 2013.

50. Evans and Schmidt 2012.

51. Katzenstein 1985.

52. Berman 2006.

53. Sejersted (2011) also makes this argument.

54. Tilton 1990.

55. Marshall (1964) makes this argument, as do many others.

56. This point has been made in many pieces on Swedish social democracy, including Berman 2006; Sejersted 2001; Brandal, Bratberg, and Thorsen 2013.

57. Bergegren and Trädgårdh 2006.

58. Pierson 2001; Quadagno 1987.

59. Korpi 1983; Shalev 1983; Esping-Anderson 1985, 1990.

60. Baldwin 1990.

61. Swenson 2002; Korpi 2003.

62. Hicks 1999.

63. E.g., Skocpol 1985a; Amenta 1998.

64. Rothstein (1998) makes this point.

65. E.g., Lin and Carroll 2006.

66. Childs 1936.

67. Trägårdh 1990.

68. See, e.g., Åmark 2005; Lundberg and Åmark 2001.

69. Kildal and Kuhnle 2005; Stråth 2005. Kahl (2005) also points to the church as a source of social-democratic ideals, i.e., Scandinavian Lutheranism's emphasis on *both* work and equality.

70. Offe 1996.

71. Löfgren 1993; Korsgaard 2002.

72. Pierson 2001.

73. Green-Pedersen and Haverland 2002; Kuhnle 2000; Bergh and Erlingsson 2009.

74. Korpi and Palme 2003; Korpi 2003.

75. Hicks 1999; Kitschelt 2001.

76. F. Castles 2001; Huber and Stephens 2001.

77. Lindbom 2008.

78. Korpi and Palme 2003; Korpi 2003, 606.

79. Offe 1996, 171.

80. S. Castles and Miller 2009.

81. Ryner 2000.

82. See also Ekberg 1990; Hjerm 2005; Valenta and Bunar 2010; Trondman 2006.

83. Orum, Feagin, and Sjoberg 1991, 6.

84. For a timeline of Swedish governments, see table 1.

85. Baldwin 1990.

86. Westin 2006.

87. For examples of such histories, see Åmark 2005. On social insurances, see Naumann 2007. On social assistance, see Lin and Carroll 2006.

88. See Nord 2001 for more on Swedish daily newspapers.

89. Miles and Huberman 1994; Riffe and Freitag 1997.

90. Sewell 1996, 273.

1. 1928–1932: Ethnic Nation and Social Democratic Consolidation

1. The history of SAP that appears here primarily follows Tingsten (1941).
2. Hentilä 1978; Gunnarsson 1971.
3. Tingsten 1941, 460.
4. See Gunnarsson 1971.
5. Tingsten 1941.
6. Hentilä 1978.
7. Baldwin 1990.
8. Berman 2006.
9. Ibid.
10. Gramsci 1971.
11. Berman 2006.
12. A full transcript of Hansson's speech, "People's Home—Citizen's Home," is available at http://www.svenskatal.se/19280011-per-albin-hansson-folkhemstalet/.
13. Åsard and Bennett 1997, 95.
14. *ARB* January 8, 1931.
15. Offe 1984.
16. Wallerstein 1991, 85.
17. *DN* May 2, 1928.
18. *ARB* May 2, 1928.
19. Social Democratic Party 1928.
20. *ARB* June 27, 1930.
21. *ARB* July 19, 1930.
22. *DN* June 4, 1930.
23. *ARB* October 10, 1930.
24. *ARB* August 27, 1929.
25. *DN* May 1, 1928.
26. *DN* September 22, 1930.
27. *DN* July 3, 1928.
28. *SvD* August 12, 1928; *SvD* September 1, 1928; *DN* September 3, 1928.
29. *ARB* December 3, 1928.
30. *ARB* May 2, 1930.
31. *ARB* March 26, 1932.
32. *ARB* December 31, 1932.
33. Tingsten 1941, 458–460; Berman (2006) makes this same observation.
34. *ARB* July 11, 1932.
35. *DN* January 22, 1928.
36. *ARB* January 2, 1931.
37. *ARB* June 4, 1928.
38. *ARB* June 22, 1932.
39. *DN* September 8, 1930; see also *SvD* September 6, 1930.
40. *DN* May 23, 1931.
41. *DN* July 2, 1928.
42. *DN* August 20, 1928.

43. *ARB* October 10, 1930.
44. *ARB* December 31, 1930.
45. *ARB* June 22, 1932.
46. *ARB* July 28, 1930.
47. *Fosterländskhet* means "patriotism," though with a connotation of traditionalism and blind loyalty. *Folklikghet* is patriotism rooted in community and a feeling being of the people.
48. *ARB* July 12, 1932.
49. See, e.g., *ARB* November 5, 1932.
50. *DN* January 21, 1928.
51. *ARB* January 3, 1931.
52. Hernes 1988; Stråth 2004.
53. Stråth 2004.
54. Arthur Engberg, quoted in Blomkvist 2006, 61.
55. Cf., e.g., the iconic "daily plebiscite" description of nations in Renan 1994.
56. Herder 2002.
57. Arthur Engberg, quoted in Blomkvist 2006.
58. Spektorowski and Mizrachi 2004.
59. Vougt 1925, 2.
60. Lundborg and Linders 1926, 41.
61. This view toward Slavic peoples was not unusual in socialist movements. Engels considered the Slavs "'historyless peoples' whose only mission was to disappear in the future revolutionary holocaust that would sweep them away with other 'waste products' such as the Bretons, Basques and Scottish Highlanders"; quoted in Wistrich 1982, 33.
62. Blomkvist 2006, 200–219.
63. *DN* February 17, 1928.
64. Ibid.
65. *NSD*, April 23, 1926.
66. See Spektorowski 2004.
67. See, e.g., Broberg and Tydén 1996; Svanberg and Tydén 1992.
68. Lundborg 1926, 145–147; see also Broberg and Tydén 1996.
69. Lundborg 1926, 71.
70. Spektorowski 2004, 84–106.
71. Löfgren 1989; Lundborg 1926; Trägårdh 1990.
72. Lundborg 1926, 42.
73. Stråth 2004, 10–11.
74. Löfgren 1989, 10.
75. Ibid., 21.
76. *ARB* November 4, 1929.
77. *ARB* February 10, 1931.
78. Svanberg and Tydén 1992.
79. *Karlstads-Tidningen*, a Liberal paper, quoted in Blomkvist 2006, 211–212.
80. *ARB* April 12, 1904.
81. *ARB* October 27, 1930.
82. E.g., *ARB* June 12, 1931; *DN* November 1, 1930.

83. *ARB* October 27, 1930.
84. Brubaker 1992.
85. *DN* May 22, 1928; *DN* June 26, 1929.
86. *DN* January 7, 1929.
87. Stråth 2004, 8.
88. Stråth 2005.
89. Spektorowski and Mizrachi 2004.
90. Marshall 1964.
91. Marshal 1964; see also Olson 2006, which talks about a "codification of social cooperation" (182).
92. I.e., Anderson 1983.

2. 1945–1950: Making the "People's Home"

1. For more on the "cow trade" agreement, see Baldwin 1990; Åmark 2005.
2. See Swenson 2002 on the effect of labor-capital agreements on social policy development.
3. Åmark 2005.
4. *DN* July 17, 1947.
5. Ruin 1990.
6. Nordlund 1999.
7. Koblik 1987.
8. Kvist 2002.
9. Ibid.; Svanberg and Tydén 1992, 283.
10. See Svanberg and Tydén 1992, 279–287, for more details on this migration.
11. E.g., Byström 2006; Koblik 1987; Nordlund 1999.
12. Kushner and Knox 1999; Kreis 2000.
13. Levine 1996.
14. Byström 2006.
15. Svanberg and Tydén 1992.
16. See, e.g., *DN* July 18, 1946.
17. See, e.g., *DN* November 24, 1945.
18. *ARB* January 16, 1945.
19. Paulson was later revealed to be a Nazi double agent who, in concert with Lönnegren, revealed the name of 538 refugees who had fled Germany. Both were imprisoned for their actions.
20. *ARB* January 8, 1945.
21. *DN* January 16, 1945.
22. See, e.g., *DN* January 18, 1945; *ARB* January 8, 1945.
23. *DN* August 15, 1946.
24. *ARB* January 16, 1945.
25. See, e.g., Blomkvist 2006; Carlsson 2004; Andersson 2000; Nordlund 1999.
26. E.g., *DN* July 25, 1947; *DN* August 15, 1946; *DN* February 25, 1945. See also *ARB* January 21, 1946.

27. *DN* August 15, 1946 (emphasis in the original).

28. *DN* December 26, 1946.

29. E.g., *DN* May 26, 1945.

30. Lamont and Molnar 2002.

31. Note that the same policies that were applied to Nordic refugees were also applied to the so-called Estlandssvenskar—ethnically Swedish Estonians who fled Estonia in great numbers toward the end of World War II.

32. See, e.g., *DN* March 23, 1947.

33. *DN* August 7, 1946.

34. Svenska Riksdagen 1945, 29/12.

35. Byström 2006.

36. Lomfors 2005.

37. Ibid.

38. E.g., *DN* June 20, 1945; *ARB* May 15, 1945; *SvD* March 14, 1945.

39. *DN* January 16, 1945; *SvD* February 13, 1945.

40. Ekholm 1984.

41. See, e.g., Svenska Riksdagen 1945, 23/45.

42. Ibid.

43. See Salminen and Campling 1999 on self-censorship of anti-Soviet material in the Finnish press as an example.

44. *DN* March 10, 1948.

45. The tension between neutrality and Nordism evident in the case of the Karelian refugees provided a recurring point of debate, particularly in regard to Sweden's decision not to join NATO while Norway and Denmark joined. The idea that even a labor-market union among the Nordic countries "might not be seen as so harmless by the Soviet Union" was even considered. *DN* February 25, 1946.

46. *ARB* January 16, 1945.

47. See, e.g., *ARB* November 24, 1945.

48. *DN* November 11, 1949.

49. See Byström 2006. Sweden's refugee policy from 1951 on was largely dictated by the Geneva Convention on Refugees, which was followed but in a comparatively narrow interpretation. How to interpret this convention becomes a key political question much later in the century as refugee migration becomes salient again.

50. *DN* June 12, 1946; *ARB* August 11, 1946.

51. *ARB* August 7, 1946.

52. *DN* March 10, 1948.

53. *ARB* March 23, 1947.

54. See, e.g., *DN* December 22, 1945.

55. See, e.g., *DN* November 21, 1947. Some of these Finns were migrants, but many were native Finnish-speaking Swedish citizens. As noted in chapter 1, distinctions between these two groups were often blurred by the fact that communities stretched across state boundaries in the northernmost parts of Sweden and Finland.

56. *DN* January 31, 1946.

57. E.g., *ARB* August 11, 1946; *SvD* August 29, 1946. The requirement for work visas for those Baltic refugees who had not been deported in 1945 was lifted. This change

in policy indicates, perhaps, an in-between status between the Nordics, whose path to citizenship was easy, and workers from southern Europe, who were considered unsuitable for membership.

58. *ARB* July 8, 1946.

59. *ARB* August 11, 1946.

60. *DN* May 18, 1949.

61. *DN* August 28, 1946; *ARB* November 8, 1946.

62. Durkheim 1983, 219. It should be noted that Durkheim did not necessarily consider "social legislation" as productive of justice or solidarity, either, but thought of it as a sort of society-level charity or enforced fraternity.

63. Schoenfeld and Meštrović 1989.

64. *ARB* January 23, 1946. See also *DN* October 19, 1946.

65. *SvD* September 6, 1948.

66. *DN* January 7, 1945.

67. *ARB* May 2, 1950.

68. E.g., *DN* August 15, 1946.

69. *DN* March 20, 1946.

70. *ARB* April 7, 1946.

71. Rickard Schwartz, letter, March 1948, Arbetarrörelsens flyktinghjälp (The Labour Movement Refugee Relief), series F1, Arbetarrörelsens arkiv och Bibliotek.

72. In practice, though the law said "citizen," many noncitizens received their *folkpension* exactly as Swedish citizens did. Nonetheless, officially, both pensions and child allowances were restricted to citizens, and only later extended to legal permanent, and then to temporary, residents.

73. E.g., *DN* February 17, 1946; *DN* March 13, 1946; *ARB* December 1, 1946; *SvD* March 13, 1946 (my emphasis). The same formulation is found in regard to child allowances (*DN* October 19, 1946) and to health care (*DN* October 11, 1946; *DN* February 1, 1946; *ARB* May 2, 1946).

74. E.g., Stråth 1994.

75. *ARB* March 21, 1946. See also *DN* June 3, 1946, for some of the Liberals' "credit taking."

76. "Bertil Ohlin," in Folkpartiets Riksorganisations arkiv, vol. 1.

77. See, e.g., Åmark 2005 for the party political struggles within parliament regarding social insurances.

78. E.g., *ARB* March 21, 1946; *ARB* June 20, 1946.

79. *ARB* May 2, 1947.

80. *ARB* August 10, 1948.

81. See, e.g., *DN* July 28, 1948.

82. *DN* September 9, 1946.

83. *DN* January 17, 1950; *DN* April 2, 1949.

84. Svenska Riksdagen 1949/1950, 29/2. See also *DN* July 9, 1947; *DN* August 15, 1949, and May 29, 1949.

85. *DN* January 2, 1950.

86. *DN* August 5, 1949. See also *DN* September 9, 1946, and *DN* January 3, 1949, which express much the same sentiment.

87. *SvD* January 11, 1949.

88. *DN* January 21, 1948.

89. *ARB* March 21, 1946.

90. *ARB* January 23, 1946.

91. Social Democratic Party 1946.

92. Svenska Riksdagen 1947, 24/13. See also *ARB* November 5, 1947.

93. E.g., Per Edvin Sköld, former Social Democratic trade minister, quoted in *DN* August 17, 1947.

94. *DN* July 11, 1948.

95. *DN* September 15, 1948; *DN* September 15, 1950; *DN* March 1, 1949.

96. *DN* July 30, 1946.

97. *DN* July 12, 1946; *DN* October 16, 1947; *ARB* July 18, 1947.

98. *DN* September 2, 1947.

99. Glover 2009.

Interlude 1

1. Cf. Wimmer 2002.

2. Gramsci 1971.

3. 1968–1975: Security, Equality, and Choice

1. In 1969, the Conservatives changed their name from the Right Party (Högerpartiet) to the Moderate Party (Moderata Samlingspartiet), perhaps in recognition of the general shift to the left in Swedish politics and their own acceptance of a number of welfare-state reforms commonly thought to belong to the left parties. I follow general international consensus in continuing to call them "Conservatives" despite the change in their Swedish name.

2. Ruin 1990.

3. Ibid.

4. Palme, in fact, was hired, not as a political secretary, but as an assistant. The person who recommended him for the job stated that he was "unsure of whether [Palme] is a Social Democrat." Once in the job, however, it became clear that Palme was not only a Social Democrat but talented politically. It was largely thanks to Erlander's influence that Palme rose quickly in the party.

5. A new unicameral system replaced the former two-chamber system. Furthermore, the new system had a single set of elections every three years that required reconfirmation of governments more frequently than previously, making the government more vulnerable to temporary shifts in political opinion.

6. Olof Palme, quoted in *DN* August 6, 1973.

7. Ibid.

8. *Trygghet* entails not so much physical safety, but social, psychological, and especially economic security.

9. *DN* September 16, 1970. As stated in the introduction, the relationship between newspapers and parties is somewhat different during this period than during previous periods. *DN* and *SvD*, while still officially Liberal and Conservative, respectively, increasingly publish opinion pieces by writers who are either politically unaffiliated or who are affiliated with a different political party than the paper itself. *DN*, in particular, published a large number of unaffiliated writers, most importantly several immigrant writers without ties to the organized parties. I have noted in the analysis when writers' affiliations differ from that of the party. As before, *ARB* remains a mainstream Social Democratic paper, closely tied to SAP.

10. *DN* January 7, 1975.

11. See *SvD* February 13, 1972.

12. *DN* September 11, 1973.

13. *DN* August 7, 1973, profiles all four parties' election posters, featuring these slogans. The article proclaims *tryggheten* the watchword of the 1973 election.

14. *DN* September 15, 1973.

15. Åmark 2005.

16. Thorbjörn Fälldin, quoted in *DN* August 6, 1973.

17. *DN* October 17, 1973.

18. *DN* August 6, 1975.

19. Svenska Riksdagen 1973, 108/64.

20. Svenska Riksdagen 1973, 108/65.

21. See, e.g., Svenska Riksdagen 1972, 102/33.

22. Holmberg and Gilljam 1987. See also Svallfors 1989.

23. *DN* August 22, 1973.

24. *DN* August 29, 1973.

25. E.g., *DN* May 16, 1969; *DN* June 24, 1970. See also *SvD* January 13, 1968, for similar arguments from the Conservatives.

26. *ARB* June 18, 1969; *ARB* August 11, 1969.

27. *ARB* September 3, 1973; *Svenska Riksdagen* 1973: 108/59.

28. *DN* August 23, 1971.

29. Social Democratic Party (SAP) 1971.

30. SAP 1969, Internal Party Minutes, September 7.

31. *DN* October 21, 1972; *DN* February 5, 1975; *DN* February 12, 1975.

32. Social Democratic Party and Landsorganisation (SAP-LO) 1969.

33. *ARB* August 5, 1968.

34. Palme, quoted in SAP 1969, Internal Party Minutes, July 9; Erlander makes the same point in the same meeting as well.

35. Ibid.

36. Erlander, quoted in SAP 1969, Internal Party Minutes, July 9.

37. Palme, in SAP 1969, Internal Party Minutes, June 27.

38. Bergegren, quoted in SAP 1969, Internal Party Minutes, September 7.

39. Hirdman 1998.

40. Tingsten 1941.

41. Myrdal, quoted in SAP 1969. Internal Party Minutes, September 7. See also Hansen 2001.

42. Mats Hellström, quoted in SAP 1972. Party Congress, April 6.

43. Myrdal, quoted in SAP 1969, Internal Party Minutes, June 27.

44. Gunnar Lange, quoted in ibid.

45. Palme, quoted in SAP 1969, Internal Party Minutes, September 7.

46. SAP-LO 1969.

47. Petersson 1991.

48. A. Myrdal 1968–1971.

49. Ibid.

50. Klinth 2005.

51. *ARB* February 13, 1968.

52. Nettelbrandt 1969.

53. *DN* January 26, 1975.

54. *DN* January 28, 1975.

55. *ARB* January 13, 1974; *ARB* March 21, 1975.

56. *ARB* November 26, 1972.

57. Klinth 2005; cf. Wetterberg 1997.

58. Five thousand Czech refugees arrived in 1968. Eventually, as many as 18,000 Chileans came to Sweden. However, this migration was spread over several years and during the period under study, the numbers remained small compared with labor migration (Svanberg and Tydén 1992, 342; Lindqvist 1991). A considerable amount of press was devoted to Sweden's decisions to grant asylum and material aid to a small number of Americans—mostly Vietnam War deserters, but also some civil rights activists—in the late 1960s and 1970s. These discussions were almost entirely divorced from any other discussions of migrants or refugees.

59. *DN* January 13, 1968.

60. See Hultén 2006 for a more precise overview of the types of issues addressed.

61. This shift has also been noted in Hansen 2001 and Svanberg and Tydén 1992.

62. See, e.g., *ARB* July 8, 1968; *ARB* July 28, 1968; *DN* January 22, 1975.

63. *ARB* July 17, 1968.

64. Yalcin 2010.

65. *ARB* July 8, 1968. See also *ARB* August 15, 1969.

66. Ivar Lind, quoted in *ARB* July 28, 1968.

67. *DN* January 22, 1975.

68. Ibid.

69. *ARB* August 14, 1973.

70. *ARB* September 2, 1973.

71. *DN* August 25, 1973.

72. E.g., *ARB* November 14, 1970; *ARB* October 7, 1971. See also Hultén 2006.

73. *DN* September 5, 1973.

74. *DN* September 7, 1973.

75. *DN* September 1, 1973. The Center Party argued in favor of restrictions along much the same lines as SAP, a fact that their coalition partners, the Liberals, generally only acknowledged in passing. See, e.g., *DN* July 24, 1973.

76. This argument was not foreign to SAP. In their discussion of immigration policy at their 1972 party congress, this was a recurrent theme. Yet, this idea of "open-market" immigration policy was not a part of their public contributions to debate.

77. *DN* January 22, 1975.

78. See, e.g., *DN* June 23, 1975.

79. Palme, May 1, 1971, speech, Palmearkivet.

80. Lars Alvarsson, quoted in *ARB* July 20, 1968.

81. SAP-LO 1972, "Invandrarfrågor, Motionerna nr I 1-I 9."

82. See Yalcin 2010 for more on this.

83. *DN* August 14, 1969.

84. *DN* September 15, 1971. The Liberals were not entirely opposed to immigrant-directed policy, however. This policy was primarily cultural, not economic.

85. E.g., *SvD* September 12, 1968; *SvD* May 16, 1969; *SvD* September 13, 1969.

86. E.g., *SvD* August 15, 1972; *SvD* January 14, 1973.

87. E.g., *DN* August 26, 1972.

88. Reported in Wallengren 2014.

89. Myrdal, quoted in SAP 1969, Internal Party Minutes, April 24.

90. Alva Myrdal, despite her illustrious race-scholar husband Gunnar Myrdal and her involvement in the exploration of the "population problem," seemed relatively uninterested in the problems of immigrants at home.

91. "Handlingar från Alva Myrdals verksamhet i jämlikhetsfrågor, 1968–1971." Arbetarrörelsens arkiv och Bibliotek, 4/1/14/007.

92. SAP-LO 1969, 53.

93. Ibid., 120.

94. SAP-LO 1972, 96.

95. Ibid., 97.

96. Ibid., 107.

97. Ibid., 81.

98. E.g., *DN* January 28, 1970.

99. Korpi 1970.

100. Yalcin 2010.

101. Arbetarrörelsens arkiv och Bibliotek, SAP Internal Party Minutes 1971, 13/14.

102. Román 1994.

103. Hultén 2006.

104. *DN* February 13, 1968.

105. See also Román 1994.

106. Ryner (2000) makes this suggestion.

107. See Hirdman 1998, 1992.

108. Cf., e.g., Hirdman 1992; Hultén 2006.

109. Hansen 2001.

110. E.g., Hammar 1985.

111. Wadensjö 1973.

112. Claes-Adam Wachmeister, quoted in *DN* March 16, 1968.

113. Michael Wächter, quoted in *DN* March 4, 1966.

114. This phrase ("the right to equality included the right to be different") recurs in Schwarz's writing, but originates in *DN* February 25, 1966. See Román 1994.

115. For Reinans, see *DN* March 27, 1968; for Kivaed, see *DN* April 14, 1969.

116. Schwarz 1971.

117. See, e.g., SAP Member of Parliament Göran Johansson's contribution to the Immigrant Policy debate at the 1972 Party Congress. SAP 1972, Party Congress, "Invandrarfrågor, Motionerna nr 11-19."

118. Yalcin 2010.

119. Ibid.

120. *DN* August 25, 1973. Many believe, perhaps correctly, that these requirements had the unintended consequence of creating discrimination against immigrants given the associated cost. See Wadensjö 1973.

121. *ARB* September 13, 1968.

122. Knocke 1981, 189.

123. Lars Sköld, quoted in *DN* January 9, 1968.

124. Sveriges socialdemokratiska arbetareparti 1978.

125. *ARB* December 27, 1972.

126. E.g., *DN* August 25, 1973; *ARB* June 12, 1972.

127. SAP-LO 1972, 81.

128. Although it was not obligatory for immigrant workers to join their union, it was perceived as such by most. See Kjellberg 2000.

4. 1991–1995: People's Home No Longer?

1. Berman 2006.

2. These are the official unemployment rates of the Swedish Employment Office. Different sources give slightly different rates, but the trends are similar. For Sweden's labor-market data, see the International Labour Organization's ILOSTAT Database, http://laborsta.ilo.org/applv8/data/SSM4A/E/SE.html.

3. Unlike previous chapters, the analysis in this chapter does not use each of the three newspapers as representatives of their affiliated party. The reason is that both *DN* and *SvD* were no longer institutionally tied to their respective parties (although they retained the labels of "independent liberal" and "independent conservative") and consequently published a wider array of political viewpoints. In many cases, the political party affiliation of the writer is known, and in these cases I have indicated that affiliation. Where the political stance of the writer is unknown, no label is attached. *ARB* remains institutionally affiliated with SAP, but even *ARB* writers are sometimes not SAP members, and therefore their affiliations are noted in the text.

4. Reinfeldt, *SvD* November 11, 1995.

5. See Håkansson 1987, 61–79.

6. Fryklund 1994.

7. E.g., *DN* September 13, 1991; *SvD* September 14, 1991.

8. E.g., Håkansson 1994.

9. Ibid.

10. There is some evidence that social-democratic parties, in general, have experienced electoral defeats following "moderations" in recent years. See Karreth, Polk, and Allen 2012.

11. Edgerton, Fryklund, and Peterson 1994.

12. Westlind 1994; Korpi 1993.

13. *DN* June 29, 1993.

14. *DN* September 16, 1991. See also *DN* September 20, 1991.

15. Lindbeck and Thygesen 1993, 16.

16. The report praised the Swedish model as a good solution to the economic problems of the mid-twentieth century, but argued that the model was increasingly outdated.

17. *DN* December 20, 1992.

18. *DN* July 3, 1993. See also *DN* June 29, 1993.

19. *DN* July 3, 1993.

20. *DN* January 14, 1993.

21. *DN* December 21, 1992.

22. *DN* December 21, 1992; *DN* November 13, 1991; *SvD* July 22, 1994.

23. E.g., Bäck, *SvD* September 13, 1994.

24. *SvD* February 14, 1994.

25. Rourke O'Brien (2015) suggests that this high rate is in part due to a broader understanding of what "disability" is in generous welfare states, not necessarily fraud or an increased incidence of fraud.

26. E.g., Henriksson, *DN* March 11, 1992.

27. Reinfeldt quoted in Kratz, *SvD* January 13, 1994.

28. *SvD* January 4, 1994. See also Reinfeldt, *SvD* November 11, 1995.

29. *SvD* November 3, 1992.

30. Grejder quoted in *SvD* January 13, 1994.

31. *DN* June 9, 1993.

32. *SvD* July 18, 1993.

33. *DN* December 18, 1995.

34. *DN* July 28, 1993.

35. *DN* February 5, 1995.

36. E.g., *ARB* March 2, 1991.

37. E.g., *SvD* January 4, 1994.

38. *DN* August 29, 1993.

39. *DN* October 13, 1992.

40. *DN* April 3, 1993; *DN* March 18, 1993.

41. See *DN* January 30, 1993.

42. *DN* April 3, 1993. See also Linde, *DN* November 8, 1995.

43. *DN* June 3, 1993.

44. *DN* December 27, 1992.

45. *DN* December 11, 1992. See also Wegestål, *ARB* October 30, 1991.

46. *ARB* April 14, 1993.

47. *DN* May 2, 1995.

48. E.g., Jonsson, *DN* October 22, 1995.

49. Lundby-Wedin, *DN* April 12, 1995.

50. Palme and Wennemo 1998; Scruggs 2006.

51. Palmer 2000.

52. See Karlsson, *DN* January 25, 1994.

53. See, e.g., *DN* December 16, 1995; *ARB* August 17, 1994.

54. Bratt, *DN* January 26, 1993.

55. Ibid.

56. Svallfors 2011.

57. Hansen 1993.

58. Tham, *ARB* May 18, 1991.

59. Paulson, *ARB* July 23, 1995. See also Sundström, *ARB* June 18, 1992; Ljunggren, *ARB* March 22, 1994; Kratz, *SvD* January 3, 1994.

60. Karlsson quoted in Forslind, *SvD* December 7, 1992.

61. Westerståhl, *DN* November 20, 1991.

62. Vänsterpartiet (Left Party) 1993.

63. Kristdemokraterna (Christian Democrats) 1993.

64. Moderaterna (Moderates) 1993.

65. The one exception to the Conservatives' weak resistance to expansionary immigration policies is former Conservative Sten Andersson. During his tenure as a member of parliament with the Conservatives (between 1983 and 2002), Andersson consistently provided an anti-immigration viewpoint in parliament. He launched attacks on multiculturalism, attributing social tensions to increased cultural clashes, as well as Sweden's "unique and unsupported refugee policy," which he believed Sweden did not have the resources to support (Svenska Riksdagen 1994, 13/14). However, the effects of his anti-immigration rhetoric on the immigration discourse were muted by the fact that he was rarely backed by his fellow Conservatives and was considered an exception by the other parties. His status as an outsider in the party was confirmed when Andersson left the Conservatives before the 2002 elections and stood for election as a Sweden Democrat. Andersson cited the Conservatives' loss of their conservative values in general sometime in the late 1980s, as well as a disagreement over the nature of the Conservative immigration policy as the cause of his defection to the Sweden Democrats.

66. E.g., Svenska Riksdagen 1992, 93/60; Svenska Riksdagen 1991, 92/57; Svenska Riksdagen 1993, 94/5.

67. E.g., Karlsson, *DN* January 12, 1992.

68. Rydgren 2002; Widfelt 2000.

69. Riks-SOM 1993.

70. Riks-SOM 1991–1995.

71. Riks-SOM 1993.

72. Riks-SOM 1991–1995.

73. See Dahlström 2007.

74. *DN* May 3, 1992.

75. See, e.g., Rydgren 2002; Widfeldt 2000.

76. Hammar 1991.

77. Freeman 1992.

78. Svenska Riksdagen 1993, 94/39.

79. Appelqvist 2000, 37.

80. *DN* October 22, 1993.

81. *DN* March 4, 1992.

82. Albons, *ARB* May 5, 1992.

83. Alam and Host, *DN* July 5, 1992.

84. *ARB* April 13, 1993.
85. See, e.g., *SvD* May 13, 1991; *SvD* September 18, 1994.
86. *DN* October 2, 1993.
87. *DN* October 16, 1993.
88. *DN* August 7, 1992.
89. See also Dahlström 2007; Odmalm 2011.
90. *DN* August 13, 1993.
91. *DN* September 15, 1993.
92. *ARB* September 24, 1993.
93. *DN* August 21, 1992.
94. *DN* September 24, 1994.
95. Schorri, *ARB* April 9, 1993.
96. Narti, *DN* August 21, 1992.
97. "Non-European" was common despite the fact that the largest refugee groups were from the former Yugoslav republics.
98. Ginsburg, *DN* March 23, 1995.
99. *DN* November 20, 1991.
100. *ARB* November 4, 1991.
101. *DN* October 2, 1993.
102. *DN* July 8, 1992.
103. See, e.g., *DN* July 8, 1992; *SvD* March 9, 1992.
104. *DN* October 1, 1995.
105. *DN* February 10, 1993.
106. Eger 2010.
107. Ginsburg, *DN* March 23, 1995.
108. *DN* September 15, 1993. See also Carlsson and Selander, *SvD* October 4, 1993, for norms regarding women and family life.
109. *DN* April 14, 1992.
110. Albons, *DN* September 18, 1993.
111. *DN* July 11, 1992.
112. *DN* January 10, 1992.
113. Quoted in Naumann, *DN* January 20, 1992.
114. Wahlström, *DN* December 8, 1994.
115. Keller, *DN* September 14, 1994.
116. *SvD* March 28, 1992; *DN* October 24, 1994.
117. E.g., Malmborg, *DN* April 5, 1992.
118. *ARB* June 13, 1994.
119. E.g., *DN* May 3, 1993.
120. *DN* July 17, 1993.
121. Behtoui and Neergaard 2010; Hansen and Lofstrom 2009; Kesler 2010.
122. Amin and Björkman, *DN* February 5, 1994.
123. Diaz quoted in Öhrström, *DN* July 2, 1993.
124. *DN* February 10, 1993.
125. Alam and Host, *DN* July 5, 1992.
126. *SvD* November 12, 1992.

127. Begler, Mossler, and Bergström, *DN* September 19, 1995.
128. See, e.g., *DN* January 16, 1994.
129. *ARB* October 16,1993. In actuality, Sweden was doing a reasonably good job of integrating immigrants, compared to elsewhere in Europe. See Hjerm 2005.
130. *SvD* February 16, 1992.
131. Rojas, *DN* November 11, 1992.
132. Fonseca, *ARB* April 14, 1994.
133. Begler, Mossler, and Bergström, *DN* September 19, 1995.
134. *ARB* October 19, 1994.
135. Persson and Blomberg 1997: 98/16.
136. Ibid., pp. 1–2, 15–16.
137. Ibid., pp. 20–25.
138. This interpretation of shifts is not necessarily a conventional one. Many academic commentators have noted that immigrants were segregated into their own institutions for a long time and that *this* segregation was the cause of integration problems (see, e.g., Ålund and Schierup 1991). Part of the confusion comes from a lack of separation between *cultural* policy, which had long been targeted, and *economic* policy, which had not.
139. *DN* July 2, 1993.
140. Von Essen quoted in Kratz, *SvD* September 22, 1993.
141. E.g., *SvD* August 13, 1993.
142. *DN* November 11, 1992.
143. *ARB* February 13, 1996.
144. *DN* October 16, 1993.
145. Enander and Fogelbäck 1994.
146. Antman 1993. Perhaps also worth mentioning is Björkman 1993, a work not of academic but of poetic societal critique.
147. Rojas, *DN* November 11, 1992.
148. *SvD* October 19, 1994.
149. *ARB* May 15, 1994.
150. *ARB* June 13, 1992.
151. Gröning 1993, 14.

5. The End of Social-Democratic Hegemony

1. Östberg 2012.
2. "Alliance for Sweden" is generally shortened to Alliansen (The Alliance). The parties involved in the coalition include the Conservatives, Liberals, Center Party, and Christian Democrats.
3. Aylott and Bolin 2007. The exodus of SAP voters for the Greens and, indeed, the Greens' continued willingness to act, at times, as a "pivot" party rather than as SAP Jr. calls into question this interpretation, however.
4. *SvD* August 26, 2005.
5. Oscarsson and Holmberg 2008.

6. Agius 2007. Other sources, relying on Organisation for Economic Co-operation and Development (OECD) data, put the number at around 18% ("Swedish Oust Persson as Right Wins Poll," *Financial Times*, September 18, 2006).

7. *SvD* May 1, 2006.

8. *SvD* August 24, 2006.

9. Gustavsson 2012.

10. *SvD* September 14, 2006.

11. *SvD* September 14, 2006.

12. Lindbom 2008, 16–17.

13. Oscarsson and Holmberg 2009.

14. *SvD* November 15, 2006.

15. See *SvD* May 8, 2007; *SvD* May 9, 2007; *DN* June 22, 2007.

16. *SvD* October 21, 2006.

17. *SvD* December 2, 2008.

18. ROT stands for "Reparation, Ombyggnad, Tillbyggnad" (Repair, Renovation, Extension), and RUT for "Rengöring, Underhåll och Tvätt" (Cleaning, Maintenance, Laundry). The latter is intended, broadly, for any domestic services.

19. *SvD* July 30, 2010.

20. *NSD* November 16, 2010.

21. Interview on *P1 Radio* by Kaliber, February 11, 2012, http://sverigesradio.se /sida/ artikel.aspx?programid=1316&artikel=4946667. There is something in what Carlsson said, though clumsily expressed. Sweden does still have a relatively robust middle class. Nonetheless, the increase of inequality from bottom to top is likely to, eventually, threaten the middle class as well.

22. *SvD* May 15, 2013.

23. *DN* October 21, 2006.

24. See the interview with Andreas Borg in Wiklund 2006 for examples of framing neoliberalism as pragmatic problem solving.

25. *DN* October 21, 2006.

26. Karreth, Polk, and Allen 2012.

27. Lindbom 2008.

28. Marshall 1964.

29. *DN* March 26, 2006.

30. *DN* April 19, 2006.

31. *DN* April 20, 2006.

32. Pred 2000; Wigerfelt and Wigerfelt 2000; Lindström 2002; Lange and Westin 1993.

33. *DN* March 21, 2006.

34. Widfeldt 2008.

35. *SvD* December 10, 2006.

36. Rydgren 2002.

37. *SvD* September 21, 2006.

38. Kvist 2012.

39. *NSD* August 20, 2010.

40. Weibull, Oskarsson, and Bergström 2013.

41. Wennberg, quoted in *NSD* September 20, 2010.

42. *NSD* August 22, 2010. See also Mehlin 2010.

43. Aylott and Bolin (2007) predicted this in their analysis of the 2006 election.

44. See, e.g., *NSD* September 20, 2010.

45. The figures are from the Election Authority of Sweden (Valmyndigheten), http://www.val.se.

46. Spehar, Bucken-Knapp, and Hinnfors 2011.

47. *SvD* March 2, 2011.

48. Göransson 2011.

49. *SvD* January 26, 2012.

50. Svenska Riksdagen 2008/09: 37.

51. Svenska Riksdagen 2008/09: SfU3. This line of reasoning is a popular one in the academic study of European welfare states. See, e.g., Ekberg 2011.

52. Svenska Riksdagen 2008/09: SfU3.

53. *DN* March 13, 2013.

54. Ibid.

55. Ibid.

56. Nyamko 2006.

57. Mella and Palm 2012.

58. This scandal involved party members Erik Almqvist and Christian Westling, who left their posts, but not their party, shortly after the scandal. Kent Ekeroth was given a "time-out" for his involvement and rejoined his party in January 2013.

59. EU Migrant Integration Policy Index, http://www.mipex.eu/sweden.

60. Edling and Rydgren 2012; Semyonov and Glikman 2009; Rydgren 2004.

61. A sampling of recent governmental reports on integration shows this shift. See, e.g., Kamali et al. 2006, 79; Skans 2010, 88; Arbetsmarknadsdepartementet 2012, 69; Westerberg and Bohlin 2012, 74.

62. *SvD* May 13, 2013.

63. *SvD* April 13, 2013; *SvD* February 13, 2013; *SvD* May 1, 2013.

64. See, e.g., *SvD* September 1, 2014.

65. Ibid.

66. Schierup and Ålund 2011.

67. *SvD* August 5, 2014.

68. *DN* September 13, 2014.

69. Reinfeldt, quoted in *DN* August 16, 2014.

70. *DN* January 30, 2015.

71. Åkesson, quoted in *DN* September 14, 2014.

72. See, e.g., *DN* August 21, 2014; *SvD* September 9, 2014.

73. See, e.g., *DN* September 28, 2014.

74. See, e.g., *DN* January 10, 2015; *DN* January 30, 2015.

75. *DN* November 18, 2014.

76. *DN* December 11, 2014.

77. Ibid.

78. Karlsson and Sjöstedt 2015.

79. *DN* December 4, 2014.

80. *DN* May 5, 2015.
81. See, e.g., Aylott 2014.
82. Schmidt and Evans 2012.
83. Schall 2014.
84. Schierup and Ålund 2011.

Conclusions: Who Belongs in the Swedish People's Home?

1. Conversi 2007.
2. Wimmer 2002.
3. Cohen 1972.
4. Geertz 1998; Appadurai 1996.
5. In fact, it is perhaps in just this area of cultural hegemony and what that means for new members that the Nordic states are least alike. Both Norway and Denmark have far-right parties with histories of success dating back to the 1970s. Even on the welfare front, it may only be institutions—and not the cultures that support them—that look similar (see, e.g., Sejersted 2011; Åmark 2005).

6. With some notable exceptions, as discussed in the introduction to this book. Marcus Crepaz (2008) in his chapter on Sweden in *Trust beyond Borders* offers, perhaps, the best example. Even Crepaz's work, however, is inattentive to the ways that the trust-building welfare state was created in contexts of homogeneity.

REFERENCES

Archives

Arbetarrörelsens arkiv och bibliotek (The Labor Movement Archives and Library), Stockholm, SE. Contains material from Party Congresses listed in the references, as well as SAP Internal Party Minutes. Available at http://www.arbark.se.

Folkpartiets Riksorganisations arkiv (Archive of the Liberal National Organization), Stockholm, SE. Contains material from the personal archives of Liberal leaders and documents internal to the Liberal Party. Available at https://www.riksarkivet.se.

Palmearkivet. A digital archive of documents relating to Olof Palme. Available at http://www.olofpalme.org.

Riksarkivet (The National Archives). Contains documents relating to the functioning of the Swedish government, as well as documents of the Conservative and Liberal parties. Available at https://www.riksarkivet.se.

Svenska Riksdagen (The Swedish Parliament), Stockholm, SE. Transcripts of debates within the Swedish parliament. References list the year, session, and section of the debates. Available at http://www.riksdagen.se.

Newspapers

Arbetet (*ARB*, Social Democratic)
Dagens Nyheter (*DN*, Liberal)
Karlstads-Tidningen (Liberal)
Norrländska Social-Demokraten (*NSD*, Social Democratic)
Svenska Dagbladet (*SvD*, Conservative)

Books and Articles

Adamson, Walter L. 1980. *Hegemony and Revolution: Gramsci's Political and Cultural Theory*. Berkeley, CA: University of California Press.
Agius, Christine. 2007. "Sweden's 2006 Parliamentary Election and After: Contesting or Consolidating the Swedish Model?" *Parliamentary Affairs* 60 (4): 585–600.
Alesina, Alberto, and Edward Glaeser. 2004. *Fighting Poverty in the US and Europe: A World of Difference*. Oxford: Oxford University Press.
Ålund, Aleksandra, and Carl-Ulrik Schierup. 1991. *Paradoxes of Multiculturalism: Essays on Swedish Society*. Aldershot, UK: Avebury.
Åmark, Klas. 2005. *Hundra år av välfärdspolitik: Välfärdsstatens framväxt i Norge och Sverige*. Umeå, SE: Boréa.
Amenta, Edwin. 1998. *Bold Relief: Institutional Politics and the Origins of Modern American Social Policy*. Princeton, NJ: Princeton University Press.
Anderson, Benedict. 1983. *Imagined Communities: Reflections on the Origin and Spread of Nationalism*. London: Verso.
Andersson, Lars. 2000. *En jude är en jude är en jude: Representationer av juden i svensk skämtpress omkring, 1900–1930*. Lund, SE: Nordic Academic Press.
Antman, Peter, ed. 1993. *Systemskiftet: Fyra folkhemsdebatter*. Stockholm: Carlssons Förlag.
Appadurai, Arjun. 1996. *Modernity at Large: Cultural Dimensions of Globalization*. Minneapolis: University of Minnesota Press.
Appelqvist, Maria. 2000. "Flyktingmottagandet och den svenska välfärdsstaten under 1990-talet." In *Välfärdens förutsättningar: Arbetsmarknad, demografi och segregation*, edited by Johan Fritzell. Stockholm: Statens Offentliga Uttryck.
Arbetarrörelsens flyktinghjälp. Series F1, Arbetarrörelsens arkiv och bibliotek. Stockholm, SE.
Arbetsmarknadsdepartementet. 2012. *Med rätt att delta: Nyanlända kvinnor och anhöriginvandrare på arbetsmarknaden*. Stockholm: Statens Offentliga Utredningar.
Åsard, Erik, and W. Lance Bennett. 1997. *Democracy and the Marketplace of Ideas: Communication and Government in Sweden and the United States*. Cambridge: Cambridge University Press.
Aylott, Nicholas. 2014. "Why Did Sweden's New Government Call an Extraordinary Election?" https://maktochpolitik.wordpress.com/2014/12/18/why-did-swedens-new-government-call-an-extraordinary-election.

Aylott, Nicholas, and Niklas Bolin. 2007. "Towards a Two-Party System? The Swedish Parliamentary Election of September 2006." *West European Politics* 30 (3): 621–633.

Baldwin, Peter. 1990. *The Politics of Social Solidarity: Class Bases of the Welfare State.* Cambridge: Cambridge University Press.

Bask, Miia. 2005. "Welfare Problems and Social Exclusion among Immigrants in Sweden." *European Sociological Review* 21 (1): 73–89.

Behrenz, Lars, Mats Hammarstedt, and Jonas Månsson. 2007. "Second-Generation Immigrants in the Swedish Labour Market." *International Review of Applied Economics* 21 (1): 157–174.

Behtoui, Alireza, and Anders Neergaard. 2010. "Social Capital and Wage Disadvantages among Immigrant Workers." *Work, Employment and Society* 24 (4): 761–779.

Bengtson, Tommy, and Kirk Scott. 2005. "Why Is Sweden's Population Aging? What Are We Able and Unable to Do about It?" *Sociologisk Forskning* (3): 3–12.

Bennich-Björkman, Li, Per Adman, Per Strömblad, and Branka Likic-Brboric. 2007. "Citizens at Heart? Political Integration in Comparative Perspective." *Statsvetenskaplig Tidskrift* 109 (2): 123–127.

Berggren, Henrik, and Lars Trägårdh. 2006. *Är Svensken Människa? Gemenskap och Oberoende in den Moderna Sverige.* Stockholm: Norstedt.

Bergh, Andreas, and Gissur Ó. Erlingsson. 2009. "Liberalization without Retrenchment: Understanding the Consensus on Swedish Welfare State Reforms." *Scandinavian Political Studies* 32 (1): 71–93.

Bergmark, Åke, and Olaf Bäckman. 2004. "Stuck with Welfare? Long-Term Social Assistance Recipiency in Sweden." *European Sociological Review* 20 (5): 425–443.

Bergmark, Åke, Mats Thorslund, and Elisabet Lindberg. 2002. "Beyond Benevolence: Solidarity and Welfare State Transition in Sweden." *International Journal of Social Welfare* 9 (4): 238–249.

Berman, Sheri. 1998. "Ideas, Norms, and Culture in Political Analysis." *Comparative Politics* 33 (2): 231–250.

———. 2006. *The Primacy of Politics: Social Democracy and the Making of Europe's Twentieth Century.* New York: Cambridge University Press.

Billig, Michael. 1995. *Banal Nationalism.* Thousand Oaks, CA: Sage.

Björkman, Peter. 1993. *Det döende folkhemmet.* Haparanda, SE: Flowers of Bellis Are Still Alive.

Blomkvist, Håkan. 2006. *Nation, ras och civilisation i svensk arbetarrörelse före nazismen.* Stockholm: Carlssons Förlag.

Bosniak, Linda. 2000. "Citizenship Denationalized." *Indiana Journal of Global Legal Studies* 7: 447–509.

Brandal, Nik, Øyvind Bratberg, and Dag Einer Thorsen. 2013. *The Nordic Model of Social Democracy.* London: Palgrave Macmillan.

Brett, Judith. 1997. "John Howard, Pauline Hanson and the Politics of Grievance." In *The Resurgence of Racism*, edited by Geoffrey Gray and Christine Winter. Melbourne: Monash Publications in History.

Broberg, Gunnar, and Mattias Tydén. 1996. "Eugenics in Sweden: Efficient Care." In *Eugenics and the Welfare State: Sterilization Policy in Denmark, Sweden, Norway and Finland*, edited by Gunnar Broberg and Nils Roll-Hansen. East Lansing: Michigan State University Press.

Brubaker, Rogers. 1992. *Citizenship and Nationhood in Germany and France*. Cambridge, MA: Harvard University Press.

———. 2004. "The Manichean Myth: Rethinking the Distinction between 'Civic' and 'Ethnic' Nationalism." In *Nation and National Identity: The European Experience in Perspective*, edited by Hanspeter Kriesi, Klaus Armingeon, Hannes Siegrist, and Andreas Wimmer. West Lafayette, IN: Purdue University Press.

Byrne, David. 1999. *Social Exclusion*. Buckingham, UK: Open University Press.

Byström, Mikael. 2006. *En bröder, gäst och parasit: Uppfattningar och föreställningar om utlänningar, flyktingar och flyktingpolitik i svensk offentlig debatt, 1942–1947*. Stockholm: Almqvist & Wiksell International.

Carlsson, Carl. 2004. *Medborgarskap och diskriminering: Östjudar och andra invandrare i Sverige, 1860–1920*. Uppsala: Studia Historica Upsaliensia.

Castles, Francis G. 2001. "On the Political Economy of Recent Public Sector Development." *Journal of European Social Policy* 11 (3): 195–211.

Castles, Stephen, and Mark Miller. 2009. *The Age of Migration: International Population Movements in the Modern World*. New York: Palgrave Macmillan.

Childs, Marquis. 1936. *Sweden: The Middle Way*. London: Heinemann.

Cohen, Stanley. 1972. *Folk Devils and Moral Panics: The Creation of the Mods and Rockers*. London: MacGibbon & Kee.

Connor, Walker. 1993. "Beyond Reason: The Nature of the Ethnonational Bond." *Ethnic and Racial Studies* 1 (4): 377–400.

Conversi, Daniele. 2007. "Homogenisation, Nationalism, and War: Should We Still Read Ernest Gellner?" *Nations and Nationalism* 13 (3): 371–394.

Crepaz, Markus. 2008. *Trust beyond Borders: Immigration, the Welfare State, and Identity in Modern Societies*. Ann Arbor: University of Michigan Press.

Dahlström, Carl. 2007. "Rhetorical Objectives and Program Efficiency in Swedish Policy about Immigrants." *Journal of Public Policy* 27 (3): 319–340.

Durkheim, Emile. 1983. *Professional Ethics and Civic Morals*, edited by Bryan S. Turner. London: Routledge.

Edgerton, David L., Björn Fryklund, and Tomas Peterson. 1994. "Systemvalet." In *Det politiska missnöjets Sverige: Statsvetare och sociologer ser på valet 1991*, edited by Bo Bjurulf and Björn Fryklund. Lund, SE: Lund University Press.

Edling, Christofer, and Jens Rydgren. 2012. "Neighborhood and Friendship Composition in Adolescence." *SAGE Open* 2: 1–10.

Eger, Maureen A. 2010. "Even in Sweden: The Effect of Immigration on Support for Welfare State Spending." *European Sociological Review* 26 (2): 203–221.

Ekberg, Jan. 1990. *Invandrare på Arbetsmarknaden: Rapporer från Högskolan i Växjö*. Växjö, SE: CAPO.

———. 2011. "Will Future Immigration to Sweden Make It Easier to Finance the Welfare System?" *European Journal of Population/Revue Europeenne de Demographie* 27 (1): 103–124.

Ekholm, Curt. 1984. *Balt- och tyskutlämningen, 1945–1946: Omständigheter kring interneringen i läger i Sverige och utlämningen till Sovjetunionen av f. d. tyska krigsdeltagare.* Stockholm: Almqvist & Wiksell International.

Enander, Crister, and Jan Fogelbäck. 1994. *Uppbrottstider: En brevväxling om det rämnande folkhemmet.* Klavreström, SE: Hägglunds Förlag.

Esping-Anderson, Gösta. 1985. *Politics against Markets: The Social Democratic Road to Power.* Princeton, NJ: Princeton University Press.

———. 1990. *The Three Worlds of Welfare Capitalism.* Princeton, NJ: Princeton University Press.

Evans, Bryan, and Ingo Schmidt, eds. 2012. *Social Democracy after the Cold War.* Athabasca, CAN: Athabasca University Press.

Faist, Thomas. 1996. "Immigration, Integration, and the Welfare State." In *The Challenge of Diversity Integration and Pluralism in Societies of Immigration,* edited by Rainer Bauböck, Agnes Heller, and Aristide R. Zolberg. Aldershot, UK: Avebury.

Fox, Cybelle. 2012. *Three Worlds of Relief: Race, Immigration and the American Welfare State from the Progressive Era to the New Deal.* Princeton, NJ: Princeton University Press.

Freeman, Gary P. 1986. "Migration and the Political Economy of the Welfare State." *Annals of the American Academy of Political and Social Science* 485: 51–63.

———. 1992. "Migration Policy and Politics in the Receiving States." *International Migration Review* 26: 1144–1167.

Fryklund, Björn. 1994. "Inledning." In *Det politiska missnöjets Sverige: Statsvetare och sociologer ser på valet 1991,* edited by Bo Bjurulf and Björn Fryklund. Lund, SE: Lund University Press.

Geertz, Clifford. 1998. "The World in Pieces: Culture and Politics at the End of the Century." *Focaal: Tijdschrift voor Antropologie* 32: 91–117.

Gilens, Martin. 1995. *Why Americans Hate Welfare: Race, Media and the Politics of Antipoverty Policy.* Chicago: University of Chicago Press.

Glover, Nikolas. 2009. "Imaging Community: Sweden in 'Cultural Propaganda' Then and Now." *Scandinavian Journal of History* 34 (3): 246–263.

Goldberg, Chad Alan. 2007. *Citizens and Paupers: Relief, Rights, and Race, from the Freedmen's Bureau to Workfare.* Chicago: University of Chicago Press.

Göransson, Ingemar E. L. 2011. *Arbetarrörelsens kris: Mellan reformism och marknadsliberalism.* Linghem, SE: Ord och Kulturs Förlag.

Goul Andersen, Jörgen, and Tor Björklund. 2000. "Radical Right-Wing Populism in Scandinavia: From Tax Revolt to Neo-liberalism and Xenophobia." In *The Politics of the Extreme Right: From the Margin to the Mainstream,* edited by Paul Hainsworth. London: Pinter.

Gramsci, Antonio. 1971. *Selections from the Prison Notebooks.* Edited by Quintin Hoare and Geoffrey Nowell-Smith. New York: International.

Greenfeld, Liah. 1992. *Nationalism: Five Roads to Modernity.* Cambridge: Harvard University Press.

Green-Pedersen, Christoffer, and Markus Haverland. 2002. "The New Politics and Scholarship of the Welfare State: A Review Essay." *Journal of European Social Policy* 12 (1): 43–51.

Gröning, Lotta. 1993. "En ideologisk debattbok om socialdemokratin." In *I mökret blir alla katter grå*, by Lotta Gröning et al. Borås, SE: Tidens Förlag.

Gunnarsson, Gunnar. 1971. *Socialdemokratiskt idearv: Utopism, Marxism, Socialism*. Stockholm: Carlssons Förlag.

Gustavsson, Jakob. 2012. *Rationalitetens tyranni: En kritisk textanalys av politiska uttalanden i offentligheten gällande sjukförsäkringen*. Kristianstad, SE: Högskolan Kristianstads Tryck.

Håkansson, Anders. 1994. "Det socialdemokratiska valnederlaget och utvecklingen mot 'dealignment' i Sverige." In *Det politiska missnöjets Sverige: Statsvetare och sociologer ser på valet 1991*, edited by Bo Bjurulf and Björn Fryklund. Lund, SE: Lund University Press.

——. 1987. "Samband mellan ekonomisk och politisk utveckling i Sverige: En forskningsöversikt." *Statsvetenskaplig Tidskrift* 90 (1): 61–79.

Hammar, Tomas. 1991. "Managing International Migration: Past, Present and Future Trends." *Regional Development Dialogue* 12: 183–191.

——. 1985. *Sverige åt svenskarna: Invandringspolitik, utlänningskontroll och asylrätt, 1900–1932*. Stockholm: Almqvist & Wiksell International.

Hansen, Erik Jørgen, ed. 1993. *Welfare Trends in the Scandinavian Countries*. New York: M. E. Sharpe.

Hansen, Jorgen, and Magnus Lofstrom. 2009. "The Dynamics of Immigrant Welfare and Labor Market Behavior." *Journal of Population Economics* 22 (4): 941–970.

Hansen, Lars-Erik. 2001. *Jämlikhet och valfrihet: En studie av den svenska invandrarpolitikens framväxt*. Stockholm: Almqvist & Wiksell International.

Heclo, Hugh. 1974. *Modern Social Politics in Britain and Sweden: From Relief to Income Maintenance*. New Haven, CT: Yale University Press.

Heilbroner, Robert L., and William S. Milberg. 1995. *The Crisis of Vision in Modern Economic Thought*. Cambridge: Cambridge University Press.

Hentilä, Seppo. 1978. "The Origins of the 'Folkhem' Ideology in Swedish Social Democracy." *Scandinavian Journal of History* 3: 323–345.

Herder, Johann Gottfried. 2002. *Herder: Philosophical Writings*. Edited and translated by Michael N. Forster. Cambridge: Cambridge University Press, 2002.

Hernes, Helga M. 1988. "Scandinavian Citizenship." *Acta Sociologica* 31: 199–215.

Hjerm, Mikael. 2005. "Integration into the Social Democratic Welfare State." *Social Indicators Research* 70 (2): 117–138.

Hicks, Alexander. 1999. *Social Democracy and Welfare Capitalism*. Ithaca, NY: Cornell University Press.

Hirdman, Yvonne. 1998. *Att lägga livet till rätta: Studier i svensk folkhemspolitik*. Stockholm: Carlssons Förlag.

——. 1992. *Den socialistiska hemmafrun och andra kvinnohistorier*. Stockholm: Carlssons Förlag.

Hobsbawm, Eric J. 1983. Introduction to *The Invention of Tradition*, edited by Eric J. Hobsbawm and Terrence Ranger. Cambridge: Cambridge University Press.

Holmberg, Sören, and Mikael Gilljam. 1987. *Väljare och val i Sverige*. Stockholm: Bonniers.

Huber, Evelyn, and John D. Stephens. 2001. *Development and Crises of the Welfare State: Parties and Policies in Global Markets*. Chicago: University of Chicago Press.

Hultén, Gunilla. 2006. *Främmande sidor: Främlingskap och nationell gemenskap i fyra svenska dagstidningar efter 1945*. Valdemarsvik, SE: Akademitryck.

Hutchinson, John. (1987) 1994. "The Dynamics of Cultural Nationalism." In *Nationalism: A Reader*, edited by John Hutchinson and Anthony D. Smith. London: Routledge.

Ignatieff, Michael. 1993. *Blood and Belonging: Journeys into the New Nationalism*. Toronto: Viking.

Kahl, Sigrun. 2005. "The Religious Roots of Modern Poverty Policy: Catholic, Lutheran and Reformed Protestant Traditions Compared." *European Journal of Sociology* 46 (1): 91–126.

Kamali, Masoud, Andrián Groglopo, Marcus Lundgren, and Simon Andersson. 2006. *Integrationens svarta bok: Jämlikhet och social sammanhålling*. Stockholm: Statens Offentliga Utredningar.

Karlsson, Mattias, and Oscar Sjöstedt. 2015. "Budgetpresentation Sverigedemokraterna," https://www.youtube.com/watch?v=qGOMN9OznZw.

Karreth, Johannes, Jonathan T. Polk, and Cristopher S. Allen. 2012. "Catch All or Catch and Release? The Electoral Consequences of Social Democratic Parties' March to the Middle in Western Europe." *Comparative Political Studies* 46 (7): 791–822.

Katzenstein, Peter. 1985. *Small States in World Markets: Industrial Policy in Europe*. Ithaca, NY: Cornell University Press.

Kesler, Christel. 2010. "Immigrant Wage Disadvantage in Sweden and the United Kingdom: Wage Structure and Barriers to Opportunity." *International Migration Review* 44 (3): 560–592.

Kildal, Nanna, and Stein Kuhnle, eds. 2005. *Normative Foundations of the Welfare State: The Nordic Experience*. New York: Routledge.

Kitschelt, Herbert A. 2001. "Partisan Competition and Welfare State Retrenchment: When Do Politicians Choose Unpopular Policies?" In *The New Politics of the Welfare State*, edited by Paul Pierson. Oxford: Oxford University Press.

Kitschelt, Herbert A., and Anthony J. McGann. 1995. *The Radical Right in Western Europe: A Comparative Analysis*. Ann Arbor: University of Michigan Press.

Kjaer, Peter, and Ove K. Pedersen. 2001. "Translating Liberalization: Neoliberalism in the Danish Negotiated Economy." In *The Rise of Neoliberalism and Institutional Analysis*, edited by John L. Campbell and Ove K. Pedersen. Princeton, NJ: Princeton University Press.

Kjellberg, Anders. 2000. "Facklig organisering och arbetsmarknad: marginalisering av ungdomar och invandrare?" In *Har den svenska modellen överlevt krisen? Utvecklingstendenser i arbetslivet inför 2000-talet*, edited by Stig Tegle. Stockholm: Arbetslivsinstitutet.

Klinth, Roger. 2005. "Pappaledighet som jämställdhetsprojekt: Om den svenska pappaledighetens politiska historia." In *Forskarrapporter till Jämställdhetspolitiska*. Stockholm: Statens Offentliga Utredningen.

Knocke, Wuokko. 1981. *Invandrare möter facket: Betydelse av hemlandsbakgrund och hemvist i arbetslivet; Forskningslägesrapport kompletterad med intervjuer*. Stockholm: Arbetslivscentrum.

Koblik, Steven. 1987. *"Om vi teg, skulle stenarna ropa": Sverige och judeproblemet, 1933–1945*. Stockholm: Norstedt.

Kohn, Hans. 1948. *The Idea of Nationalism: A Study in Its Origins and Background.* New York: Macmillan.

Korpi, Walter. 1983. *The Democratic Class Struggle.* London: Routledge & Kegan Paul.

———. 1970. *Varför strejkar arbetarna?* Stockholm: Tidens Förlag.

———. 1993. "Ville väljarna ha systemskifte 1991?" In *I mörkret blir alla katter grå*, by Lotta Gröning et al. Borås, SE: Tidens Förlag.

———. 2003. "Welfare-State Regress in Western Europe: Politics, Institutions, Globalization, and Europeanization." *Annual Review of Sociology* 29: 589–609.

Korpi, Walter, and Joakim Palme. 2003. "New Politics and Class Politics in the Context of Austerity and Globalization: Welfare State Regress in 18 Countries, 1975–95." *American Political Science Review* 97 (3): 425–446.

Korsgaard, Ove. 2002. "A European Demos? The Nordic Adult Education Tradition—*folkeoplysning*—Faces a Challenge." *Comparative Education* 38 (1): 7–16.

Kreis, Georg. 2000. "Swiss Refugee Policy, 1933–45." In *Switzerland and the Second World War*, edited by Georg Kreis. Portland, OR: Frank Cass.

Kristdemokraterna. 1993. *Principprogram.* Stockholm: Kristdemokraterna.

Kuhnle, Stein, ed. 2000. *Survival of the European Welfare State.* London: Routledge.

Kushner, Tony, and Katharine Knox. 1999. *Refugees in an Age of Genocide: Global, National and Local Perspectives during the Twentieth Century.* London: Frank Cass.

Kvist, Karin. 2002. "A Study of Antisemitic Attitudes with Sweden's Wartime Utlänningsbyrå." In *Bystanders to the Holocaust: A Re-Evaluation*, edited by David Cesarani and Paul A. Levine. New York: Routledge.

Kvist, Jon. 2012. "Retrenchment or Social Investments? The Great Recession, the European Union and Policies of Austerity in Europe." Working Paper. Center for Welfare State Research, Odense, DK.

Kymlicka, Will. 1995. *Multicultural Citizenship: A Liberal Theory of Minority Rights.* Oxford: Oxford University Press.

Laitin, David D. 1986. *Hegemony and Culture: Politics and Religious Change among the Yoruba.* Chicago: University of Chicago Press.

Lamont, Michele, and Virag Molnar. 2002. "The Study of Boundaries in the Social Sciences." *Annual Review of Sociology* 28: 167–195.

Lange, Anders, and Charles Westin. 1993. *Förhållningssätt till Invandring och Invandrare 1993.* Stockholm: Centrum för Invandringsforskning.

Levine, Paul A. 1996. *From Indifference to Activism: Swedish Diplomacy and the Holocaust, 1938–1944.* Uppsala: Studia Historica Upsaliensis.

Lin, Ka, and Eero Carroll. 2006. "State Institutions, Political Power and Social Policy Choices: Reconstructing the Origins of Nordic Models of Social Policy." *European Journal of Political Research* 45: 345–367.

Lindbeck, Assar, and Niels Thygesen. 1993. *Nya villkor för ekonomi och politik: Ekonomikommissionens förslag: betänkande.* Stockholm: Statens Offentliga Utredning.

Lindbom, Anders. 2008. "The Swedish Conservative Party and the Welfare State: Institutional Change and Adapting Preferences." *Government and Opposition* 43 (4): 539–560.

Lindqvist, Beatrix. 1991. *Drömmar om vardag i exil: Om chilenska flyktingars kulturella strategier.* Stockholm: Carlssons Förlag.

Lindström, Anders. 2002. *Inte har dom gjort mig nåt: En studie av ungdomars attityder till invandrare och flyktingar i två mindre svenska lokalsamhällen*. Umeå, SE: Umeå Tryckeri.

Löfgren Orvar. 1993. "Materializing the Nation in Sweden and America." *Ethnos: Journal of Anthropology* 58 (3–4): 161–196.

——. 1989. "The Nationalization of Culture." *Ethnologia Europaea* 19: 5–23.

Lomfors, Ingrid. 2005. *Blind fläck: Minne och glömska kring svenska Röda korsets hjälpinsats i Nazityskland 1945*. Stockholm: Atlantis.

Lundberg, Urban, and Klas Åmark. 2001. "Social Rights and Social Security: The Swedish Welfare State, 1900–2000." *Scandinavian Journal of History* 26 (3): 157–176.

Lundborg, Herman, and Frans Josua Linders, eds. 1926. *The Racial Characters of the Swedish Nation*. Uppsala: Almqvist & Wiksell.

Mann, Michael. 2001. "Democracy and Ethnic War." In *Democracy, Liberalism and War: Rethinking the Democratic Peace Debate*, edited by Tarak Barkawi and Mark Laffey. Boulder, CO: Lynne Riener.

Marshall, Thomas Humphrey. 1964. "Citizenship and Social Class." In *Class, Citizenship and Social Development*. Garden City, NY: Doubleday.

Mella, Orlando, and Irving Palm. 2012. *Mångfaldsbarometern 2012*. Uppsala: Uppsala University.

Mehlin, Lena. 2010. "Sahlin—En Sjunkbomb." *Aftonbladet*, April 4.

Migrant Integration Policy Index. 2011. Sweden: MIPEX. Accessed June 20, 2011. http://integrationindex.eu/sweden.

Miles, Matthew B., and A. Michael Huberman. 1994. *Qualitative Data Analysis: An Expanded Sourcebook*. Thousand Oaks, CA: Sage.

Moderaterna. 1993. *Moderaternas handlingsprogram 1993*. Stockholm: Moderata Samlingspartiet.

Montesino, Norma. 2010. "Social Integration and New Realities in the Swedish Welfare Society." *Social Work and Society* 8 (1): 94–103.

Mood, Carina. 2011. "Lagging Behind in Good Times: Immigrants and the Increased Dependence on Social Assistance in Sweden." *International Journal of Social Welfare* 20 (1): 55–65.

Myrdal, Alva. 1968–1971. "Jämlikhet och valfrihet." In *Handlingar från Alva Myrdals verksamhet i jämlikhetsfrågor, 1968–1971*. Stockholm: Arbetarrörelsens arkiv och bibliotek, 4/1/14/007.

Myrdal, Gunnar. 1960. *Beyond the Welfare State*. New Haven, CT: Yale University Press.

Naumann, Ingela. 2007. "From the 'Women's Question' to 'New Social Risks': One Hundred Years of Social Policy Discourse on the Reconciliation of Motherhood and Work." Paper presented at the Fifth ESPAnet Conference, Vienna, Austria, September 20–22.

Nettelbrandt, Cecilia. 1969. In "PM om folkpartiet och skattetrycket." Stockholm: Arbetarrörelsens arkiv och bibliotek, 1889/F/11/A/39.

Nord, Lars. 2001. *Vår Tids Ledare: En studie av den Svenska Dagspressens Politiska Opinionsbildning*. Stockholm: Carlssons Förlag.

Nordlund, Sven. 1999. "'The War Is Over—Now You Can Go Home!' Jewish Refugees and the Swedish Labour Market in the Shadow of the Holocaust." *Holocaust Studies: A Journal of Culture and History* 9: 171–198.

Nyakamo, Sabuni. 2006. "Kontrollera underlivet på alla högstadieflickor." *Expressen*, July 17.

O'Brien, Rourke L. 2015. "Disability and the Worlds of Welfare Capitalism." *Sociological Science* 2: 1–19.

Odmalm, Pontus. 2011. "Political Parties and 'the Immigration Issue': Issue ownership in Swedish Parliamentary Elections, 1991–2010." *West European Politics* 34 (5): 1070–1091.

Offe, Claus. 1984. "Competitive Party Democracy and the Keynesian Welfare State." In *Contradictions of the Welfare State*, edited by John Keane. Cambridge: MIT Press.

———. 1996. "Democracy against the Welfare State?" In *Modernity and the State: East, West*. Cambridge, MA: MIT Press.

Olson, Kevin. 2006. *Reflexive Democracy: Political Equality and the Welfare State*. Cambridge, MA: MIT Press.

Orum, Anthony M., Joe R. Feagin, and Gideon Sjoberg. 1991. "The Nature of the Case Study." In *A Case for the Case Study*, edited by Joe R. Feagin, Anthony M. Orum, and Gideon Sjoberg. Chapel Hill: University of North Carolina Press.

Oscarsson, Henrik, and Sören Holmberg. 2009. "Därför vann Alliansen: En sammanfattning av några resultat från valundersökning 2006." Stockholm: Statistiska Centralbyrå.

———. 2008. *Regeringsskifte: Väljarna och valet 2006*. Stockholm: Norsteds Juridik.

Östberg, Kjell. 2012. "Swedish Social Democracy after the Cold War: What Happened to the Movement?" In *Social Democracy after the Cold War*, edited by Bryan Evans and Ingo Schmidt. Edmonton, CAN: Athabasca University Press.

Palme, Joakim, and Irene Wennemo. 1998. *Swedish Social Security in the 1990s: Reform and Retrenchment*. Stockholm: Printing Works of the Cabinet Office and the Ministers.

Palmer, Edward. 2000. "The Swedish Pension Reform Model: Framework and Issues." Social Protection Discussion Paper No. SP 0012. World Bank, Washington, DC.

Persson, Göran, and Leif Blomberg. 1997. *Sverige, framtiden och mångfalden: Från invandrarpolitik till integrationspolitik*. Stockholm: Statens Offentliga Utredningen. Available at http://www.regeringen.se/rattsdokument/proposition/1999/09/prop.-19979816.

Petersson, Olof. 1991. "Democracy and Power in Sweden." *Scandinavian Political Studies* 14 (2): 173–191.

Pierson, Paul. 1994. *Dismantling the Welfare State? Reagan, Thatcher, and the Politics of Retrenchment*. Cambridge: Cambridge University Press.

———. 1996. "The New Politics of the Welfare State." *World Politics* 48 (2): 143–179.

———. 2001. *The New Politics of the Welfare State*. New York: Oxford University Press.

Polanyi, Karl. 2001. *The Great Transformation: The Political and Economic Origins of Our Time*. Boston: Beacon Press.

Pred, Allan. 2000. *Even in Sweden: Racisms, Racialized Spaces, and the Popular Geographical Imagination*. Los Angeles: University of California Press.

Putnam, Robert D. 2007. "E Pluribus Unum: Diversity and Community in the Twenty-first Century: The 2006 Johan Skytte Prize Lecture." *Scandinavian Political Studies* 30 (2): 137–174.

Quadagno, Jill. 1994. *The Color of Welfare: How Racism Undermined the War on Poverty.* New York: Oxford University Press.

———. 1987. "Theories of the Welfare State." *Annual Review of Sociology* 13: 109–128.

Renan, Ernest. (1882) 1994. "What Is a Nation?" In *Nationalism: A Reader,* edited by John Hutchinson and Anthony D. Smith. London: Routledge.

Riffe, Daniel, and Alan Freitag. 1997. "A Content Analysis of Content Analyses: Twenty-Five Years of Journalism Quarterly." *Journalism and Mass Communication Quarterly* 74 (3): 515–524.

Riks-SOM. 1991–1995. *Nationella Samhälle Opinion Medier 1991–1995.* Gothenburg, SE: SOM-Institutet.

———. 1993. *Nationella Samhälle Opinion Medier 1993.* Gothenburg, SE: SOM-Institutet.

Riley, Dylan. 2010. *The Civic Foundations of Fascism in Europe: Italy, Spain, and Romania, 1870–1945.* Baltimore: Johns Hopkins University Press.

Román, Henrik. 1994. *En invandrarpolitisk oppositionell: Debattören David Schwarz syn på svensk invandrarpolitik åren, 1964–1993.* Uppsala: Uppsala Multiethnic Papers.

Rothstein, Bo. 1998. *The Social Democratic State: The Swedish Model and the Bureaucratic Problem of Social Reforms.* Pittsburgh, PA: University of Pittsburgh Press.

Ruin, Olaf. 1990. *Tage Erlander: Serving the Welfare State, 1946–1969.* Pittsburgh, PA: University of Pittsburgh Press.

Rydgren, Jens. 2004. "Mechanisms of Exclusion: Ethnic Discrimination in the Swedish Labour Market." *Journal of Ethnic and Migration Studies* 30 (4): 697–716.

———. 2002. "Radical-Right Populism in Sweden: Still a Failure, but for How Long?" *Scandinavian Political Studies* 25: 27–56.

Ryner, Magnus. 2000. "Transformation and Migration." In *Immigration and Welfare: Challenging the Borders of the Welfare State,* edited by Michael Bommes and Andrew Geddes. London: Routledge.

Salminen, Esko, and Jo Campling. 1999. *The Silenced Media: The Propaganda War between Russia and the West in Northern Europe.* New York: St. Martin's Press.

Sassoon, Anne S. 2000. *Gramsci and Contemporary Politics: Beyond Pessimism of the Intellect.* London: Routledge.

Schall, Carly Elizabeth. 2014. "Multicultural Iteration: Swedish National Day as Multiculturalism-in-Practice." *Nations and Nationalism* 20 (2): 355–375.

———. 2012. "(Social) Democracy in the Blood? Ethnic and Civic Idioms of Swedish Nationhood and the Consolidation of Social Democratic Power, 1928–1932." *Journal of Historical Sociology* 25 (3): 440–474.

Schierup, Carl-Ulrik, and Aleksandra Ålund. 2011. "The End of Swedish Exceptionalism? Citizenship, Neoliberalism and the Politics of Exclusion." *Race and Class* 53 (1): 45–64.

Schmidt, Ingo, and Bryan Evans. 2012. "The End of Social Democracy." In *Social Democracy after the Cold War,* edited by Bryan Evans and Ingo Schmidt. Athabasca, CAN: Athabasca University Press.

Schoenfeld, Eugen, and Stjepan G. Meštrović. 1989. "Durkheim's Concept of Justice and Its Relationship to Social Solidarity." *Sociology of Religion* 50 (2): 111–127.

Schumpeter, Joseph A. 2010. *Capitalism, Socialism and Democracy*. New York: Rout-ledge.

Schwarz, David. 1971. *Svensk invandrar- och minoritespolitik, 1945–1968*. Stockholm: Prisma.

Scruggs, Lyle. 2006. Generosity Index. Welfare State Entitlements Data Set: A Com-parative Institutional Analysis of Eighteen Welfare States, Version 1.2. Available at http://www.sp.uconn.edu/~scruggs/#links.

Sears, David O., and Jack Citrin. 1985. *Tax Revolt: Something for Nothing in California*. Enlarged edition. Cambridge, MA: Harvard University Press.

Sears, David O., and Tom Jessor. 1996. "Whites' Racial Policy Attitudes: The Role of White Racism." *Social Science Quarterly* 77 (4): 751–759.

Sejersted, Francis. 2011. *The Age of Social Democracy: Norway and Sweden in the Twen-tieth Century*. Princeton, NJ: Princeton University Press.

Semyonov, Moshe, and Anya Glikman. 2009. "Ethnic Residential Segregation, Social Contacts, and Anti-minority Attitudes in European Societies." *European Sociological Review* 25 (6): 693–708.

Sewell, William H., Jr. 1996. "Three Temporalities: Toward an Eventful Sociology." In *The Historic Turn in the Human Sciences*, edited by Terrence J. McDonald. Ann Arbor: University of Michigan Press.

———. 1980. *Work and Revolution in France: The Language of Labor from the Old Regime to 1848*. Cambridge: Cambridge University Press.

Shalev, Michael. 1983. "The Social Democratic Model and Beyond: Two Generations of Comparative Research on the Welfare State." *Comparative Social Research* 6: 315–351.

Skans, Oskar Nordström. 2010. *Vägen till arbete: Arbetsmarknadspolitik, utbildning och arbetsmarknadsintegration*. Stockholm: Statens Offentliga Utredningar.

Skocpol, Theda. 1985a. "Bringing the State Back In: Strategies of Analysis in Current Research." In *Bringing the State Back In*, edited by Peter Evans, Dietrich Rueschmeyer, and Theda Skocpol. Cambridge: Cambridge University Press.

———. 1985b. "Cultural Idioms and Political Ideologies in the Revolutionary Recon-struction of State Power: A Rejoinder to Sewell." *Journal of Modern History* 57: 86–96.

Smith, Anthony D. 1986. *The Ethnic Origins of Nation*. Oxford, UK: Blackwell.

———. 2001. *Nationalism: Theory, Ideology, History*. Cambridge, UK: Polity.

Smith, Rogers. 2003. *Stories of Peoplehood: The Politics and Morals of Political Member-ship*. Cambridge: Cambridge University Press.

Social Democratic Party (SAP). 1946. Internal Party Minutes. Stockholm: Arbetar-rörelsens arkiv och bibliotek, SE/ARAB/auk/1140/1946.

———. 1969. Internal Party Minutes. Stockholm: Arbetarrörelsens arkiv och bibliotek, SE/ARAB/auk/1140/1969.

———. 1971. Low-Income Committee. "Handlingar från utredning av låginkomst-frågorna ur facklig synpunkter." Stockholm: Arbetarrörelsens arkiv och bibliotek, 189/F/11/A/37.

———. 1928. *Partipolitiska Program*. Stockholm: Arbetarrörelsens arkiv och bibliotek, October 10.

———. 1972. Party Congress. "Invandrarfrågor, Motionerna nr 1 1-1 9." Stockholm: Ar-betarrörelsens arkiv och bibliotek, 2599/1/758/1972.

Social Democratic Party and Landsorganisation (SAP-LO). Committee on Equality. 1972. *Jämlikhet: Allas deltagande i arbetsliv och politik.* Stockholm: Prisma.

———. 1969. *Jämlikhet: Första rapport från SAP-LOs arbetsgrupp för jämlikhetsfrågor.* Stockholm: Prisma.

Spehar, Andrea, Gregg Bucken-Knapp, and Jonas Hinnfors. 2013. "Ideology and Entry Policy: Why Non-Socialist Parties in Sweden Support Open Door Migration Policies." In *The Politics of Migration: Citizenship, Inclusion and Discourse in Europe,* edited by Umut Korkut, Gregg Bucken-Knapp, Aidan McGarry, Jonas Hinnfors, and Helen Drake. New York: Palgrave-MacMillan.

Spektorowski, Alberto. 2004. "The Eugenic Temptation in Socialism: Sweden, Germany and the Soviet Union." *Comparative Studies in Society and History* 46 (1): 84–106.

Spektorowski, Alberto, and Elisabet Mizrachi. 2004. "Eugenics and the Welfare State in Sweden: The Politics of Social Margins and the Idea of a Productive Society." *Journal of Contemporary History* 39 (3): 333–352.

Stråth, Bo. 2004. "Nordic Modernity: Origins, Trajectories and Prospects." *Thesis Eleven* 77: 5–23.

———. 2005. "The Normative Foundations of the Scandinavian Welfare States in Historical Perspective." In *Normative Foundations of the Welfare State: The Nordic Experience,* edited by Nanna Kildal and Stein Kuhnle. New York: Routledge.

———. 1994. "The Swedish Path to National Identity in the Nineteenth Century." In *Nordic Paths to National Identity in the Nineteenth Century.* Oslo: The Research Council of Norway.

Sutherland, Claire. 2005. "Nation-building through Discourse Theory." *Nations and Nationalism* 11 (2): 185–202.

Svallfors, Stefan. 2011. "A Bedrock of Support? Trends in Welfare State Attitudes in Sweden, 1981–2010." *Social Policy and Administration* 45 (7): 806–825.

———. 1989. *Vem älskar välfärdsstaten? Attityder, organiserade intressen och svensk välfärdspolitik.* Lund: Arkiv Förlag.

Svanberg, Ingvar, and Mattias Tydén. 1992. *Tusen år av invandring: En svensk kulturhistoria.* Stockholm: Gidlunds Bokförlag.

Sveriges socialdemokratiska arbetareparti. Arbetsgruppen för invandrarfrågor. 1978. *Jämlikhet. Valfrihet. Samverkan: förslag till invandringspolitiskt handlingsprogram.* Stockholm: Socialdemokraterna.

Swenson, Peter A. 2002. *Capitalists against Markets: The Making of Labor Markets and Welfare States in the United States and Sweden.* New York: Oxford University Press.

Swidler, Ann. 1986. "Culture in Action: Symbols and Strategies." *American Sociological Review* 51 (2): 273–286.

Tilton, Timothy Alan. 1990. *The Political Theory of Swedish Social Democracy: Through the Welfare State to Socialism.* New York: Oxford University Press.

Tingsten, Herbert. 1941. *The Swedish Social Democrats: Their Ideological Development.* Translated by Greta Frankel and Patricia Howard-Rosen. Totowa, NJ: Bedminster Press.

Trägårdh, Lars. 2002. "Crisis and the Politics of National Community: Germany and Sweden 1933–1994." In *Culture and Crisis: The Case of Germany and Sweden,* edited by Lars Trägårdh and Nina Witoszek. New York: Berghahan Books.

———. 1990. "Swedish Model or Swedish Culture?" *Critical Review* 4 (4): 569–590.

Trondman, Mats. 2006. "Disowning Knowledge: To Be or Not To Be 'the Immigrant' in Sweden." *Ethnic and Racial Studies* 29 (3): 431–451.

Valenta, Marko, and Nihad Bunar. 2010. "State Assisted Integration: Refugee Integration Policies in Scandinavian Welfare States; The Swedish and Norwegian Experience." *Journal of Refugee Studies* 23 (4): 463–483.

Van der Waal, Jeroen, Peter Achterberg, Dick Houtman, Willem de Koster, and Katerina Manevska. 2010. "Some Are More Equal than Others: Economic Egalitarianism and Welfare Chauvinism in the Netherlands." *Journal of European Social Policy* 20 (4): 350–363.

Vänsterpartiet. 1993. *För en solidarisk värld. Principprogram antaget av vänsterpartiets 30:e congress.* Stockholm: Vänsterpartiet.

Vasta, Ellie 2004. "Community, the State and the Deserving Citizen: Pacific Islanders in Australia." *Journal of Ethnic and Migration Studies* 30 (1): 195–213.

Viroli, Maurizio. 1995. *For Love of Country: An Essay on Nationalism and Patriotism.* Oxford: Clarendon Press.

Virtanen, Simo, and Leonie Huddy. 1998. "Old-fashioned Racism and New Forms of Racial Prejudice." *Journal of Politics* 60: 311–332.

Voss, Kim. 1993. *The Making of American Exceptionalism: The Knights of Labor and Class Formation in the Nineteenth Century.* Ithaca, NY: Cornell University Press.

Vougt, Allan. 1925. *Rasbiologi och socialism.* Eskilstuna, SE: Frihet.

Wadensjö, Eskil. 1973. *Immigration och samhällsekonomi.* Lund, SE: Studentlitteratur.

Wallengren, Hans. 2014. *Socialdemokrater möter invandrar: Arbetarrörelsen, invandrarna och främlingsfientlighet i Landskrona.* Lund, SE: Nordic Academic Press.

Wallerstein, Immanuel. 1991. "The Construction of Peoplehood: Racism, Nationalism, Ethnicity." In *Race, Nation, Class: Ambiguous Identities*, edited by Etienne Balibar and Immanuel Wallerstein. London: Verso.

Weber, Max. 1978. *Economy and Society.* Edited by Guenther Roth and Claus Wittich. Berkeley: University of California Press.

Weibull, Lennart, Henrik Oskarsson, and Annika Bergström. 2013. *Vägskäl: 43 kapitel om politik, medier och samhälle.* Bohus, SE: Ale Tryckteam.

Westerberg, Bengt, and Christina Olsson Bohlin. 2012. *Främlingsfienden inom oss.* Stockholm: Statens Offentliga Utredningar.

Westin, Charles. 2004. "Racism and Multiculturalism: The Swedish Response to Immigration." In *Racism, Xenophobia and the Academic Responses: European Perspectives*, edited by Charles Westin. Stockholm: CEIFO.

———. 2006. *Sweden: Restrictive Immigration Policy and Multiculturalism.* Stockholm: Migration Policy Institute.

Westlind, Dennis. 1994. "Politisk missnöje och uppkomsten av nya partier." In *Det politiska missnöjets Sverige: Statsvetare och sociologer ser på valet 1991*, edited by Bo Bjurulf and Björn Fryklund. Lund, SE: Lund University Press.

Wetterberg, Eva. 1997. "Med eller utan fader och bröder? Kvinnor i 1900-talets politiska liv." In *Mot halva makten: elva historiska essäer om kvinnors strategier och mäns motstånd*, edited by Ingrid Hagman. Stockholm: Statens Offentliga Utredning.

Widfeldt, Anders. 2008. "Party Change as a Necessity: The Case of the Sweden Democrats." *Representation* 44 (3): 265–276.

———. 2000. "Scandinavia: Mixed Success for the Populist Right." *Parliamentary Affairs* 43: 486–500.

Wigerfelt, Anders, and Bertil Wigerfelt. (2000). "'Det var ju bara en neger . . .': Rasism och nazism i ett lokalsamhälle." In *Det lokala våldet: Om rädsla, rasism och social kontroll,* edited by Ingrid Sahlin and Malin Åkerström. Stockholm: Liber.

Wiklund, Mats. 2006. *En av oss? En bok om Fredrik Reinfeldt.* Rimbo, SE: Bokförlaget Fischer.

Wilensky, Harold. 1975. *The Welfare State and Equality: Structural and Ideological Roots of Public Expenditures.* Berkeley: University of California Press.

Wimmer, Andreas. 2002. *Nationalist Exclusion and Ethnic Conflict: Shadows of Modernity.* Cambridge: Cambridge University Press.

Wistrich, Robert S. 1982. *Socialism and the Jews: The Dilemmas of Assimilation in Germany and Austria-Hungary.* Rutherford, NJ: Fairleigh Dickinson University Press.

Xu, Qingwen. 2007. "Globalization, Immigration and the Welfare State: A Cross-National Comparison." *Journal of Sociology and Social Welfare* 34 (2): 87–106.

Yalcin, Zeki. 2010. *Facklig gränspolitik: Landsorganisationens invandrings- och invandrarpolitik, 1946–2009.* Örebro, SE: Örebro Universitet.

Index